WITHDRAWN

W9-BCF-447

Gramley Library
Salem Academy and College
Winston-Salem, N.C. 27108

SOUTHERN LITERARY STUDIES
Fred Hobson, Editor

# Contents

# Illustrations

*To Absent Friends*

Copyright © 2002 by Louisiana State University Press
All rights reserved
Manufactured in the United States of America
First printing
11  10  09  08  07  06  05  04  03  02
5  4  3  2  1

Designer: Melanie O'Quinn Samaha
Typeface: Adobe Garamond
Typesetter: Coghill Composition Co. Inc.
Printer and binder: Thomson-Shore, Inc.

Library of Congress Cataloging-in-Publication Data

Marrs, Suzanne.
    One writer's imagination : the fiction of Eudora Welty / Suzanne Marrs.
        p.   cm.
    Includes bibliographical references and index.
    ISBN 0-8071-2801-5 (cloth : alk. paper)
    1. Welty, Eudora, 1909—Criticism and interpretation.   2. Women and
literature—Southern States—History—20th century.   3. Creation
(Literary, artistic, etc.)   4. Southern States—In literature.
5. Imagination.   I. Title.
PS3545.E6 Z773 2002
813'.52—dc21

                                                        2002067133

The paper in this book meets the guidelines for permanence and durability of the Committee on Production Guidelines for Book Longevity of the Council on Library Resources. ⊗

 One Writer's Imagination

*The Fiction of Eudora Welty*

SUZANNE MARRS

LOUISIANA STATE UNIVERSITY PRESS )( *Baton Rouge*

Gramley Library
Salem Academy and College
Winston-Salem, N.C. 27108

One Writer's Imagination

# Preface

In the summer of 1975, I visited my mother's college roommate. She inquired about my teaching and suggested that Eudora Welty's novel *Losing Battles* would be a good addition to the reading list I had planned for a class on women writers. In that brief conversation, Elva Lewis changed the course of my life, and I owe her a world of gratitude. She started me on what is now a twenty-seven-year course of study that has been a joy and a passion and that promises new discoveries and opportunities ahead.

When in 1983 I planned to come to Jackson, Mississippi, in order to examine the Eudora Welty Collection at the Mississippi Department of Archives and History, my high-school English teacher Frances Dunham and especially her husband, the noted scholar Lowell Dunham, insisted that I meet Eudora Welty. They would tolerate no pleas of shyness. Accordingly, I wrote to Miss Welty. I received no response, but when I reached Jackson, Charlotte Capers, Miss Welty's close friend and the former director of the Mississippi Department of Archives and History, interceded on my behalf. Charlotte would subsequently introduce me to Mississippi and to many Mississippians, and she would convince me to move to Jackson and to Millsaps College. Charlotte Capers, storyteller extraordinaire, was a wonderful sponsor and an even better friend.

From the time I met her in 1983, Eudora Welty was my friend and mentor. When I moved to Jackson, she helped me to find doctors, dentists, shops, and housing. She introduced me to her pals, who became mine. We talked together about politics, Mississippi culture, American literature, European travel, the London and the Broadway stage, murder mysteries, Bea Lillie, Fats Waller, Danny Kaye, and the Marx brothers. And Eudora talked with me about her fiction, about her life, and about the writing of fiction. My debt to her and affection for her are beyond measure.

Eudora Welty, Charlotte Capers, Lowell Dunham, and Elva Lewis have now died. Jane Petty and Beth Jones, two of Eudora Welty's friends who became my own and who helped me to understand the Welty canon, are also gone now. So too are Laura Crouch and Peter Murray, two far-flung colleagues who encouraged my work. But these absent friends are not forgotten. Jack Renfro in *Losing Battles* says as he passes his grandfather's grave, "I miss him, I miss his frowning presence." The word *frowning* does not in any way describe Welty, Capers, Lewis, Dunham, Petty, Jones, Crouch, and Murray, but Jack's sense of loss is one shared by their legion of admirers: "We miss them, we miss their smiling presences."

Let me pay homage to many other friends and colleagues in Jackson, Mississippi. They welcomed me here, talked with me about Mississippi and Eudora Welty, read and commented on my work, and assisted in my research. In particular, Patti Carr Black and Ann Morrison have offered valuable advice about the content and style of this book; I hope I have avoided the literary jargon they both dislike so much. To Mary Alice White, Elizabeth Thompson, Mittie Welty, Hank Holmes, Forrest Galey, Charles Sallis, Nicole Donald, Caroline Ellender, Greg Miller, and Jon Peede, I also extend heartfelt thanks.

In addition, I am indebted to those colleagues and writers beyond the borders of Mississippi who have provided assistance and encouragement as I worked on this project. Harriet Pollack has given many hours to reading and suggesting revisions to my text. In addition, Mary Hughes Brookhart, Susan Ketchin, Peggy Prenshaw, Michael Kreyling, John Shelton Reed, Wayne Flynt, and Louis Rubin have in various ways provided counsel. Eudora Welty's friends William Jay

Smith, John Ferrone, and Reynolds Price have my abiding gratitude for discussing Welty's life and work with me, and her friend and agent Timothy Seldes my abiding gratitude for examining the manuscript of this book and providing sage advice in publishing matters.

Millsaps College, the Mississippi Department of Archives and History, the Harry Ransom Humanities Research Center, and the University of Maryland Libraries have all provided me with much-needed and much-appreciated support.

Thanks to my family for their interest, enthusiasm, and help—and special thanks to Rowan Taylor, who has long been my champion, who read and commented on drafts at every stage, and who pushed me to complete this project.

Above all, I again and again thank Eudora Welty for her fiction, for her friendship and support, and for teaching me as much as I could absorb about the reading and writing of stories.

# Acknowledgments

Excerpts from Eudora Welty's letters to Katherine Anne Porter (Papers of Katherine Anne Porter, Special Collections, University of Maryland Libraries) are reprinted by permission of the University of Maryland Libraries and by permission of Russell & Volkening, Inc., as agents for the author. Copyright © 1941, 1942, 1943, 1948. Excerpt from Eudora Welty's letter to Elizabeth Bowen is reprinted by permission of the Harry Ransom Humanities Research Center at the University of Texas at Austin, and by permission of Russell & Volkening, Inc., as agents for the author. Copyright © 1951. Excerpts from Eudora Welty's letters to Diarmuid Russell, Mary Louise Aswell, and John F. Robinson (Eudora Welty Collection, Mississippi Department of Archives and History) are reprinted by permission of Russell & Volkening, Inc., as agents for the author. Copyright © 1940, 1941, 1943, 1945, 1946, 1948, 1949, 1950, 1951, 1963. Excerpts from Eudora Welty's manuscripts (Eudora Welty Collection, Mississippi Department of Archives and History) are reprinted by permission of Russell & Volkening, Inc., as agents for the author. Copyright © 1934, 1936, ca. 1939/1940, 1942, 1947, 1961, 1963, 1964, 1966, 1967, 1969, 1983.

Excerpts from *The Bride of the Innisfallen and Other Stories*, copyright ©
1955 and renewed 1983 by Eudora Welty, reprinted by permission of Harcourt,
Inc., and of Russell & Volkening, Inc., as agents for the author. Excerpts from
*A Curtain of Green and Other Stories*, copyright © 1941 and renewed 1969 by
Eudora Welty, reprinted by permission of Harcourt, Inc., and of Russell &
Volkening, Inc., as agents for the author. Excerpts from *Delta Wedding*, copyright © 1946, 1945 and renewed 1974, 1973 by Eudora Welty, reprinted by
permission of Harcourt, Inc., and of Russell & Volkening, Inc., as agents for the
author. Excerpts from "The Demonstrators," copyright © 1966 and 1980, used
by permission of Russell & Volkening, Inc., as agents for the author. Excerpts
from *The Eye of the Story* by Eudora Welty, copyright © 1978 by Eudora Welty,
used by permission of Random House, Inc., and of Russell & Volkening, Inc.,
as agents for the author. Excerpts from *The Golden Apples*, copyright © 1949,
1948, 1947 and renewed 1977, 1976, 1975 by Eudora Welty, reprinted by permission of Harcourt, Inc., and of Russell & Volkening, Inc., as agents for the
author. Excerpts from *Losing Battles*, copyright © 1970 by Eudora Welty, used
by permission of Russell & Volkening, Inc., as agents for the author. Excerpts
from *One Time, One Place*, copyright © 1971 by Eudora Welty, used by permission of Russell & Volkening, Inc., as agents for the author. Excerpts from *One
Writer's Beginnings*, copyright © 1984 by Eudora Welty, used by permission of
Russell & Volkening, Inc., as agents for the author. Excepts from *The Optimist's
Daughter* by Eudora Welty, copyright © 1969, 1972 by Eudora Welty, used by
permission of Random House, Inc., and of Russell & Volkening, Inc., as agents
for the author. Excerpts from *The Ponder Heart*, copyright © 1954, 1953, and
renewed 1982, 1981 by Eudora Welty, reprinted by permission of Harcourt,
Inc., and of Russell & Volkening, Inc., as agents for the author. Excerpts from
*The Robber Bridegroom*, copyright © 1942 and renewed 1970 by Eudora Welty,
reprinted by permission of Harcourt, Inc., and of Russell & Volkening, Inc., as
agents for the author. Excerpts from *The Wide Net and Other Stories*, copyright
© 1943 and renewed 1971 by Eudora Welty, reprinted by permission of Harcourt, Inc., and of Russell & Volkening, Inc., as agents for the author. Excerpts
from "Where is the Voice Coming From?", copyright © 1963 and 1980, used
by permission of Russell & Volkening, Inc., as agents for the author. Excerpts
from Diarmuid Russell's letters to Eudora Welty, copyright © 1941, 1943,

1944, 1945, 1952, used by permission of Pamela Russell Jessup and by Russell & Volkening, Inc.

Parts of chapters 2, 5, and 7 are reprinted by permission of Louisiana State University Press from my essay "'The Huge Fateful Stage of the Outside World': Eudora Welty's Life in Politics," in *Eudora Welty and Politics: Did the Writer Crusade?*, edited by Harriet Pollack and Suzanne Marrs, copyright © 2001 by Louisiana State University Press. Parts of chapter 4 appeared in a somewhat different form as "'The Treasure Most Dearly Regarded': Memory and Imagination in *Delta Wedding*," *Southern Literary Journal* 25, no. 2 (1993): 79–91. Most of chapter 6 appeared as "Place and the Displaced in Eudora Welty's *The Bride of the Innisfallen*," *Mississippi Quarterly* 50, no. 4 (Fall 1997): 647–68. The following essays have been incorporated in somewhat different forms into chapter 8: "Eudora Welty: The Southern Context," *Perspectives on the South* 4 (1987): 19–37; "The Making of *Losing Battles*: Plot Revision," *Southern Literary Journal* 18 (Fall 1985): 40–9; "The Making of *Losing Battles*: Jack Renfro's Evolution," *Mississippi Quarterly* 37 (Fall 1984): 469–74; "The Making of *Losing Battles*: Judge Moody Transformed," *Notes on Mississippi Writers* 17 (1985): 47–53. The text also includes brief excerpts from the following of my works: *The Welty Collection: A Guide to the Eudora Welty Manuscripts and Documents at the Mississippi Department of Archives and History*, copyright © 1988 by University Press of Mississippi; "The Conclusion of Eudora Welty's 'First Love': Historical Backgrounds," *Notes on Mississippi Writers* 13, no. 2 (1981): 73–8; "The Metaphor of Race in Eudora Welty's Fiction," *Southern Review*, n.s. 22 (1986): 697–707. All are used by permission.

# Abbreviations

One Writer's Imagination

I

# En Route to *A Curtain of Green*

In 1931, after spending two years at the University of Wisconsin and another year at the Columbia University School of Business, twenty-two-year-old Eudora Welty returned to Jackson, Mississippi, to live—called back by her father's illness and by her own inability to find work in New York City. Shortly after her return, Welty's father died, and this devastating loss changed the course of her life. At a young age she came face to face with the transient nature of human existence and the powerful bonds and responsibilities of family life.

She would spend the next thirty-five years living with her mother in Jackson, and her life there would inevitably prove more restricted than it had been in Madison and Manhattan. Only on long trips could she go to the Cotton Club or Small's Paradise in Harlem, see an African American cast perform *Macbeth* under the direction of a young Orson Welles, take advantage of the Broadway stage, or stroll through exhibitions of Georgia O'Keeffe's paintings.[1] The artistic

1. The biographical information here and throughout much of this study comes from inter-

opportunities available in New York City obviously could not be matched in a southern town. And even Welty's trips back to New York—trips taken first in an attempt to find a job, then to sell her stories—would be tinged with guilt. Welty reported that whenever her train left Jackson for New York, "my mother was already writing to me at her desk, telling me she missed me but only wanted what was best for me. She would not leave the house till she had my wire, sent from Penn Station the third day from now, that I had arrived safely. I was not to worry about her or things at home, about how she was getting along. She anxiously awaited my letter after I had tried my stories on the publishers" (*OWB*, 94).

Her mother's anxiety troubled Welty, but her need to pursue a writing career was more compelling. As Welty has noted, "The torment and the guilt—the torment of having the loved one go, the guilt of being the loved one gone—comes into my fiction as it did and does into my life. And most of all the guilt then was because it was true: I had left to arrive at some future and secret joy, at what was unknown, and what was now in New York, waiting to be discovered. My joy was connected with writing; that was as much as I knew" (*OWB*, 94). It was back in Jackson, however, where Welty wrote away, producing many a story that she saw as a failure. And perhaps those early, never-published stories *were* failures, because Welty had not yet discovered how to incorporate her most profound emotions, her sense of loss and guilt, into fiction. "The Children," an unpublished typescript probably written in 1934 and now held by the Mississippi Department of Archives and History, hints at a tension between mother and daughter, but that relationship is not developed. Such tensions would be fully developed in Welty's mature work, but the nature of those tensions is quite different from what many feminist scholars expect to see.

According to Carolyn Heilbrun, women of Welty's generation typically felt and repressed antagonisms toward a mother who supported the patriarchal family structure. Heilbrun writes,

> What was the function of mothers toward daughters before the current women's movement, before, let us say, 1970? Whatever the drawbacks, whatever the

---

views and conversations that I had with Eudora Welty, conversations and interviews dating from 1983 until her death in 2001.

frustrations or satisfactions of the mother's life, her mission was to prepare the daughter to take her place in the patriarchal succession, that is, to marry, to bear children (preferably sons), and to encourage her husband to succeed in the world. But for many women, mothers and daughters alike, there moved in their imaginations dreams of some other life: of personal accomplishment, of the understanding and control of hard facts and complex problems, of a place in a community where women were in sufficient numbers to render the accomplished woman neither lonely nor an anomaly. Above all, the dream of taking control of one's life without the intrusion of a mother's patriarchal wishes for her daughter, without the danger of injuring the much loved and pitied mother.

A superficial examination of Eudora Welty's relationship with her mother might tend to support Heilbrun's view, or at least suggest that Mrs. Welty sought a socially appropriate role for her daughter. For instance, on June 22, 1930, the *Jackson Daily Clarion-Ledger* reported that "the handsome home of Mr. and Mrs. C. W. Welty, Pinehurst Place, was on Thursday afternoon at three-thirty o'clock the scene of beautiful entertaining when Mrs. Welty was hostess at eight tables of bridge honoring her attractive daughter Miss Eudora Welty." But such typical Jackson entertainments were highly unusual in the Welty household.[2]

The 1930 bridge party notwithstanding, conflicts between Eudora Welty and her mother were seldom based upon the expectation that Welty play a conventional female role but paradoxically stemmed from the deep love mother and daughter felt for each other. Chestina Welty desired to shield and protect her daughter from harm. That desire could be heroic and supportive: On the eve of surgery for breast cancer, Mrs. Welty attended her young daughter's piano recital, never mentioning the danger she faced. When as an adult Eudora Welty learned of her mother's act, she felt deep admiration and gratitude. But the very quality Welty loved and admired could also become oppressive. In 1937, for instance, Welty joined her friends John, Will, and Anna Belle Robinson for a car trip over primitive roads to Mexico City. Mrs. Welty had cautioned against the trip, not because it defied convention, but because it seemed dangerous, and Welty regretted how much her mother would worry while she was gone.

2. Carolyn Heilbrun, *Writing a Woman's Life* (New York: Norton, 1988), 118–9; "Miss Eudora Welty Honored at Beautiful Bridge Party of Eight Congenial Tables," *Jackson Daily Clarion-Ledger*, 22 June 1930.

Mrs. Welty's worries were well founded, as it turned out. John Robinson was driving one day when a young Indian child darted into the path of the Jacksonians' car; the four stopped to care for the injured child and were ultimately investigated by the police. Welty had to phone her mother from the police station to request extra funds. The possibility of such events prompted the tensions between mother and daughter. The desire to protect each other, not disagreement about gender roles, was the source of conflict between the two.

Indeed, far from embracing the established social order, Chestina Welty herself was a model for defying convention. Mrs. Welty was not as soft-spoken and indirect in manner as the typical Jackson lady. When asked to contribute to a missionary society, for example, she saw no reason for evasiveness in her reply. She did not wish, she simply said, to tell people in other countries what to think. If her outspoken ways were unusual, so were her activities. A member of the Research Club, Mrs. Welty joined because she believed in the value of the research projects members actually undertook; the more usual women's luncheon clubs were anathema to her. While conventional Jackson ladies might deprecatingly refer to intellectual girls as "brains," Chestina Welty, who had put herself through Marshall College, wanted her daughter to excel in academic endeavors and sought to support Eudora's friends who were trapped in families that did not have such ambitions for young women.

Though she loved to study her Bible and was a member of Galloway Methodist Church, Chestina Welty was not a regular churchgoer, even though church attendance was socially expected. And when Chestina Welty helped to establish Jackson's first garden club and served as its president, it was a "working, digging neighborhood group"—not a club for elaborate refreshments, stylish frocks, and pleasant conversation.[3] She thus violated in very basic ways the expectations that many Jacksonians held. Neither by word nor example did Chestina Welty pressure her daughter to adhere to convention. Eudora Welty was free to set her own course in life.

And set her own course she did. Like her mother, Welty was uninterested in most women's clubs and chose not to be active in a church. She did not make

---

3. Eudora Welty, written comments on draft of an unpublished lecture by Suzanne Marrs, 19 September 1990, Marrs's personal collection.

the appropriate marriage and was not pressured to. She attended concerts, including the occasional jazz artist appearance in a black movie house, patronized a black record shop, and photographed many black Mississippians. In addition, though Welty was not a political activist, she (along with her mother) cherished liberal sentiments that were held by a rather small minority in the overwhelmingly conservative South. Like many upper-middle-class Mississippians, she abhorred the very popular Theodore Bilbo's election, and she was proud when her friend Hubert Creekmore's letter criticizing Senator Bilbo was published in *Time* magazine on October 22, 1934. This political deviance, established early in Welty's life, would continue. Finally, Welty's unusual choice of a literary career, undertaken with her mother's support, also set her apart. As Anne Goodwyn Jones notes, despite an established tradition of writing among southern women, the "'independent, self-declarative life of the writer' places the woman who writes into a special class that is in certain respects outside the norms of southern society."[4]

In certain respects, an "independent, self-declarative life" placed both Eudora Welty and her mother "outside the norms of southern society," and Welty's fiction provides a suggestive portrait of that common bond. Though Welty and her mother have quite rightly been associated with the mother and daughter in "The Winds," Chestina Welty might also be linked in spirit to the female cornetist of the story, for like the cornetist, Mrs. Welty provided her daughter with a vision of the "the other way to live."[5] (Interestingly enough, Chestina Welty actually played the cornet as a girl in West Virginia.) And Welty certainly draws upon her mother's "independent, self-declarative life" in "A Curtain of Green." In this story, the deep-seated connection between mother and daughter emerges from Welty's use of gardening, not as a conventional domestic activity but as a way of defying conventionality.

After the death of her husband, Chestina Welty found solace in the creative work of gardening, not in the social display of a garden. With Eudora as her

4. Anne Goodwyn Jones, *Tomorrow Is Another Day* (Baton Rouge: Louisiana State University Press, 1981), 39.

5. Eudora Welty, "Moon Lake," *The Golden Apples* (New York: Harcourt, Brace, 1949),138.

interested and committed "yard man," she worked long hours among her plants and flowers, year after year, finding her evolving garden "to be satisfying, though never perfect." In fact, she found the garden to be satisfying because it was *never* perfect, because it was always a work in progress. It also served as a source of consolation for life's difficulties. As she noted in a small (and never published) essay titled "The Perfect Garden," "The loved garden is always satisfyingly responsive to moods. It flaunts its colors joyously when we are glad, its peace and fragrance are soothing to frayed nerves when we are weary from contact or perhaps conflict with the everyday world, and its recurrent beauty whispers a message of comfort and hope when our hearts are lonely or sorrowful." But Chestina Welty found more than consolation in her garden. She found a creative activity, noting that "creating a garden is much like painting a picture or writing a poem, and artists and poets often make lovely gardens. But sometimes we less articulate folks, who can neither paint pictures nor write poems, yet feel the need of expressing ourselves, find a garden a very happy medium." What might be seen by some as a conventional domestic activity was far more for Chestina Welty. Her work in the garden was not unlike Eudora Welty's work in fiction.[6]

It seems somehow appropriate that the garden, which provided such a strong bond between mother and daughter, also provided a strong bond between Eudora Welty and her literary agent, Diarmuid Russell. Eudora Welty had her own passion for gardening, especially for growing camellias. She planted a wide variety of camellias in the Pinehurst Place yard and worked hard to see that they survived, stitching up covers to protect the young bushes from freezes. She even set up a sort of mini-nursery in the basement and worked at grafting the plants, and she sent Russell both camellia plants and suggestions for helping them flourish in Westchester County, New York. Russell, like the Welty women, was an avid gardener, and in his correspondence with Welty he talks about the state of his garden almost as much as he does the state of Welty's fiction. For both Welty and Russell, it seems, gardening and writing were linked at some profound level.

Welty makes this link explicit in "A Curtain of Green." In the story, the gardener, like the writer, confronts the dark irrationality of human experience and

6. Chestina Welty, "The Perfect Garden," Xerox copy, Marrs's personal collection, 2–3, 1.

attempts to deal with that irrationality. Mrs. Larkin has seen her husband killed by a falling chinaberry tree and has realized that her love could not protect him. In the depths of her grief, she then ventures deeper and deeper into gardening, becoming "over-vigorous, disreputable, and heedless" in the eyes of her neighbors (*CG*, 208). Mrs. Larkin seeks not Chestina Welty's "well designed [garden] plot," but seeks "to allow an over-flowering" (*CG*, 209); in the process, she finds that the garden provides not solace but immersion in a hostile force. She finds herself on the brink of killing Jamey, whose hopeful essence has not yet been wounded, and seeks to penetrate and participate in the mystery of nature that has killed her husband and destroyed her faith in the power of love. But at day's end, she drops the hoe she had contemplated using as a weapon, and she finds release in the afternoon rain and in the garden's "quiet arcade of identity" (*CG*, 214). Momentarily, at least, she accepts both nature's mystery and its beauty. Surely Mrs. Larkin's isolation within her community, her grief, her venturing into the garden, and her discovery of some consolation there draw in oblique ways upon Chestina Welty's own experience. Mrs. Larkin's love, which like Chestina Welty's seeks to but cannot protect the beloved, sprang from a key source of tension between Welty and her mother, but the story found its starting point in the depth of Mrs. Welty's love for her husband, in her abiding grief at his loss (a grief that loomed over a concerned daughter), in her intellectual and creative toughness, and in her inability to retreat into a mindlessly conventional consolation.

In *One Writer's Beginnings*, Welty writes that "all serious daring starts from within" (104), but she also shows that her inner life was nourished by a mother who was a model of serious daring. Eudora Welty was extremely fortunate, as are we her readers, that she found that model first thing and at home. She also found at home a group of friends who exemplified intellectual daring in many ways and who supported her work in fiction. As Howard Gardner observes in his distinguished study of creative people ranging from Albert Einstein to Martha Graham, "creators" typically need a "special relation to one or more supportive individuals." Eventually, in Welty's case, this role would be played, as Michael Kreyling's *Author and Agent* has so persuasively shown, by Diarmuid Russell. But Welty did not meet Russell until 1940, and prior to that time his supportive role was filled by a number of Welty's friends who lived in Jackson or who regularly returned there for visits. Friends like Aimee Shands, Leone Shotwell, Mary Frances Horne, and Joe Skinner had, like Welty, returned from Columbia University's graduate schools. And Jackson was also home to artists Karl Wolfe, William Hollingsworth, and Helen Jay Lotterhos, all of whom were Welty's friends and one of whom literally led her to a story. Indeed, as Welty tagged along on a Lotterhos sketching trip, she saw the woman who prompted her to create Phoenix Jackson and "A Worn Path." Even more important support perhaps came from Frank Lyell, Lehman Engel, Nash Burger, Hubert Creekmore, and John Robinson, who provided Welty with an easy, good-humored, imaginatively stimulating community in which to begin writing and with advice, encouragement, and friendship throughout her career.[7]

Frank Lyell took a Ph.D. in English from Princeton University, taught first at North Carolina State University and then at the University of Texas at Austin, traveled widely, and was an afficionado of fine food, opera, and theater throughout his life. Lehman Engel left Jackson to study music at the Cincinnati College-Conservatory, went on to New York City, and became an important composer of concert music and of incidental music for the stage, a choral conductor, and a music director for the Broadway stage. Nash Burger took a master's degree in English from the University of Virginia, taught English at Jackson's Central High School, and went on to become an editor for the *New York Times Book Review*. Hubert Creekmore, a graduate of the University of Mississippi, studied playwriting with George Pierce Baker at Yale University, worked for the Mississippi Highway Department, wrote scripts for local theatrical productions, and eventually settled in New York City, where he was an editor, a literary agent, and an author in his own right. He published three novels and several volumes of poetry. John Robinson, with whom Welty was for many years romantically involved and who was her longtime friend, graduated from Jackson's Central High School and from the University of Mississippi, worked in New Orleans as an adjuster for an insurance company, returned from World War II to study at the University of California, published stories in *Harper's* and the *New Yorker*, and eventually settled in Italy.

This group of friends had many good times together, viewing their own

7. Howard Gardner, *Creating Minds* (New York: Basic Books, 1993), 369.

world with the affection, imagination, and irony that would eventually characterize such Welty stories as "Why I Live at the P.O.," "Lily Daw and the Three Ladies," "Petrified Man," and "Old Mr. Marblehall." Lyell, Creekmore, Engel, and Welty were all in residence in Jackson for a number of summers early in the thirties. Engel reports that "Each summer all of us went home to swelter. . . . There were about five such summers before I began staying on in New York with work to occupy and to pay me. But at home Frank [Lyell], Eudora, Hubert Creekmore, and I used to meet at Eudora's, and we formed what we called the Night-Blooming Cereus Club, the total membership of which sat up to see the glorious white flower with the yellow feathery center bloom." Lyell, Creekmore, Engel, and Welty named themselves in the camp spirit of their summer activities. In those days Jackson ladies would advertise the coming bloom of a cereus in the newspaper and invite anyone interested to drop by for the blooming. This group, observing the admonition "Don't take it 'cereus,' life's too mysterious" (turning on the lyric from Rudy Vallee's "Life Is Just a Bowl of Cherries"), visited one open house where a lady informed them that in the morning the flowers would look like "wrung chickens' necks." Years later, in "The Wanderers," Welty would use the "naked, luminous, complicated" (*GA*, 235) cereus as an emblem of life's beauty and brevity, and she would have an old country woman tell Virgie Rainey that "tomorrow it'll look like a wrung chicken's neck." But in the early thirties none of the Night-Blooming Cereus Club members anticipated such symbolic implications of their activities. For them the cereus was and remained an emblem of good fellowship, of the pleasure imaginative individuals could share if they embraced the world around them. In 1956, recalling the happy past and hoping that a dramatization of *The Ponder Heart* would meet with success, Engel sent Welty on opening night the closest thing he could find to a cereus bloom, and when Welty later used the cereus as an image in *Losing Battles*, she informed Engel she had done so for him.[8]

These friends lived up to their motto; they did not take their society too seriously. They mocked an emphasis upon beauty and cosmetics when Frank Lyell

8. Lehman Engel, *This Bright Day* (New York: Macmillan, 1974), 40; Eudora Welty to Lehman Engel, 3 August 1956, 5 August 1970, Engel Papers, Millsaps College, Jackson, Mississippi.

photographed Welty, in a Helena Rubinstein pose, about to apply pea soup, shoe polish, and household cleansers to her face. And they mocked the stock elements of literary romance when Lehman Engel photographed a disdainful Welty in a Spanish shawl being courted by a devoted Lyell in a sombrero; Welty was, Engel asserts in his autobiography, "the unwitting inventor of camp."[9]

Comic sensibilities notwithstanding, these friends were serious about the importance of the arts, even the comic ones. They loved to talk about literature and the theater—and they did more than talk. Creekmore was a published writer before Welty. He kept a long and detailed record of his submissions to a wide variety of periodicals and established a literary magazine. He and Burger were contributors to the one issue of Creekmore's own *Southern Review* (1934), though Welty was relegated to the staff. Three years later, Welty would join Creekmore, Burger, and Peter Taylor on equal terms in contributing stories to another local publication—Dale Mullen's *River* magazine in Oxford, Mississippi.

Welty's friendships fostered an already well-established love of travel. Creekmore, Welty recalled, was the hub of a group she labeled Jackson-in-New York, and this group enjoyed the hospitality of fellow Mississippians like editor Herschel Brickell and actress Ruth Ford. Welty visited New York once or twice a year after leaving Columbia, attending concerts and the theater, taking advantage of art museums and the New York Public Library.[10] And in 1937 Welty joined John Robinson and his siblings on a trip to Mexico. As a traveler, then, Welty knew far more freedom than a southern woman earlier in the twentieth century might have. Although her early unpublished stories do not deal with journeys, Welty's travels in the 1930s reinforced an emotion that had long been hers. During childhood trips to West Virginia, Welty had discovered "a fierce independence that was suddenly mine, to remain inside no matter how it scared me when I tumbled" (*OWB*, 60), and this association of travel and independence would eventually find its way into Welty's fiction, into stories of travelers who are free to break from established roles and create their own identities.

---

9. Eudora Welty, *Photographs* (Jackson: University Press of Mississippi, 1989), xxi, xx; Engel, 41.

10. Eudora Welty to Suzanne Marrs, n.d., Marrs's personal collection.

As one might expect, the group with whom Welty socialized and traveled was positively disposed toward her career as a writer and toward the creative endeavors of women generally. Creekmore recommended that Welty submit "Death of a Traveling Salesman" and "Magic" to *Manuscript*, which readily accepted both stories for publication. Burger had written a master's thesis about Sherwood Bonner, the first serious woman writer in Mississippi, a woman who violated all sorts of conventions to pursue her career. It was no surprise that he supported Welty in her efforts at fiction. And as years went by, Welty would correspond with Robinson, Lyell, and Engel about her literary endeavors and would value their advice. These friends, in turn, found themselves sustained and supported by Welty. In 1969, Burger recalled her devotion to the arts and to artists during his adult years in Jackson: "The large Welty home on Pinehurst, which had succeeded the earlier house near Davis School, became the center of a swarm of local writers and would-be writers, journalists, painters, practitioners in all the arts and just plain friends and disciples. All were attracted by Eudora's unflagging interest, hospitality, humor and often long-tried good manners."[11]

Welty and her friends maintained both their close emotional and professional ties with each other and their identities as southerners, but in many ways they were highly critical of southern life. Engel recalled that being a Jew and being a boy who played the piano brought him the scorn of many high-school classmates.[12] Creekmore would voice his objections to a destructive class system in *The Welcome* and to race prejudice in *The Chain in the Heart*, while Welty would make the oppressive power of racism an implicit part of "Powerhouse," "A Worn Path," and "Keela, the Outcast Indian Maiden."

Furthermore, in a number of stories, Welty, Creekmore, and Robinson would go on to describe the plight of poor, rural white southerners. Welty especially, because she chose to remain in Mississippi as many of her friends departed, would come to know a great deal about Mississippi poverty, black and white, and about the resources, material and spiritual, with which Mississippians combated it. After her father died, Welty felt the effects of the Great Depression firsthand, though the Welty family remained relatively affluent by Mississippi

11. Nash K. Burger, "Eudora Welty's Jackson," *Shenandoah* 20, no. 3 (1969): 13.
12. Engel, 23.

Gramley Library
Salem Academy and College
Winston-Salem, N.C. 27108

standards. The insurance policies and Lamar Life Insurance stock that Christian Webb Welty had expected to secure his family from financial worry failed to do so. During the course of the Depression, Welty and her mother took in a boarder—Miss Fannye Cook, head of the Mississippi Wildlife Museum. Edward Welty, Eudora's brother, designed and built a duplex on the large Pinehurst Street lot where the family home was already located. The duplex generated income for his mother, and Mrs. Welty briefly gave bridge lessons as a way of further enhancing the family finances. And of course daughter Eudora worked at the WJDX radio station, then for the Works Progress Administration, and later for the Mississippi Advertising Commission, writing stories for the *Memphis Commercial Appeal* along the way. But these financial hard times were mild indeed compared to the economic suffering Welty observed elsewhere around Mississippi.

During the months she spent working for the Works Progress Administration, publicizing its 1936 projects about the state, Welty encountered a poverty she had never known as an upper-class white Mississippian. Both whites and blacks in Depression-era Mississippi knew the physically and spiritually debilitating effects of poverty—though poverty in Mississippi was a longtime condition, not a recent development. Welty's photographs of this period document the tattered clothing, shabby housing, hard work, and unbroken spirits that characterized Mississippi in the thirties. Her stories like "Death of a Traveling Salesman," "The Hitch-Hikers," "Clytie," "A Worn Path," "A Piece of News," and "The Whistle" tell us of the primitive roads, ramshackle hotels, dogtrot houses, oil lamps, open hearths for cooking and heating, and desperation that were often typical of rural and small-town Mississippi life. In 1930 Mississippi had the nation's lowest ten-year average for farm income and the nation's lowest average for days spent in school; in the thirties 50 to 90 percent of children in large areas of the South suffered from an inadequate diet; and in 1930 Mississippi had fewer than ten physicians for every ten thousand citizens. James Loewen and Charles Sallis, in vividly describing the lives of Mississippi sharecroppers, give us some indication of what Welty was seeing during her WPA work.

Most of the unpainted wooden houses . . . had only three rooms. With families of from five to fifteen people living in them, the houses were terribly crowded.

Few houses had screens and almost none had indoor plumbing. Sharecroppers usually heated their homes with wood or coal stoves.

The sharecropper's diet centered around flour, cornmeal, sorghum, salt pork, lard, and dry peas. Many sharecroppers tried to grow vegetables to improve their diet, but some landowners discouraged gardening because they preferred to use the land for cotton. A better-than-average sharecropper's menu included other items such as chitterlings ("chitlins"), rabbit, molasses, butter, milk, and sweet potato pie. The poorest sharecroppers, however, lived on only two meals a day—rice, cornbread, and coffee for breakfast, and peas and cornbread for dinner.[13]

Such conditions were the ones Welty came to know, to photograph, and to write about. Her story "The Whistle" in particular indicts a one-crop, cash-crop tenant farming system for destroying the lives of tenant farmers. But Welty's WPA work had taught her that the desperate plight of tenant farmers did not unrelentingly typify all of Mississippi's poor, and her photographs of Mississippi offer cause for hope. They often focus upon individual faces, upon expressions of joy despite economic oppression. The temperate climate of Mississippi and the possibility even for those living in town to plant gardens, own chickens, maybe even have a cow—these factors meliorated the effects of poverty in an essentially rural state as they could not in a northeastern urban center. So too did the smallness of Mississippi's population. As Welty writes in the introduction to *One Time, One Place*: "In New York there had been the faceless breadlines; on Farish Street in my home town of Jackson, the proprietor of the My Blue Heaven Café had written on the glass of the front door with his own finger dipped in window polish: 'AT 4:30 *AM* WE OPEN OUR DOORS. WE HAVE NO CERTAIN TIME TO CLOSE. THE COOK WILL BE GLAD TO SERVE U. WITH A 5 *And* 10¢ STEW.' The message was personal and particular. More than what is phenomenal, that strikes home. It happened to me everywhere I went, and I took these pictures" (*OTOP*, 3). And in stories like "Death of a Traveling Salesman" and "A Worn Path," poverty is a backdrop, a limiting

13. Statistics from Howard Odum, *Southern Regions* (Chapel Hill: University of North Carolina Press, 1936), 20, 51–3, 103, 370; James W. Loewen and Charles Sallis, *Mississippi Conflict and Change*, rev. ed. (New York: Pantheon Books, 1980), 204.

but not a controlling factor, in the lives of her characters who find sources of meaning and fulfillment despite economic deprivation.

As Welty has noted, Mississippi was not the only place where she saw people afflicted by unemployment and poverty. Probably in 1935 or 1936, on one of her regular visits to New York City, she photographed rather ordinary-looking people who during traditional business hours were sitting on Union Square park benches or gathering for protests because they had no jobs to occupy their days and provide them with purpose and with sustenance. These photographs seldom focus upon a single face but instead depict numerous individuals typically over-shadowed by massive city buildings. Welty sensed that the impersonal, concrete-and-steel world of the city was in some sense responsible for the suffering she saw all about her, and her relatively faceless pictures of the city's unemployed suggest the anonymity they experienced. As Welty told interviewers Hunter Cole and Seetha Srinivasan in 1989, "These people of the Great Depression kept alive on the determination to get back to work and to make a living again. I photographed them in Union Square and in subways and sleeping in subway stations and huddling together to keep warm, and I felt, then, sort of placed in the editorial position as I took their pictures. Recording the mass of them did constitute a plea on their behalf to the public, their existing plight being so evident in the mass."[14]

The same city that offered the relatively affluent Welty a vital personal and cultural life, she realized, denied others both the physical and emotional means to exist. She would write about this situation in her story "Flowers for Marjorie," showing the desperation that the city, with its massive population, impersonality, and distance from the natural world bring to Howard and Marjorie, who have migrated north from Victory, Mississippi. The effects of the Great Depression, Welty recognized, spanned the nation from farm to city.

Welty's focus upon race and poverty and her decision to become a writer point toward two paradoxes that seem central to her achievement. Paradox one: Though being a writer, especially a writer who focused upon poverty and racial

14. Hunter McKelva Cole and Seetha Srinivasan, "Eudora Welty and Photography: An Interview," in *More Conversations with Eudora Welty*, ed. Peggy W. Prenshaw (Jackson: University Press of Mississippi, 1996), 194–5.

discrimination, set Welty apart from most upper-class white Mississippians, it did not leave her isolated or alienated in her community. For earlier women writers this might have been the case. Anne Goodwyn Jones certainly believes it was, and in *Tomorrow Is Another Day: The Woman Writer in the South, 1859–1936*, she discusses the way many of these women resorted to subterfuge rather than openly defying convention. For the woman who cherished an independent habit of mind in a South that expected "dependence, submission, and deference" from its women, Jones argues, the life of a writer had special advantages. Fiction provided a "way to circumvent the barrier between private thought and public utterance, between diary and platform." Jones thus concludes that "fiction can become a strategy for speaking truths publicly."[15]

Eudora Welty's Jackson, however, did not expect the degree of "dependence, submission, and deference" that the South may once have demanded of its women. In Welty's South, as in England, a good deal of eccentricity was tolerated and even welcomed, especially within class boundaries. As many a southerner has said, "the only sin is being boring." Southern students often relished going North to school so that they might be "characters"; in the South their relatively slight eccentricities had caused no stir. William B. Hamilton, Welty's friend and a Mississippian who taught history at Duke University, referred to the South as "the last stronghold of eccentricity." At the very least, we should note that this South was not a monolith. As John Shelton Reed has observed, neither the southern city nor the small southern town was "simply one community": "The two racial groupings are only the most obvious of the many subcommunities within most southern towns, subcommunities with the ability to mind their own business and to cooperate when circumstances require. The monolithic small-town community may be a New England or a Midwestern phenomenon, but the southern reality has usually been more complicated than that."[16] Southerners, Reed notes, object not so much to differences as to the attempt to convince them that they should do differently. Reed does not directly

15. Jones, *Tomorrow Is Another Day*, 39.

16. Welty, written comments on draft of an unpublished lecture by Suzanne Marrs, 19 September 1990; John Shelton Reed, *One South* (Baton Rouge: Louisiana State University Press, 1982), 178–9.

address the freedom enjoyed by women, but he suggests that women were often able to be both socially acceptable and unconventional in behavior. This is not to say that Welty was radically unconventional or ill at ease with the code of behavior the upper-class South held dear. She valued good manners, graciousness, concern for the feelings of others, and she was quite gentle in manner. Indeed, Welty was willing to grant her friends the freedom to differ from her views just as they were willing to return that favor. Yet though she would not be willing to violate the rules of hospitality and begin a controversy at a dinner party given by friends of opposing philosophies, Welty was quite able to speak openly and frankly in less social situations. Except for occasions during the racially tense sixties, Mississippi provided Welty with a place from which to write, not in an atmosphere of hostility, but in an atmosphere of acceptance even as she challenged society's assumptions.

Paradox two: Even as she wrote about the destructive effects of poverty and racism, Welty experienced the exhilarating power of the imagination. When she turned seriously to writing, she drew upon her imagination to transform the world of Mississippi into her own fictional world—one removed from the randomness of daily experience, a world that would be shaped by and centered upon issues she deemed crucial. As she would later write in her essay "Place in Fiction": "The writer must accurately choose, combine, superimpose upon, blot out, shake up, alter the outside world for one absolute purpose, the good of his story. To do this, he is always seeing double, two pictures at once in his frame, his and the world's, a fact that he constantly comprehends; and he works best in a state of constant and subtle and unfooled reference between the two. It is his clear intention—his passion, I should say—to make the reader see only one of the pictures—the author's—under the pleasing illusion that it is the world's; this enormity is the accomplishment of a good story" (*ES*, 124–5). As she set about creating her own fictional worlds, Welty focused upon issues that were often disheartening, but the creative process itself brought her tremendous joy. Indeed, for Welty, the life of the imagination was always one of joy. When an interviewer once observed that "you clearly derive more pleasure from the act of writing than do a good many authors," Welty's response was unequivocal: "I love writing! I love it."[17] And in the 1930s, as Welty was discovering the pleasures writing would bring to her, she was also coming to believe that a shared act of imagination, however temporary, could be a source of meaning for people like the simpleminded Ruby Fisher and her husband Clyde in "A Piece of News," the desperate sharecroppers Jason and Sara Morton in "The Whistle," and the musician Powerhouse and his audiences, both black and white, in "Powerhouse." The imagination that Welty found to be her greatest joy she also found to be her pervasive theme in *A Curtain of Green*, the book in which she collected these and other stories written between 1936 and 1940.

What forces transformed a bright young college graduate into a major writer? No one can adequately answer that question. But Eudora Welty's mother, her circle of friends, and her community combined to provide an environment in which her imagination could flourish, could transcend convention and conventional beliefs, and could take its own course. The Mississippi world in which she lived and a job that took her out into it sparked that imagination. And the pleasures of the imagination led Welty to make those pleasures a central thematic issue in her first book of fiction.

17. Scot Haller, "Creators on Creating: Eudora Welty" in *Conversations with Eudora Welty*, ed. Peggy W. Prenshaw (Jackson: University Press of Mississippi, 1984), 314.

II

## Eudora Welty's Secret Sharer
### The Living World and the Writer's Imagination in *A Curtain of Green*

Eudora Welty's world after she returned to Mississippi in 1931 was one that at once disturbed and nourished her imagination, that provided the raw materials which her imaginative vision would transfigure and transform. Welty's early stories were typically prompted by her very diverse contemporary experiences of Depression-era Mississippi. Of the seventeen stories in *A Curtain of Green*, only three had their origins in any distant time. For "A Piece of News," Welty drew upon a college experience ten years past, while for "A Memory" and for "A Visit of Charity" she drew upon childhood memories. The other fourteen stories emerged from experiences and encounters of the Depression era. Welty was fascinated with and distressed by the world around her, and she set about turning into fiction what she had just heard and seen.

In her early stories, we see Welty experiencing the variety, both comic and tragic, of contemporary Mississippi, but we also see her discovering the exhilarating power of her own imagination, taking her start in actuality, moving into a world wholly her own, and occasionally pausing briefly to revise what she had written. Welty describes the double nature of this creative process in *One Writ-*

*er's Beginnings*, observing that "the outside world is the vital component of my inner life. My work, in the terms in which I see it, is as dearly matched to the world as its secret sharer. My imagination takes its strength and guides its direction from what I see and hear and learn and feel and remember of my living world" (76). The living world sparked Welty's imagination in her stories— actual events, bits of conversation, real places, are everywhere. But at the same time, Welty thoroughly reshaped the living world so that it might more effectively convey the values or emotions or sensations that had made it memorable to her. As Welty wrote in 1941 to her agent Diarmuid Russell: "What you look for in the world is not simply for what you want to know, but for more than you want to know, and more than you can know, better than you had wished for, and sometimes something draws you to a discovery and there is no other happiness quite the same." Here Welty eloquently describes her creative approach to experience. In his book *Fire in the Crucible: The Alchemy of Creative Genius*, John Briggs offers a more generalized and more academic analysis. He writes that the germ of a story "is in some way a fractal chip of vision. It is to the author like the chance discovery of a lens that holds promise of bringing the vision into focus in a concrete form. The germ contains an omnivalent nuance, a 'more'ness, a gleam of truth, a sense of wholeness. The wholeness of a germ is one of its most important characteristics."[1] As Welty began seriously writing in the 1930s, she excitedly made this very discovery; she recognized that fragmentary bits of an actual experience or place could prompt an imaginative vision of wholeness. And for many of her early stories—"The Whistle," "Powerhouse," and "A Piece of News," for example—Welty drew upon and transformed the world around her in order to focus upon the significance of the imagination, that crucial element of her inner life. Writing about the poverty and racism she had observed in Mississippi, Welty suggests that they may wound or destroy the imagination, but she further suggests that for some individuals the imagination may be resilient enough to combat even the physical suffering and psychological

---

1. Welty to Russell, n.d. [early October 1941], restricted papers, Welty Collection, Mississippi Department of Archives and History (hereafter referred to as MDAH), Jackson, and as cited by Michael Kreyling, *Author and Agent* (New York: Farrar, Straus, and Giroux, 1991), 11; John Briggs, *Fire in the Crucible* (New York: St. Martin's Press, 1988), 282.

despair that poverty and racism foster. She suggests that the most profound barriers between people spring from a lack of imagination and that imagination can provide moments of connection and communication that help compensate for material deprivation and challenge racial divisions. Imagination thus becomes a subject as well as a source of her stories, a subject and a source drawn from her most profound contemporary experiences. The result is a fiction that is the outside world's secret sharer, its second and more essential self.

In taking the imagination as her central subject, Welty set herself apart from the two poles of literary criticism that, as Alfred Kazin observed in 1942, were competing for followers in the thirties. Never did she or would she see fiction as a vehicle for advancing an ideology, as Marxist writers and critics did. Distressed as she was by the poverty and the racial oppression she encountered, Welty did not place her faith in an ideological solution. On the other hand, neither did she retreat from the world and embrace a formalist view of literature. For Welty, the literary imagination did not involve "an image of some perfect discipline and harmony, some perfect assemblage of movements, which gave the critic [or author] the advantage of a personal sense of order, a primary conception by which to read the world's folly and error."[2] Instead it involved encountering and embracing those who lived lives far different from her own. For Welty, works of the imagination or even moments of imaginative insight provided a means of parting "a curtain, that invisible shadow that falls between people, the veil of indifference to each other's presence, each other's wonder, each other's human plight" (*OTOP*, 8). And in parting that veil of indifference, Welty may well have done more both to call for reform and to establish the significance of the imagination than either the Marxists or the formalists could have conceived.

Welty's story "The Whistle" is based on actual events. A friend of Welty's lived in Utica, Mississippi, a truck farming center near Jackson, and Welty occasionally visited her there. In the thirties, during an overnight stay, Welty heard a piercing whistle warn local tenant farmers of a coming freeze. The uncle of Welty's friend, in fact, was the man who owned the tenants' land and who sounded

2. Alfred Kazin, *On Native Grounds* (New York: Reynal and Hitchcock, 1942), 400–52, 431.

the whistle. Though she had heard the whistle from the comfort of a fine house, the next morning Welty encountered visible signs of a poverty and a desperation she had never imagined: The fields were covered with clothes and bedclothes, anything the tenants could muster to protect their fragile crops. At her own home Welty had often gone out into the night to cover the camellias she so loved to grow, but never had her actions been crucial to her family's very existence. The distinction between her sheltered life and the lives of Mississippi's tenant farmers left an indelible impression upon her, and it soon inspired the plot of a story.[3]

Plot, Welty has written, "forms a kind of metaphor. . . . But a living metaphor. From the simplest to the most awesomely complicated, a plot is a device organic to human struggle designed for the searching out of human truth" (*ES*, 167). Certainly plot in "The Whistle" forms a kind of metaphor. The warning whistle wakes Jason and Sara Morton in the middle of a long, cold night. It commands them to rise and go into the moonlit fields. It requires that they use the pallets on which they sleep and the quilts they need for warmth to cover their tomato plants; it requires that even the clothes from their backs be removed and placed on the plants. The whistle represents an arbitrary and alien force, and Jason and Sara feel helpless and vulnerable in response to it.

That arbitrary and alien force, as W. U. McDonald has argued, is in large part a sharecropping system. The whistle "is known everywhere as Mr. Perkins' whistle" (*CG*, 111). And Mr. Perkins is the man who owns what was once the tenants' land and reaps the profits from it. He need not come into the fields himself; he merely blows the summoning whistle. His power as landowner seems absolute, and Jason and Sara's labors have left them without the energy to engage in protests like those waged by the Mississippi farmers who had joined organizations such as the Southern Tenant Farmers Union.

Moreover, Jason and Sara's despair is intensified because it is not Mr. Perkins alone who controls their lives. They are also victims of the natural world, and the whistle suggests the power that world holds over them. The natural world itself can be exceedingly arbitrary. Sara recognizes this fact as she recalls the history of their farming endeavors: "Now, according to the Almanac, it was spring.

3. Eudora Welty, interview by Marrs, 19 September 1985.

. . . But year after year it was always the same. The plants would be set out in their frames, transplanted always too soon, and there was a freeze. . . . When was the last time they had grown tall and full, that the cold had held off and there was a crop?" (*CG*, 109). The cold that threatens Sara and Jason is "like a white pressing hand"; it is as uncaring as the "hard, quick hand" Mr. Perkins extends at harvest time. The cold sinks into Jason and Sara "like the teeth of a trap" (*CG*, 111, 110, 113). Both the economic system of the thirties and the power of the natural world hold them prisoner. Jason and Sara Morton have little control over their own lives and have no way to contest that fact.

The whistle Welty actually heard, the man who sounded it, the farmers who responded to it thus all appear in "The Whistle," but Welty presents a selective account of her experience in Utica, Mississippi. She writes not about herself or her friend or her friend's fine house. She includes only those details that emphasize the injustice of a sharecropping system and the hard terms that nature inevitably imposes upon farmers. These concepts shine through what might have been only realistic description and exemplify the process Welty discusses in her essay "Words into Fiction." In that essay she first describes the pitch blackness of a cave, and she then writes that "without the act of human understanding— and it is a double act through which we make sense to each other—experience is the worst kind of emptiness; it is obliteration, black or prismatic, as meaningless as was indeed that loveless cave. Before there is meaning, there has to occur some personal act of vision. And it is this that is continuously projected as the novelist writes, and again as we, each to ourselves, read" (*ES*, 136–7).

Welty's selective vision, however, does more than illuminate an actual experience. Her ability to pierce the darkness of experience is matched by her ability to create actions that complement and complete the meaning she had seen in that experience. Perhaps the most striking event in "The Whistle" is one entirely of Welty's making, one she added when revising the periodical version of the story for book publication. When Jason and Sara return to their cabin, having left quilts and clothes in the fields, Jason rekindles their fire. And when they burn the last of their wood supply, he breaks up their wooden chair and their kitchen table and burns them. Alfred Appel suggests that the fire is an emblem of hope,[4] but this creation of Welty's imagination is also an emblem of memory and of imagination itself. The fire, the Mortons' one means of combating the cold, their one means of exerting control over their lives, suggests that they may not be totally helpless victims, that their barren past may in part be redeemed:

> And all of a sudden Jason was on his feet again. Of all things, he was bringing the split-bottomed chair over to the hearth. He knocked it to pieces. . . . It burned well and brightly. Sara never said a word. She did not move. . . .
>
> Then the kitchen table. To think that a solid, steady four-legged table like that, that had stood thirty years in one place, should be consumed in such a little while! Sara stared almost greedily at the waving flames.
>
> Then when that was over, Jason and Sara sat in darkness where their bed had been, and it was colder than ever. The fire the kitchen table had made seemed wonderful to them—as if what they had never said, and what could not be, had its life, too, after all. (*CG*, 114)

The fire suggests that "what could not be" can exist at least in the imagination.

Just as the fire in the story is associated with imaginative vision, it is also linked to memory. Earlier in the evening, lying in the cold house, Sara remembers the summer harvest time much as Welty herself actually remembered it:

> There in her mind, dusty little Dexter became a theater for almost legendary festivity, a place of pleasure. On every road leading in, smiling farmers were bringing in wagonloads of the most beautiful tomatoes. The packing sheds at Dexter Station were all decorated—no it was simply that the May sun was shining. . . . The music box was playing in the café across the way, and the crippled man that walked like a duck was back taking poses for a dime of the young people with their heads together. With shouts of triumph the men were getting drunk, and now and then a pistol went off somewhere. In the shade the children celebrated in tomato fights. A strong, heady, sweet smell hung over everything. Such excitement! (*CG*, 109–10)

4. Alfred Appel, *A Season of Dreams* (Baton Rouge: Louisiana State University Press, 1965), 11.

But Sara cannot sustain these happy summer memories. They come to her "only in brief snatches, like the flare-up of the little fire" (*CG*, 110). And ultimately the sound of the whistle outlasts the roaring blaze of the furniture. Imagination, memory, hope—the fire quite naturally suggests these three, for the fire frees Jason and Sara from the trap of the present moment and of the cold, but that freedom is fleeting. In creating the episode of the fire, Welty thus matched the flames of her imagination to a cold and very real Utica, Mississippi, night—her inner vision is matched to the living world as its secret sharer—and Welty's story is far more compelling as a result.

Finally, in "The Whistle" Welty finds a shared act of imagination to be crucial to communication and relationship. Sara and Jason have long been married, have long shared a one-room house, and have long failed to communicate: "Every night they lay trembling with cold, but no more communicative in their misery than a pair of window shutters beaten by a storm. Sometimes many days, weeks went by without words. They were not really old—they were only fifty; still, their lives were filled with tiredness, with a great lack of necessity to speak, with poverty which may have bound them like a disaster too great for any discussion but left them still separate and undesirous of sympathy. Perhaps, years ago, the long habit of silence may have been started in anger or passion. Who could tell now?" (*CG*, 108). The terms of their existence have destroyed any emotion that might have bound them together. But, as we have already seen, when Jason makes the fire, they know a moment of communication: "The fire the kitchen table had made seemed wonderful to them—as if what they had never said, and what could not be, had its life, too, after all" (*CG*, 114). Their common past, their desperate present, do not bind Jason and Sara together, but the fire helps them jointly to imagine the relationship they have missed, a relationship that momentarily seems to live, but that will not endure.

In "Powerhouse," a shared act of imagination is a way of momentarily overcoming the separation induced, not by poverty, but by racism and vocation. "Powerhouse" is a story that sprang both from Welty's outside world and from the depths of her inner life. In interviews Welty frequently recounted the story of a Fats Waller concert in Jackson, and she dealt most precisely with this source in a lecture she gave at Harvard University in 1983. She told the audience of her third Harvard lecture:

In "Powerhouse," I tried to turn the impromptu, frantic and abandoned playing together of a jazz pianist and his musicians into an exchange in words—something with its own rhythmic beat and crazy references, in the same onrush of performance. It was an attempt, like any other from a storywriter, to turn one sort of experience into another in order to convey it. During the '40s I was present at such a concert by Fats Waller; I hadn't dreamed I'd go home after it was over compelled to put down words. The story, all my invention, is nothing but the result of that evening: "Powerhouse" came from Fats Waller, and the story Powerhouse tells sprang from Fats Waller's *music*, out of his *performance* that night on stage. It was a one-time thing. I was not musically qualified to write it, but at the time of writing, I felt I was outside musical qualifications; it was a sort of combustion; I was writing about a demon.

In her attempt to "turn one sort of experience into another," Welty includes only a few details about the concert she actually heard, but those few details are crucial to the story's development. The story's opening and closing sections describe an event much like the one Welty attended: "It's a white dance, and nobody dances, except a few straggling jitterbugs and two elderly couples. Everybody just stands around the band and watches Powerhouse" (*CG*, 257). Though whites will not allow blacks to join them as members of the audience, they are fascinated by black musicians and their music. The irony of this typical situation clearly struck Welty, who during her student days in New York City had so often been to black nightclubs like Small's Paradise and the Cotton Club. And Welty intensifies the irony by locating the story's point of view in the white audience: "The point of view of this story," she noted, "is floating around somewhere in the concert hall—it belongs to the 'we' of the audience."[5] That audience is both attracted to and repelled by Powerhouse, by his artistry and by his blackness. "You know people on a stage—and people of a darker race—," the story's narrator observes, "so likely to be marvelous, frightening" (*CG*, 253–4). Of course, Powerhouse, whether marvelous or frightening, is "other" to his white southern audience. That audience will certainly not invite him to share their refreshments; he must walk to the World Café in Negrotown if he is to have a beer at intermis-

5. Eudora Welty, William E. Massey Lecture III, 6, Welty Collection, MDAH.

sion. The separation between black and white at the dance and at the café clearly betokens the larger separation that tragically governed southern society, its educational and religious institutions, professional opportunities, medical care, and political system.

But ultimately, Welty told interviewer Linda Kuehl, Powerhouse's role as "the traveling artist and performer—not Fats Waller himself, but any artist" separates him from the audience as absolutely as does his race.[6] "When somebody, no matter who, gives everything," the narrator says, "it makes people feel ashamed for him" (*CG*, 257). The fictional audience is not willing to take the kind of risks Powerhouse takes; its members are not willing to show their deepest emotions. Point of view thus emphasizes the alienation of the audience from the performer, for the white narrator finds Powerhouse's willingness to give everything to be as overwhelming a barrier as race, even in the segregated American South. Welty herself said that she was driven by "the love of her art and the love of giving it, the desire to give it until there is no more left" (*OWB*, 101). In this way she created Powerhouse out of her own inner life and used the actual situation of the concert to emphasize the separateness of the artist.

Much of what Welty wrote in "Powerhouse," of course, varies from events Welty had observed. In an attempt to capture the meaning of her experience, for instance, Welty shifted her story's setting away from actuality. Waller's concert took place in Welty's home town of Jackson. Though her fictional Mississippi River town called Alligator is Jackson in its size and ability to host touring concerts, its name was drawn from a small Mississippi Delta hamlet. A town called Alligator surely seems more provincial than a state capital, and a one-night stand in a town called Alligator emphasizes the transient life the musicians must lead, emphasizes how thoroughly they are cut off from home and loved ones and roots, emphasizes how much they have sacrificed for their profession.

Displaced though the musicians are, the African American community of Mississippi gave birth to the blues and might be expected to understand these black musicians. Certainly, Powerhouse and his band receive a warm reception at the World Café, but even there the artist is set apart from his audience. The

6. Linda Kuehl, "The Art of Fiction XLVII: Eudora Welty," in *Conversations with Eudora Welty*, ed. Peggy W. Prenshaw (Jackson: University Press of Mississippi, 1984), 85.

waitress, who delights in "talk and scares" (*CG*, 261), wants to know if the story Powerhouse tells of Gypsy is factual; she does not see its metaphoric import. The black hero Sugar Stick Thompson (whose name and exploits are based upon an actual hero named Sugarman), who "dove down to the bottom of July Creek and pulled up all those drownded white people fall out of a boat" (*CG*, 266), is totally inarticulate. And Powerhouse, for his part, is absolutely unwilling to relinquish center stage to the hapless Thompson. Welty has created this situation to reinforce what her actual experience had allowed her to see: The separateness that Powerhouse feels is as much a function of his vision and creativity, and his absorption in that vision and creativity, as it is of his race. He is set apart even in the World Café in Negrotown.

Most of what Welty wrote in "Powerhouse," of course, was an attempt to translate a musical experience into literary terms, and the act of translation is itself a way of overcoming the separateness imposed by language barriers. Alfred Appel long ago analyzed Welty's success in making this translation.[7] A brief reexamination of the musical qualities he identified in the story should thus suffice here. The characters' words in the story, for instance, are as rhythmic as had been the music that Welty heard. In the midst of playing a song, Powerhouse tells his fellow musicians about a telegram he had supposedly received, and his words match the tempo of the music he plays: "'Telegram say—here the words: Your wife is dead.' He puts 4/4 over the 3/4" (*CG*, 257). And when Powerhouse questions why his wife might have committed suicide, the rhythmic words continue to echo the music he is playing: "'Tell me, tell me, tell me.' He makes triplets, and begins a new chorus" (*CG*, 258). The rhythmic language of music and of the storyteller merge. In addition, Welty translates the improvisational nature of jazz into literary terms. Welty did not hear Fats Waller tell any stories about his wife, and she certainly never saw Waller go to a café like the World Café. But she invented this story and a location where Powerhouse could tell it in order to re-create a sense of Waller's improvisational genius. When Powerhouse tells his musicians about Gypsy's suicide, he is improvising:

"Listen how it is. My wife gets missing me. Gypsy. She goes to the window. She looks out and sees you know what. Street. Sign saying Hotel. People walking.

7. Appel, 153–8.

Somebody looks up. Old man. She looks down, out of the window. Well? . . . *Sssst! Plooey!* What she do? Jump out and bust her brains all over the world."

He opens his eyes. "That's it," agrees Valentine. "You gets a telegram."

"Sure she misses you," Little Brother adds.

"No, it's nighttime." How softly he tells them! "Sure. It's the nighttime. She say, What do I hear? Footsteps walking up the hall? That him? Footsteps go on off. It's not me. I'm in Alligator, Mississippi, she's crazy. Shaking all over. Listens till her ears and all grow out like old music-box horns but still she can't hear a thing. She says, All right! I'll jump out the window then." (*CG*, 263–4)

Powerhouse has received no telegram, and even if he had, he could not know how Gypsy had behaved. Clearly, he is shaping a story as he goes along just as Fats Waller would have improvised at the piano. And this improvised story re-creates for Welty's readers both the comic and tragic impact of Waller's music. The story of Uranus Knockwood finding Gypsy's body, for instance, causes everybody in the World Café to moan with pleasure (*CG*, 265), but when the waitress asks Powerhouse, "All that the truth?" he replies, "Truth is something worse, I ain't said what, yet" (*CG*, 266). Though Powerhouse's story of love and separation and death becomes comic in the telling, its import is tragic nonetheless. Welty's translation of the Waller concert is a very effective one—the rhythm, the improvisation, the mood of the concert are all captured in her story. And her translation in a sense penetrates the separateness about which she writes. She sees Waller in emblematic terms. In creating Powerhouse and having him tell the story of Gypsy's suicide, Welty depicts Powerhouse as more than a musician—he is the artist who is willing to contemplate the most unpalatable truths, the artist who is willing to endure separation, isolation, in order to practice his art, but who nevertheless is bound to other artists.

In "Powerhouse," therefore, we see both the external world of Welty's contemporary experience—the white dance with a black band—and the world of her own creation, and these two worlds are perfectly matched. The elements Welty drew from an actual concert and the events she created work harmoniously together to establish the fear and insecurity at the roots of racial prejudice, the nature and separateness of the artist, and the close connection between musician and storyteller. The living world and the created world combine also to sug-

gest that a shared act of imagination can bridge, if only momentarily, the separateness between individuals. Just as the story shows Powerhouse as set apart
from his audiences, it also shows the ways in which he does make contact.
Though neither the whites at their dance nor Alligator's black citizens whom
Powerhouse encounters at the World Café in Negrotown consciously recognize
themselves in his lyrics or tall tales, this "inspired" musician, this fanatic, gives
his white audience "the only time for hallucination" and leaves his black audience in a "breathless ring" (CG, 254, 265). At the dance he sends "everybody
into oblivion," and at the World Café "everybody in the room moans with pleasure" (CG, 254, 265). The song that closes Welty's story, the song she included
only because censors had rejected "Hold Tight, I Want Some Seafood Mama,"
seems particularly relevant to this issue of communication and imagination.[8]
"Somebody loves me, . . ." Powerhouse sings, "Maybe it's you" (CG, 269).
Maybe, just maybe, Powerhouse will have a deep and lasting effect upon a member of his audience—the probability seems slight. Still, the story's very existence
suggests that it is possible for a shared act of imagination to overcome barriers
between artist and audience, between black and white, and to extend beyond the
moment of performance. Fats Waller's Jackson concert, made "by the imagination for the imagination" (ES, 145), brought forth a rare, enduring, and imaginative response from a young white woman living in the Deep South. In the
story of "Powerhouse," the creative act came full circle, and Welty's outside
world became "a vital component" of her "inner life."

"A Piece of News" is based not upon a contemporary experience but upon
an experience Eudora Welty had as a University of Wisconsin student. During
the Christmas vacation of her junior year, Welty visited the Lewistown, Montana, home of a college friend. This girl's father edited the local newspaper and
was happy to hire Welty as a reporter for the duration of her visit. While Welty
was at the newspaper office one day, a local woman snow-shoed into town to
demand a retraction: The report that her husband had shot her, she declared,
was absolutely false.[9] The humor of the situation struck nineteen-year-old Eudora Welty, but the incident also elicited a more serious and enduring reaction.

8. Kreyling, *Author and Agent*, 54.
9. Eudora Welty, interview by Marrs, 7 December 1985.

Ten years later Welty would use this event as the basis for "A Piece of News." The power of the written word to evoke an emotional response and the Montana woman's fear that readers would believe whatever they had seen in print—this more than the humor of the occurrence—stayed with Welty and became the germ for her story. Drawing upon distant memories was a process that eventually would become very important to Welty's writing, but it is quite unusual in *A Curtain of Green*, and it is not surprising that Welty chose to set the story in a locale more congenial to her imagination, a locale much like ones she had recently visited when traveling through North Mississippi for the Works Progress Administration. And as she describes isolated, poor, and largely uneducated individuals like those she so often encountered on her WPA travels, Welty implicitly suggests the importance of the printed word, the role only it can play in overcoming a poverty of experience and spirit.

In "A Piece of News" Mississippian Ruby Fisher, hale, hearty, and unwounded, reads in a newspaper that "Mrs [sic] Ruby Fisher had the misfortune to be shot in the leg by her husband this week," but Ruby does not realize that the paper has been brought from Tennessee by a traveling salesman and that the newspaper's Ruby Fisher merely shares her name. Instead she thinks, "That's me" and becomes angry with her husband. Though she soon realizes that "it was unlike Clyde to take up a gun and shoot her" (*CG*, 23, 24), she pushes that knowledge from her mind and goes on to imagine her death and burial.

In this story there is no newspaper office, there is no thought of a retraction demand, and emotions are not limited to indignation and anger. One reason for these differences between fact and fiction may lie in what Welty calls "a story-writer's truth": the story-writer, she explains, knows that "the thing to wait on, to reach there in time for, is the moment in which people reveal themselves" (*OTOP*, 7–8). In creating "A Piece of News," Welty intuitively recognized that she had not seen the Montana woman at the right moment, that the moment of revelation had already occurred. Had Welty set her story in a newspaper office and focused upon a retraction demand, her character could have revealed only a narrow range of emotions. The created narrative moves backward in time and allows Welty to accomplish far more with character. Ruby Fisher feels anger, elation, surprise, amazement, pain, and happiness immediately after reading the newspaper. Ruby is a simple-minded woman, living a routine and barren existence—for her a gift of coffee is a luxury, owning a nightgown, especially a new nightgown, is possible only in dreams, and seeing a newspaper is a most rare occurrence. The newspaper, however, suggests that something dramatic can happen even to her. It suggests something about the possibilities of experience. And Ruby is at first frightened, then entranced by that suggestion:

> At once she was imagining herself dying. She would have a nightgown to lie in, and a bullet in her heart. Anyone could tell, to see her lying there with that deep expression about her mouth, how strange and terrible that would be. Underneath a brand-new nightgown her heart would be hurting with every beat, many times more than her toughened skin when Clyde slapped at her. Ruby began to cry softly, the way she would be crying from the extremity of pain; tears would run down in a little stream over the quilt. Clyde would be standing there above her, as he once looked, with his wild black hair hanging to his shoulders. He used to be very handsome and strong!
>
> He would say, "Ruby, I done this to you."
>
> She would say—only a whisper—"That is the truth, Clyde—you done this to me."
>
> Then she would die; her life would stop right there. She lay silently for a moment, composing her face into a look which would be beautiful, desirable, and dead. (*CG*, 25)

Ruby here imagines her way into a melodramatic scene, and she makes herself appropriately beautiful and well clad for the scene just as she makes Clyde appropriately wild and handsome. The newspaper story strikes her imagination. Scarcely able to read, Ruby is nevertheless affected by the written word. The article brings Ruby a sense that she has lived her life with passionate intensity. She is concerned not with factual accuracy, as the Montana woman was, but with what might have been. The newspaper story reaches her imagination, as Cleanth Brooks has noted, just as Welty's story reaches ours.[10] The power of fiction, the power to make illusion seem real, the power upon which Welty was just beginning to draw, is thus a central subject of this story.

10. Cleanth Brooks, "American Literature: Mirror, Lens, or Prism?" in *A Shaping Joy* (New York: Harcourt Brace Jovanovich, 1971), 172.

Though her concept of the story had emerged from a Montana locale, Welty never thought of using Montana as its setting. Her imagination gravitated toward a world she knew far better. The small cabin in which Ruby cooks on an open fire and uses an oil lamp for light was like many Welty had seen as she traveled for the WPA in 1936, and the country of North Mississippi could well foster the isolation and lack of sophistication that make Ruby believable. North Mississippi was as remote as Montana from urban centers—if not in terms of miles, in terms of the immobility of its people. Moreover, Ruby's poverty, circumscribed experience, and near illiteracy—traits so common in Depression-era Mississippi—suggest her poverty of spirit, a poverty that can be enriched only by access to the written word. And Welty associates the power of the written word with the elemental force of a typical Mississippi thunderstorm, not a Montana snowstorm. McDonald links the storm in the story to "the tumult of Ruby's emotions,"[11] but the storm seems more importantly to reinforce the tremendous imaginative reaction Ruby has to the newspaper story. When Ruby first recognizes her own name in the story, she goes straight to her cabin door and opens it: "A shudder of cold brushed over her in the heat, and she seemed striped with anger and bewilderment. There was a flash of lightning, and she stood waiting, as if she half thought that would bring him in, a gun leveled in his hands"(CG, 23). But Clyde, as Ruby knows, is afraid of storms. Only in her imagination can he be equated with the force of the thunderstorm. Still Ruby persists in imagining her way into a melodrama. And when she imagines her funeral, rain is an important element: "The white rain splashed down. She could hardly breathe, for thinking that this was the way it was to fall on her grave, where Clyde would come and stand, looking down in the tears of some repentance. A whole tree of lightning stood in the sky. She kept looking out the window, suffused with the warmth from the fire and with the pity and beauty and power of her death. The thunder rolled" (CG, 26). But the violent spectacle of what might have been and of the thunderstorm cannot last. When Clyde realizes that the newspaper story is about another Ruby Fisher, imagination ceases. Its cessation is matched by the cessation of the storm: "Ruby folded her still

11. W. U. McDonald, "Eudora Welty's Revisions of 'A Piece of News,'" *Studies in Short Fiction* 7 (Spring 1970): 245.

trembling hands into her skirt. She stood stooping by the window until every-thing, outside and in, was quieted before she went to her supper. It was dark and vague outside. The storm had rolled away to faintness like a wagon crossing a bridge" (*CG*, 29).

Clearly, Welty has drawn upon the real world in creating "A Piece of News," but she is truer to the meaning she found implicit in that world than she is to its explicit qualities. The power of literature is seen in the power of a newspaper story; the capricious, uncontrollable force of the imagination is evident in the thunderstorm so typical of Mississippi weather. And Welty has drawn upon ac-tual experience, matching it to her imagination, in still a third respect. Implicit in the Montana experience is the notion of a relationship. The woman on snow shoes came to town to protest the misrepresentation of her relationship with her husband. Welty never saw the husband, but she must have wondered how he had reacted to the article and must have wondered if he were capable of violence. In "A Piece of News" she gives these speculations life and creates a husband and a relationship. Clyde, a large, bald-headed, unromantic man, is scarcely the man Ruby sees in her imagination, the "handsome and strong" man with "wild black hair hanging to his shoulders" (*CG*, 25). Clyde and Ruby feel no physical attrac-tion for each other; they share little more than their small, sparsely furnished cabin, and they scarcely ever see other people. When the poverty of her emo-tional life with Clyde makes Ruby melancholy, she seeks out the company of a traveling salesman, but her infidelity does not endanger their marriage. Clyde merely slaps her, and life continues apace. There seems to be little passion, little communication, in their marriage. The misleading newspaper article, however, offers the hope of communication. Clyde's first response to the article is to brand it a lie—he seems more like the Montana woman than does Ruby. But soon Clyde seems almost to share Ruby's belief in the article's veracity: "Slowly they both flushed, as though with a double shame and a double pleasure. It was as though Clyde might really have killed Ruby, and as though Ruby might really have been dead at his hand. Rare and wavering, some possibility stood timidly like a stranger between them and made them hang their heads" (*CG*, 28). A shared act of imagination brings Clyde and Ruby very close, closer than sharing the same food, the same cabin, the same bed have brought them, and we sense the existence of a third character, of a stranger who is the incarnation of a relationship between the two. But this third person is soon gone. Clyde realizes the article is from a Tennessee paper and that it does not describe them. Clyde laughs, and they return to their routine existence, meaningless as it is. For a moment Clyde and Ruby have shared shame and pleasure, but the relationship that exists for them is tragically short-lived.[12]

The power of the imagination is thus central to Welty's achievement in "A Piece of News." Imagination allowed her to develop what might have seemed just an amusing occurrence into a significant story, and within that story imagination alone brings the possibility of meaning and communication to characters whose lives have been restricted by their poverty and lack of education. In her essay "Words into Fiction" Welty says that fiction is made "by the imagination for the imagination," that it is "an illusion come full circle—a very exclusive thing, for all it seems to include a good deal of the world" (ES, 145). In "A Piece of News" the imagination comes full circle, moving from Welty through her characters and finally affecting her readers. It shows us "a good deal of the world" Welty had seen on her trip to Montana and on her more recent trips through Depression-era Mississippi, but ultimately it allows us to experience the power of the imagination as it exists in fiction and as it affects human relationships.

In "The Whistle," "Powerhouse," and "A Piece of News," we see just how the outside world functions in Eudora Welty's early fiction. Visiting Utica, Mississippi, attending a Fats Waller concert, and working in a Montana newspaper office—these activities fired Welty's imagination, and her imagination in turn transformed and bestowed significance upon them. Welty's creative process thus

---

12. In "No Place for You, My Love," two strangers take a day-long journey south of New Orleans, and as Michael Kreyling has noted in *Eudora Welty's Achievement of Order* (Baton Rouge: Louisiana State University Press, 1980), Welty describes them in the same way she describes Clyde and Ruby. Welty says of "No Place for You, My Love": "As I wrote further into the story, something more real, more essential, than the characters were on their own was revealing itself. In effect, though the characters numbered only two, there had come to be a sort of third character along on the ride—the presence of a relationship between the two" (ES, 111–2). And though the third characters in both "A Piece of News" and "No Place for You, My Love" live only briefly, they are significant. What Welty says of "No Place for You, My Love" she might have said of either story: "This third character's role was that of hypnosis—it was what a relationship *can do*, be it however brief, tentative, potential, happy or sinister, ordinary or extraordinary" (ES, 112).

seems intrinsic to the themes of her stories. Both the method of composition and the plots of "The Whistle," "Powerhouse," and "A Piece of News" suggest that imagination is crucial to human understanding and communication; it is the only means by which Jason and Sara Morton, Powerhouse and his audience, Ruby and Clyde Fisher, Welty and her readers, communicate. Individuals may seem too tired to communicate, too poorly educated to enjoy the written word, too isolated to have access to great art or great music, too prejudiced to recognize the genius of those different from themselves, but they may still possess the power of the imagination, and their lives may be metaphorically, if not literally, enriched by it. Though the living world is a "vital component" of Welty's achievement as a writer, her own transcendent imagination, which had just begun to assert its power, is that world's secret sharer, the essence of its fictional life, and the source of its most profound meaning.

The stories Eudora Welty would eventually collect in the volume called *A Curtain of Green* all saw periodical publication before they were grouped together as a book. These stories, which had typically been inspired by Welty's contemporary experiences of poverty and racism in Mississippi, were typically composed in a rather spontaneous fashion. Welty told interviewer John Griffin Jones, "That first book of stories really was spontaneous. They were almost never revised. They would've been the better for it. It never occurred to me. I thought you sat down and wrote a story sort of the way you read—you know, you just sit down and write it."[13] Welty's memory is for the most part accurate. Though the Mississippi Department of Archives and History holds revisions to many of the early stories, these revisions did not characteristically arise because Welty was dissatisfied with first or second drafts of unpublished stories or because she saw new directions or possibilities for her stories about the lives of Depression-era Mississippians. She revised most of these early stories not before periodical publication, but only when she had a final chance to rework the accepted manuscript before book publication. With the reality of a book in view, Welty wanted to polish her stories, but even these revisions, which took place some time after

13. John Griffin Jones, "Eudora Welty," in *Conversations with Eudora Welty*, ed. Peggy W. Prenshaw (Jackson: University Press of Mississippi, 1984), 325.

most of the stories had been first published, were not radical in nature. Welty might shift a setting from one Mississippi town to another, but she did not in revising move her story from one region to an entirely different one. She might add an incident to plot, but she did not develop a wholly new action to carry her meaning. She might revise to develop a character in a more consistent or more sympathetic fashion, but she did not add new characters or discard old ones. Indeed, Welty's agent Diarmuid Russell cautioned her not to alter the stories too extensively—the magazines, he said, might ask "What's This?"[14] As a result, though Welty's revisions to these early stories might be thorough—lists of textual variants between periodical and book publication are often extensive, and McDonald has demonstrated how crucial these changes can be to the artistry of a story—they usually fine-tuned the story rather than radically altering it. And the fine-tuning Welty undertook with these stories seems designed to provide for the reader the same sense of imagination's power that Welty had felt in first writing them; her revisions seem designed to stress the power that gave the stories existence in the first place.

Welty's revision of "The Whistle," as we have seen, involved the addition of the story's most crucial scene, and that scene clearly asserts the importance of imaginative union to people trapped in cycles of poverty. Revisions in "Death of a Traveling Salesman" at first seem set in counterpoint to those in "The Whistle," for in this story, revision stresses the way that imagination isolates the traveling salesman R. J. Bowman. Bowman, in attempting to reach Beulah, Mississippi, has lost his way and seen his car plunge into a ravine. He must seek help at a nearby dogtrot farmhouse, where a poor couple enjoy a most meager existence. There, in the book version of the story, he sees the farmwife holding a lamp—rural electrification has not reached her home. Later he wonders why the woman does not finish cleaning the lamp. Still later she lights the half-cleaned lamp, and the whole room turns "golden-yellow like some sort of flower" (*CG*, 245). Finally, when Bowman leaves the house, he violates the customs of hospitality and puts money under the lamp. Almost none of the lamp imagery appears in the periodical version of the story, but Welty wisely incorporated it into the

14. Russell to Welty, 18 February 1941, restricted papers, Welty Collection, MDAH, Jackson.

story's final version. This addition intensifies the symbolic or imaginative vision Bowman takes of the farmwife and her husband. To the traveling salesman, they seem in both versions of the story to withhold "some ancient promise of food and warmth and light" (*CG*, 244). But only in the *Curtain of Green* text does the woman with a lamp come to be an emblem of enlightenment and insight and meaning for Bowman. Such a vision need not be isolating—but Bowman can never communicate his vision to her, and he is reluctant to accept that the relationship between the poverty-stricken farm couple can be meaningful and mysterious without being rare or exotic. The repeated references to the lamp thus suggest that Bowman is at once more imaginative and more isolated than he had been in the earlier version. The power that enabled Welty to write this story is a power that fails to sustain her protagonist because he, unlike the writer who was finding a considerable readership, fails to trust himself or to share his vision.

Similarly, a deletion from the periodical version of the story establishes Bowman's quest for the town of Beulah and his vision of the farm couple as a more imaginative and metaphorical one than it had been. As the periodical story draws to a close, Bowman decides to leave Rafe and his wife five dollars:

> He paused then, a last surge of guilt sweeping over him. He remembered, distastefully, another time he had tiptoed, that first time, when he had not been able to pay a blackhaired girl on McKee Street enough, and had crept away while she was still asleep, leaving what he had in his pocket stacked—it was mostly in dimes and quarters—under the loud-ticking clock beside the paper rose, thinking, with the startled first valuations of manhood, I would like to give her five dollars.
>
> He had been proud and shy, then, and life had held out a fresh mystery to him.[15]

The relationship with the prostitute, though this earlier Bowman associates it with mystery, detracts from the romantic nature of Bowman's quest for the "remote and mysterious." It suggests that his need for love involves no distinction between casual sex and an ongoing relationship. Such is not the case in the re-

15. Eudora Welty, "Death of a Traveling Salesman," *Manuscript* 3 (May–June 1936): 29.

vised version of the story, for this passage is gone. Instead Bowman wishes that Sonny's unborn child were his own. He momentarily recognizes that the mysterious and the fulfilling aspects of life need not be remote, that they can be found in the commitments of "a marriage, a fruitful marriage" (*CG*, 248), but ultimately he flees that knowledge, leaving the cabin and offering payment for hospitality. He refuses to acknowledge that poor and isolated individuals may lead harmonious lives, may be able to communicate without words, may experience an intuitive or imaginative unity. His departure is an act of condescension to the couple; he finds comfort in the false assumption that their financial need betokens spiritual need; it does not.

Welty's revisions to "Clytie" complement those she made in "Death of a Traveling Salesman." Here Welty deals with the literal and psychological poverty that has descended upon a once prosperous family and its deeply disturbed daughter. From the earliest available version of the story, the problem for Clytie is not a lack of imagination, but the inability to use her imagination to create her own identity and to connect with others. And Welty revised an early draft of the story so that her protagonist's failure to join in a shared act of imagination becomes the very center of the story. Clytie is the antithesis of Eudora Welty, who in photographing Mississippians during the Depression found that she was "imagining myself into their lives" (*OTOP*, 6). Clytie cannot imagine herself into the lives of others because she has no life of her own. She cannot transcend her isolation because she has no self to transcend. The recognition of this fact destroys her. As Welty told Charles Bunting in a discussion of *Losing Battles*, "Unless you are very real in yourself, you don't know what it means to support others or to join with them or to help them."[16] Clytie's life has been a record of missed opportunities, opportunities to define the self, and this record of missed opportunities parallels her family's decline from prosperity to straitened circumstances in which, as the town postmistress observes, their bills "would never be paid any more than any anyone else's" (*CG*, 156). Her family's financial ruin suggests the poverty of personal resources that are Clytie's.

16. Charles T. Bunting, "'The Interior World': An Interview with Eudora Welty," in *Conversations with Eudora Welty*, ed. Peggy W. Prenshaw (Jackson: University Press of Mississippi, 1984), 49.

In an early version of the story, Clytie thinks about the faces of her family members and recalls, "It was their faces which had come pushing in front of the face of love, long ago, when she was young. In a sort of arbor, she had laughed, leaned forward . . . and the face of love, which was a little like all the other faces . . . —and yet different, yet far more—this face of love had been very close, almost familiar, almost accessible." Clytie, it seems, leads a grotesque, warped existence because her family has blocked her quest for love, perhaps the love of a particular man. But when Welty concludes the story by having Clytie recognize "the face of love" staring back at her from a rain barrel and by describing Clytie as "sick at heart, as though the poor, half-remembered face of love had finally betrayed her,"[17] Welty elicits a startled recognition from her readers. Only at this final moment do readers recognize that Clytie's search for the face of love has been a search for herself, a quest to imagine the possibilities for her own development.

In revising her story, Welty relinquished this moment of ironic revelation in favor of more sustained thematic development. Clytie's quest throughout the final story is more figurative than literal. No longer does Clytie seek the "face of love." Now she seeks "a face." Thus, when this Clytie recognizes her own reflection as the face from which she had become separated, surprise is not the primary effect Welty achieves. Instead the reader feels an understanding and a sympathy that the earlier version had precluded. Clytie fails to communicate and connect with others, the story suggests, because she has failed to create herself. In the published story, therefore, Clytie's recognition of her own face comes not so much as an ironic revelation as a completed pattern. Clytie has not been able to love herself or to give love. For Clytie there is no shared act of imagination. She wants the connection such an act can bring—she finds faces to be "the most moving sight in the whole world" (*CG*, 159), but she never can connect. Her meditations are always interrupted; she asks herself, "Was it possible to comprehend the eyes and the mouths of other people, which concealed she knew not what, and secretly asked for still another unknown thing?" (*CG*, 159). She clearly feels the answer is no. When Mr. Bobo comes to shave her father, there

---

17. Eudora Welty, "Clytie," in "Stories," Welty Collection, MDAH, 7, 13.

seems momentarily to be hope. She looks at his "pitiful, greedy, small face" (*CG*, 169) and responds not with repulsion but with sympathy. She compares him to a stray kitten, and she touches his cheek with "breathtaking gentleness." But this moment is cut short as both Clytie and Mr. Bobo give "despairing" cries, and afterwards Clytie can "hardly bear . . . the thought of that face" (*CG*, 170). Mr. Bobo has seemed like Hermes to Clytie, and he might have become a messenger of the gods, a messenger who could tell Clytie what she had been seeking. But instead this Hermes plays another role—he leads Clytie to her death. It is after her encounter with Mr. Bobo that Clytie sees her reflection in the rain barrel and drowns herself. In her reflection, she discovers a face full of waiting and suffering, a face that has not imagined a life for itself. She discovers a self never created, an absence that precludes relationships with others.

Peter Schmidt believes that Welty "seems to have feared that Clytie's fate may be the fate of any woman of imagination, incurring the anger of her community and perhaps even the curse of insanity."[18] But Welty suggests not that imagination is the source of Clytie's difficulties, but that her inability to imagine a life beyond the demands of family and community and her inability to identify with others are the forces that doom her. Imagination can be healing and restoring, but only if it leads to communication. In the revised "Clytie" this notion is forcefully advanced, and Eudora Welty's reverence for the imagination is once again evident.

In revising "The Hitch-Hikers" Welty added an incident to plot, an incident that involves the reader in the life of a decaying Delta town and an incident with a metaphoric purpose that links the story to "Clytie." In the periodical version of this story Harris goes to a party at his friend Ruth's house, but that party does not include a trip to Leland to pick up a date for Harris. It does in the story's final version:

> They all drove over in two cars to get her.
> She was a slight little thing, with her nightgown in some sort of little bag.
> She came out when they blew the horn, before he could go in after her. . . .

18. Peter Schmidt, *The Heart of the Story* (Jackson: University Press of Mississippi, 1991), 31.

"Let's go holler off the bridge," said somebody in the car ahead.

They drove over a little gravel road, miles through the misty fields, and came to the bridge out in the middle of nowhere.

"Let's dance," said one of the boys. He grabbed Carol around the waist, and they began to tango over the boards.

"Did you miss me?" asked Ruth. She stayed by him, standing in the road.

"Woo-hoo!" they cried.

"I wish I knew what makes it holler back," said one girl. "There's nothing anywhere. Some of my kinfolks can't even hear it."

"Yes, it's funny," said Harris, with a cigarette in his mouth.

"Some people say it's an old steamboat got lost once."

"Might be."

They drove around and waited to see if it would stop raining. (*CG*, 130–1)

This moveable feast, this traveling party, typifies life in the Mississippi Delta and seems appropriately flamboyant and high-spirited. But these high spirits mask a longing for something more, for the mysterious and unconventional. The townspeople are fascinated by the mysterious echo, and indulging their imaginations about its source brings them enjoyment. Their "mock rambles" (*CG*, 135; a phrase Welty added in revising the story), their long journeys to holler off a bridge or to see if the rain will stop, are efforts to transcend the conventional and uneventful life of their small town with its "ramshackle hospital," shabby hotel, and one ancient taxi. In fact, the townspeople seek the freedom known by the down-and-out hitchhikers whose lives are defined by actual, not mock, rambling, but they ultimately learn that the hitchhikers' actual rambles are characterized by inarticulate anger, empty conversation, theft, and murder. These professional wanderers experience no triumphs of the imagination and are unable to communicate; they lead essentially barren and empty lives, more barren and empty than those experienced by the citizens of Dulcie, Mississippi. Imagination, the story thus suggests, is not a function of rootlessness or of rootedness. Hitchhikers and townspeople alike need the sort of connection that a shared act of imagination can bring.

A similar poverty of imagination typifies Old Mr. Marblehall's Natchez, though literal poverty does not play a role here. Revisions to the periodical story titled "Old Mr. Grenada" create a narrator who desperately needs to communicate an imagined life to his unknown audience, but who seems unable to understand himself or to communicate with the people around him. As Catherine Chengges has observed, Welty altered her picture of the narrator by having his direct address of the reader become more frequent and more intense. In "Old Mr. Grenada," the narrator reports that Mr. Grenada "looks so old that you realize how precious old people get to thinking their insides are." But in "Old Mr. Marblehall," the revised version of the story, the narrator instructs the reader: "Watch and you'll see how preciously old people come to think they are made" (*CG*, 175). Later in the first paragraph, the narrator in "Old Mr. Grenada" describes the protagonist's tweed coat and reports, "Even in summer he wears it," but in "Old Mr. Marblehall," the narrator speaks directly to the reader: "You see, even in summer he wears it" (*CG*, 175). The narrator thus calls far greater attention to himself in the final version of the story, and he reveals his own dilemma. Like Mr. Marblehall, the narrator seems to value the unconventional even as he is caught in the grasp of convention. Chengges argues that the revisions show "Mr. Marblehall's special imagination . . . more fully," but in fact they emphasize the *narrator's* special imagination, his attempts to transcend a mundane world and to have us share in his feat. The narrator in "Old Mr. Grenada" describes the title character's new home in these words: "From the outside you know the inside is dark with old things about. For instance, there would be a big deathly-looking tapestry, wrinkling and thin."[19] But the narrator of "Old Mr. Marblehall" is a more inventive chap: "You have every reason in the world to imagine the inside is dark, with old things about. There's many a big, deathly-looking tapestry, wrinkling and thin, many a sofa shaped like an S. Brocades as tall as the wicked queens in Italian tales stand gathered before the windows" (*CG*, 177). This narrator explicitly tells us that his description is an imagined one, but then proceeds to set forth the description in an absolute, not hypothetical, fashion and to provide details the previous narrator did not invent. The narrator of "Old Mr. Marblehall" needs a life that allows him to exercise his imagination, but he offers us no indication that he leads such

19. Eudora Welty, "Old Mr. Grenada," *Southern Review* 3 (Spring 1938): 707, 707, 708; Catherine Chengges, "Textual Variants in 'Old Mr. Marblehall,'" *Eudora Welty Newsletter* 10, no. 2 (1986): 1.

a life. He seems instead a sort of voyeur; he views Mr. Marblehall's ineffectual attempts at rebellion with condescension, yet offers no evidence that he has coped with the problem more effectively. Thus, when he says that Old Mr. Marblehall "dreams that he is a great blazing butterfly stitching up a net; which doesn't make sense" (*CG*, 185), he reveals more about himself than he does about Mr. Marblehall. He has created this dream for Mr. Marblehall, but neither the narrator nor Mr. Marblehall is capable of understanding the dream. In their efforts to break free, they have unwittingly caught themselves in another net of convention. This revised narrator thus contributes greatly to the effectiveness of "Old Mr. Marblehall." The narrator's direct address of the reader and increased use of detail make the story more vivid, more immediate, but more importantly they redefine the story's central issues.

Both the origins of and the revisions to *A Curtain of Green* establish the importance Eudora Welty placed upon imagination and the external world that sustains it. Beginning her career as a writer, Welty clearly found that the exercise of her own imaginative powers was exhilarating. She found that contemporary Mississippi was full of meaning for the imaginative observer, and her early stories emerged from that sort of observation. But Welty was also convinced of imagination's importance to individuals other than writers. In writing of desolate, poverty-stricken, isolated, oppressed people, Welty suggests that poverty and racism can be destructive of the imagination, but she also suggests that imagination may offer individuals a way to mitigate their circumstances. And in revising her stories Welty intensified this suggestion. *A Curtain of Green* is perhaps the darkest of Welty's works, but the imagination, which illuminated Welty's own life, also provides the possibility of hope and meaning for characters who seem otherwise trapped and defeated. In recognizing and using her own imaginative powers, Welty thus found the origins of her first stories and their most profound thematic statement.

III

# "The Strength of an Instinct . . . the Power of an Art"

### History and Memory in *The Robber Bridegroom* and *The Wide Net*

When Eudora Welty wrote *The Robber Bridegroom,* before she completed *A Curtain of Green,* she found her inspiration in relatively uncharted territory, and as she wrote the stories to be collected in *The Wide Net,* she continued to explore this new territory. For these two books, Welty looked to the Natchez Trace region of Mississippi and to the past—both historical and personal. As Welty in retrospect pointed out, the world of the present served as the starting point for most stories in *A Curtain of Green*—not so for *The Robber Bridegroom* and *The Wide Net.* Early in the 1930s, William Hamilton, then a teacher at Jackson's Central High School and later a professor at Duke University, introduced Eudora Welty and other friends to a legendary history of the Natchez Trace—Robert Coates's *The Outlaw Years.* And by 1940 Welty had begun to write her Natchez Trace stories, drawing upon historical sources. She later recalled, "I had been working for the WPA or for the Mississippi Advertising Commission. In the course of my work I had to do a lot of reading on the Natchez Trace. I'm not a writer who writes fiction by research, but reading these primary sources, such as Dow's sermons, Murrell's diary and letters of the time, fired my imagination. I thought how much like fairy tales all of those things were."[1] *The Robber Bridegroom* and two stories from *The Wide Net* thus took their sources from local history, and local history in turn brought to Welty's mind childhood memories of the Brothers Grimm. Similarly, reading local history sent Welty on trip after trip along the Natchez Trace to Rodney, Mississippi, a place she photographed and about which she subsequently wrote a travel essay. There she discovered a past-haunted landscape, a landscape unlike any she had encountered before. Finally, Welty's excursions into nineteenth-century Mississippi history and the landscape where it had occurred sent her on one other journey, a journey into her own past.

As long ago as 1943 and as recently as 1998, critics have seen this focus upon the past as evasive and glamorizing. They have depicted Welty as a woman who refused to confront the political complexities of the present.[2] Yet though both *The Robber Bridegroom* and *The Wide Net* show a new focus upon the past, Welty views the past in these stories from the very distinctive perspective of the early 1940s, a time in which a war in Europe and ultimately a world war were the central concerns in her life. Reading about fascism, talking about it with friends like Katherine Anne Porter, learning of German military aggression, seeing the United States enter the war, worrying about her friends and family who served in the armed forces, sensing the horror of war itself and the horror that a fascist triumph would bring—the powerful emotions evoked by the events of 1939–1942 inevitably influenced Welty's depiction of the past. And in depicting the past, Welty created emblems of a contemporary international situation that for her resisted direct transformation into art. Indeed, in both *The Robber Bridegroom* and *The Wide Net*, violent acts of self-assertion, rejections of diversity, and quests to define the past authoritatively are embodied in plots that emerge from regional history, fairy tale, and autobiography, but that also implicitly allow Welty to challenge, in what may or may not always have been a conscious fashion, the dogma that leaders like Hitler daily espoused.

1. Nash K. Burger, "Eudora Welty's Monsieur Boule and Other Friends," *Southern Quarterly* 32, no. 1 (1993): 43; "An Interview with Eudora Welty," in *Conversations with Eudora Welty*, ed. Peggy W. Prenshaw (Jackson: University Press of Mississippi, 1984), 24.

2. See Diana Trilling, "Fiction in Review," *Nation*, 2 October 1943, 386–7 and Claudia Roth Pierpont, "A Perfect Lady," *New Yorker*, 5 October 1998, 94–104.

As Peggy Prenshaw's 1970 doctoral dissertation first established fully, Robert M. Coates's *The Outlaw Years* (1930) introduced Welty to many vivid stories about the trail from Nashville to Natchez and the outlaws who worked it in the late eighteenth and early nineteenth centuries. In *The Robber Bridegroom*, Welty was able to create Jamie Lockhart, Little Harp, and Mike Fink primarily because she had read Coates, but memories of childhood reading were equally important. Clement, Salome, and Rosamond all have their counterparts in the fairy tales young Eudora Welty had devoured. The importance of such childhood reading has been recognized by many writers. Elizabeth Bowen, a novelist whom Welty greatly admired and who became a close friend, has written, "The imagination, which may appear to bear such individual fruit, is rooted in a compost of forgotten books. The apparent choices of art are nothing but addictions, predispositions; where did these come from, how were they formed? The aesthetic is nothing but a return to images that will allow nothing to take their place. . . . All susceptibility belongs to the age of magic, the Eden where fact and fiction were the same; the imaginative writer was the imaginative child."[3] Perhaps this was one reason that *The Robber Bridegroom* was written quickly, easily, with slight revision. As Welty read about the Natchez Trace, she recalled the fairy tales she had loved as an imaginative child, and she felt compelled to turn them into fiction.

But perhaps the worlds of history and fairy tale converged most fully for Welty when she actually went to visit the Natchez Trace country. It seemed an extravagant, fantastic landscape to her. Welty describes her visits to this country as commencing in the little town of Port Gibson:

> A narrow gravel road goes into the West. You have entered the loess country, and a gate might have been shut behind you for the difference in the world. All about are hills and chasms of cane, forests of cedar trees, and magnolia. Falling

---

3. Peggy W. Prenshaw, "A Study of Setting in the Fiction of Eudora Welty" (Ph.D. diss., University of Texas, 1970), 224–33; see Charles Clark, "*The Robber Bridegroom*: Realism and Fantasy on the Natchez Trace," *Mississippi Quarterly* 26 (Fall 1973): 625–38, for a useful listing of relevant fairy tales; Elizabeth Bowen, "Out of a Book," in *The Mulberry Tree*, ed. Hermione Lee (San Diego, New York, London: Harcourt Brace Jovanovich, 1986), 53.

away from your road, at times merging with it, an old trail crosses and recrosses, like a tunnel through the dense brakes, under arches of branches, a narrow, cedar-smelling trace the width of a horseman. The road joined the Natchez Trace to the river. It, too, was made by buffaloes, then used by man, trodden lower and lower, a few inches every hundred years. (*ES*, 287)

Welty seems to describe an enchanted world, one totally different from everyday experience—a gate shuts behind you when you enter this world, and mysterious, aromatic tunnels are all about. In the Trace country, Welty continues, there are "nests for birds and thrones for owls and trapezes for snakes, every kind of bower in the world" (*ES*, 295). This country seemed to her the very place where fairy tales might actually occur, and she responded to this world with the same sort of wonder she had experienced in reading fairy tales.

History also seemed to be alive in this country. Welty writes that

Indians, Mike Fink the flatboatman, Burr, and Blennerhassett, John James Audubon, the bandits of the Trace, planters, and preachers—the horse fairs, the great fires—the battles of war, the arrivals of foreign ships, and the coming of floods: could not all these things still move with their true stature into the mind here, and their beauty still work upon the heart? Perhaps it is the sense of place that gives us the belief that passionate things, in some essence, endure. Whatever is significant and whatever is tragic in its story live as long as the place does, though they are unseen, and the new life will be built upon these things— regardless of commerce and the way of rivers and roads, and other vagrancies. (*ES*, 299)

Welty here suggests that place is a prompt to memory. But she might have added that the human mind grants place its significance; only in human perceptions can the "significant" and the "tragic" exist. Place may prompt the memory, but first the memory of history and legend must create the sense of place. More than place, it is the historian and the storyteller who ensure that passionate things endure, for they provide us with that knowledge.

If storytellers and historians first prompted Welty's journey into the Natchez Trace countryside and into a past-haunted fiction, her agent Diarmuid Russell and her editor John Woodburn encouraged her to follow this path. Having read so much about contemporary Mississippi in Welty's *Curtain of Green* stories, Russell was particularly pleased in the summer of 1940 when Welty introduced him to a book about Mississippi's past—*The Outlaw Years*. In Coates's sort of legendary history, Russell saw the possibility of another book. As Michael Kreyling notes, "Russell was prompted to imagine Johnny Appleseed as a figure ready for a written treatment in the Coates manner, and he suggested the subject to Welty." Johnny Appleseed did not appeal to Welty, but stories of her native state did. She thought about them as she returned home from the Bread Loaf Writers' Conference late in the summer of 1940 and immediately wrote to Russell about the possibilities of a "Mississippi book":

> There are some things about a state that nobody could even know about who has not lived there a long time, and those things should determine the whole approach, don't you think? . . . and I believe I could find stories, old ones & new ones, and beliefs and songs and violent events all over the place to show what the life here is, to my belief. . . . Think of all the people who would be in my book—wonderful Indians to start with, and the Indian tales are beautiful and dramatic and very touching some of them—and Aaron Burr & Blennerhassett, and Lafayette, and Audubon, and Jefferson Davis, and the bandits (you keep "The Outlaw Years," there is one around Jackson), and Lafitte the pirate, and all kinds of remarkable people.

When the first of these tales, *The Robber Bridegroom*, was complete, Welty sent it to Russell, who replied that "the mad blending of Bandits, Indians, the rich planter, the beautiful daughter is wonderful. It is as if you had spent many dreamy afternoons meditating on the romantic history of the South and on the fairy and folk tales of your youth." But Russell worried that such a story might not sell: "Publishers, as a rule, are conservative, and anything that seems out of the way fills them with deep suspicion. They are as cautious as kittens approaching an unknown object. At the moment the general war hysteria has made them even more cautious; they seem dubious of everything that does not seem too familiar and shrink with panic from the original." Russell nevertheless wrote Woodburn about his suggestion that Welty string "a series of stories on the necklace of the Natchez Trace." Woodburn agreed that the idea was a good one.

Having read *The Robber Bridegroom*, he wrote Welty to endorse the idea of "an entire book of Mississippi stories."[4] Encouraged by Russell, who was both friend and agent and whose judgment she trusted implicitly, and by Woodburn, who was to become an effective advocate and friend, Welty proceeded with the book eventually to be titled *The Wide Net*.

Although her reading about the Natchez Trace and her visits there were the primary spark leading to *The Robber Bridegroom* and *The Wide Net*, it is important to remember that these books were written even as Welty read about the war in Europe and then saw her friends and brothers join the American war effort. By the summer of 1941, when Welty was in residence at the artist colony of Yaddo, France had fallen to Germany, and the Battle of Britain had stopped Germany from invading England. Not surprisingly, Yaddo was consumed with talk of war: Katherine Anne Porter wanted the United States to enter the war immediately; Welty was more conflicted.[5] And even after the Japanese bombed Pearl Harbor, Welty's attitude toward the war remained ambivalent. On the one hand, she despised the concept and the brutality of war; on the other, she knew that the German anti-Semitism was evil, an evil that had to be countered. And although Welty hated to see those she loved enlist or be drafted into danger, she supported the war effort against German and Japanese aggression by working for the Red Cross and by undertaking wartime publicity projects. Between 1939 and 1945, much of Welty's attention was focused upon the war, and the war inevitably had an impact upon the fiction Welty wrote during these years.

Welty expressed revulsion at the idea and reality of war in her letters to both Diarmuid Russell and Katherine Anne Porter. To Russell she wrote in late December of 1941: "What the war has done to the people this time I believe will be more powerful than what the people can do in making the war, if that could be a physical fact. But it is true, it must be, that it is the outrage to the world

4. Kreyling, *Author and Agent*, 42; Welty to Russell, n.d. [early September 1940], Russell to Welty, 8 October 1940, Russell to Welty, 18 November 1940, all in restricted papers, Welty Collection, MDAH, and cited by Kreyling, *Author and Agent*, 42, 46, 51; John Woodburn to Welty, 26 November 1940, Welty Collection, MDAH.

5. Welty to Russell, 26 June 1941, restricted papers, Welty Collection, MDAH, and as cited by Kreyling, *Author and Agent*, 76.

spirit you mention that we feel above the viciousness of each single thing, and all seems to be in the solemn shadow of this violation—no, in the shadow of this spirit to which the violation is done, which is still as powerful as ever and in being denied is the more irrevocably defined." To Porter she wrote a few months later: "I hate and despise it [the war], and do not claim it for me or mine either, it is just wished on us as a bastard child." And in mid-August of 1945, after atomic bombs had been dropped on both Hiroshima and Nagasaki, Welty wrote to Russell in a spirit of profound regret: "I hope this ends before we have to do any more—before we drop another one. I am one of those that tremble about the universe—only you can't really tremble for a whole universe. In an H. G. Wells story, the scientists could have the bombs accidentally fall on their own heads and somebody would say, better that their secret died with them."[6] War, to Welty, violated the spirit that gave life meaning, denied the possibility of communication and communion, endangered the essence of humanity.

Despite her instincts about war in general and this war in particular, however, Welty firmly believed that an evil had been unleashed when Hitler came to power and that this evil had to be quelled. In a letter probably written at the end of August 1941, Welty told Porter,

> I felt worse about the war lately than I ever have since last summer—I don't know why—I was saying goodnight to my mother as she sat by the little radio in her room and she said, "The Russians just blew up one of their biggest dams——" and she looked so—I can't describe it—but the whole feeling of utter destruction & self-destruction came over me—it was the particular & the human reaction to it, which you instinctively keep down from day to day in order to endure your thoughts. The same day, a small thing—but the same feeling—came when the Little Theatre here was found broken into and everything in it smashed with a thoroughness which you couldn't believe—I used to be with sets & properties, so I felt a personal hurt—scenery had been slashed and

6. Welty to Russell, n.d. [late December 1941], restricted papers, Welty Collection, MDAH, and as cited by Kreyling, *Author and Agent*, 81; Welty to Porter, 17 March 19[42], Papers of Katherine Anne Porter, Special Collections, University of Maryland Libraries, College Park, Maryland; Welty to Russell, 13 August [1945], restricted papers, Welty Collection, MDAH, and as cited by Kreyling, *Author and Agent, 112.*

lights had been methodically broken, furniture had been thrown down through the trap door and paint poured in on top of it, the curtain had been painted all over with obscene words, every seat in the house was coated with white paint, and tools had all been stolen except for the saw, which was neatly covered with paint and left on the floor—"snowballs" of paint had been hurled at the framed paintings and photographs in the green room—a job which had taken not one night but a number of nights to do—in other words not impulse, but plain undigressing malice. I think you are right when you say it is loose in the world. [sic] and that it is all part of the same thing. And it strikes what is tender and "amateur",[sic] I think that was somehow symbolic. . . . Somehow the good people never seem to be very accomplished. Goodness is really too profound a thing to take to tricks, I guess. But if it has a chair pulled out from under it it can get up. This is getting crazy now. I hear the little quinine bells ringing in my ears.

Distracted by a malarial fever, Welty was equally feverish in her comments about war. Clearly she identified war both with destruction and with self-destruction, but just as clearly she asserted that the war fomented by Germany was an example of "undigressing malice," an instance of criminal activity on a grand scale. And she hoped against hope that the "tender and 'amateur' " victims of this malice could and would defeat it. This hope seemed more attainable once the United States became actively involved in the war. As Welty much later told an interviewer, "Everybody honestly believed we were trying to save the world from Nazism. We believed in our country; well, I still believe in my country. It was a very pure kind of wish to accomplish this victory, and we were in it heart and soul."[7]

Welty's feelings about the war, of course, were personal as well as philosophi-

7. Welty to Porter, [29 or 30 August 1941], Papers of Katherine Anne Porter, Special Collections, University of Maryland Libraries; on August 28, 1941, the *Jackson Clarion-Ledger* reported that the Russians had blown up their own Dnieper Dam ("Giant Soviet Dam Again is Reported Blasted by U.S.S.R.," *Jackson Clarion-Ledger*, 28 August 1941). And on August 29, 1941, the *New York Times* carried a fuller story about this event (Cyrus L. Sulzberger, "Dnieper Let Loose," *New York Times*, 29 August 1941); Charles Ruas, "Eudora Welty," in *More Conversations with Eudora Welty*, ed. Peggy W. Prenshaw (Jackson: University Press of Mississippi, 1996), 66.

cal. The anti-Semitism, which in Jackson had wounded her longtime friend Lehman Engel, which in Wisconsin had plagued her closest college pals, and which at Columbia University she sadly encountered yet again, Welty now saw in its most virulent form, undergirding the powerful Nazi state, and she found this fact devastating. Yet the war to combat this evil endangered many she held dear. As she told Porter, "When the draft comes up and gets the people I love and they go off and nothing can protect them, I feel as if it will kill me, and that can keep me from doing any kind of work." In the fall of 1942, she saw her brother Edward off for his military training, visited Lt. John Robinson where he was stationed in St. Petersburg, Florida, and then saw her brother Walter leave for another training camp. "This is an empty house and an empty town," she wrote Porter. In January 1943, "empty" was not a strong enough word: "The holidays," she told Porter, "seemed nightmarish with all the ones I love off at war." And by May or June of 1943, having returned from a visit to New York City, Welty was feeling melancholy indeed: "I've felt very lonely since I got back. I also feel that I may have seen my friend John Robinson, in the army, for the last time till the war is ended, and Diarmuid for the last time in a long time too."[8]

Her preoccupation with the dangers her brothers, John Robinson, and other friends faced certainly affected Welty's fictional output during the war years; so too did worry about her mother, who hated the war's destructiveness and who feared for her two sons in the service. By the end of August 1942, Welty found herself unable to write fiction. She had written *The Robber Bridegroom*, "First Love," "The Winds," "The Purple Hat," "Asphodel," and "The Wide Net" while war raged in Europe. After December 7, 1941, she had managed to bring "A Still Moment," "Livvie," and "At the Landing" to completion. But once her brothers seemed headed toward active military duty, she produced absolutely no new stories for more than a year. Instead, she put her writing efforts into publicity for the war effort, busied herself with volunteer projects like fund raising, bandage rolling, and paper drives, and worked diligently in her mother's garden. Finally, perhaps as a way of communicating with John Robinson, who had survived the Battle of Sicily but was still stationed in Africa, Welty returned to writ-

8. Welty to Porter, 17 March 194[2], 11 November [1942], [January 1943], [May or June 1943], Papers of Katherine Anne Porter, Special Collections, University of Maryland Libraries.

ing. She began "The Delta Cousins," drawing upon Robinson's family history in doing so. She would eventually mail the story to Robinson overseas and would later dedicate to him the novel based on the story.

Welty's 1943 return to writing is the subject for another chapter, but her writing between September 1940 and September 1942 is the immediate concern of this one. *The Robber Bridegroom* and *The Wide Net*, the books Welty sets along the nineteenth- and early-twentieth-century Natchez Trace, seem far removed from the European and Pacific theaters of war, but the values that animate those stories are the ones that governed Welty's attitudes toward war itself. The stories' distance in time and place from her contemporary world perhaps provided Welty with the aesthetic distance she needed to confront issues relevant to the war-torn present. In 1980, thinking back on her work of the early war years, Welty suggested as much: "That was a terrible time to live through. I couldn't write about it, not at the time—it was too personal. I *could* write or translate things into domestic or other dimensions in my writing, with the same things in mind."[9] In retrospect, at least, Welty seemed to believe that her Natchez Trace stories of the past gave her the perspective she needed to confront wartime issues.

In 1941, however, Welty acknowledged few connections between her work and those issues. Indeed, on at least one occasion, she worried that readers might too literally connect the contemporary world and the world of her stories. After she had revised "First Love," she wrote her agent Diarmuid Russell to express fear the story might be seen as pro-fascist:

I'm working on "First Love" but even though it is better now it would not do for you to send out—Do you realize that it might be interpreted as pro-fascist, poor Aaron Burr's unexplained little dream, that I meant to be only a symbol of what everyone has—some marvelous sway and magnetism that it can give—It is stupid and wild, but that is the way people seem to be thinking, everything is dynamite, suspicious. Even KAP, who wants us to enter the war instantly, sees fascism in everything she doesn't like, and while it may be a very intricate in-

9. Ruas, 66.

sight into deep relationships, I still hate that fever to creep into what we think of books or music, because eventually it will leave nothing to be itself.[10]

Here is the argument that Welty would make famous in her 1965 essay "Must the Novelist Crusade?" Welty decries the effect that ideological blinders can have upon readers of fiction. She wants a work of literature to be appreciated for its literary qualities—its language, structure, character development—and she wants literature to be as complex and ambiguous as the world it depicts. But even in her letter to Russell, Welty suggests that there is some merit in ideological or political readings.

Certainly, there is merit in such a reading of "First Love," and when viewed from a political perspective, the story seems not pro-fascist, but anti-fascist. Seeing the relationship between Burr and the young deaf-mute Joel Mayes as that between a charismatic leader and a devotee may, in fact, provide what Welty herself has called "a very intricate insight into deep relationships," even as it suggests that this particular relationship is essentially warped in nature. Joel feels committed to Burr not because Burr has proven himself to be a worthy guide, but because Burr provides some sense of direction or purpose for him. Burr, on the other hand, feels nothing for Joel or for any of the people who support him after his arrest, and Burr's plan is to become an absolute dictator. Joel does not fully recognize Burr, but we as readers surely do. The story thus implicitly tells us something about the "magnetism" and the danger of fascist leaders who encounter such needy individuals as Joel Mayes.

Just as "First Love" can be closely connected to the era in which it was written, so too can the other stories Welty wrote in the early forties. In both *The Robber Bridegroom* and *The Wide Net*, Welty examines key issues raised by the war even as she sets them in the distant past and casts them into "domestic or other dimensions." First and most centrally, Welty's concern is with an individual's exercise of power. In drawing upon American history and American concepts of self-reliance, Welty examines the same sort of self-worship that characterized fascist leaders, and she condemns self-glorifying individuals for violating

10. Welty to Russell, 26 June 1941, restricted papers, Welty Collection, MDAH, and as cited by Kreyling, *Author and Agent*, 76.

the dignity and worth of others. Indeed, the word *violate* and the concept of violation resonate through Welty's stories of the early forties and tie her fiction to her belief that war itself is a "violation," an "outrage to the world spirit." Second, Welty's stories assert the positive value of social and cultural diversity, a value antithetical to the premises of Nazism. Finally, Welty's fiction of the early forties deals with the nature of memory. In writing of the past, Welty inherently asserts the importance of memory; she states that memory "is so basic and vital a part of staying alive that it takes on the strength of an instinct of survival, and acquires the power of an art" (*ES*, 171). For Welty in the early forties that "instinct for survival" involved cherishing a definition of memory that differs greatly from the definition of the past set forth by Adolf Hitler, the man who literally endangered Welty's world. Hitler believed that an authoritative and unchanging view of the past could and should be set forth. Welty, on the other hand, suggests that the past must be constantly reexamined and reinterpreted in view of new situations and insights. No doctrinaire, static view can be viable.

In focusing *The Robber Bridegroom* and *The Wide Net* on these three issues—self-reliance, diversity, and memory—even as she wrote about nineteenth- and early-twentieth-century Mississippi history or about her own childhood, Welty may or may not have recognized the political relevance of her seemingly apolitical stories. The relevance is there nonetheless and is tribute to the transforming power of her imagination. Her imagination focuses upon the past but makes that past an affirmation of values that Welty hoped might emerge intact from the cataclysmic events taking place around the world.

Just how relevant Welty's Natchez Trace stories are to the twentieth-century international scene is evident in a close examination of the stories' central issues and in the way the stories confront those issues. In *The Robber Bridegroom* and *The Wide Net*, Welty's fundamental concern with the exercise of power is a case in point. Her characters again and again attempt to assert their will and to impose that will upon the lives of others. On the "huge fateful stage of the outside world," Adolf Hitler was such an individual. Writing in the May 19, 1940, *New York Times Magazine*, Otto Tolischus concludes that Hitler had "sincerely come to regard himself as an instrument of Providence" and that he aspired "to live in the esteem of posterity as the greatest man in history." Historian Alan Bullock agrees, writing that there is a Hegelian "echo in Hitler's belief about himself. . . . he came to believe that he was a man with a mission, marked out by Providence, and therefore exempt from the ordinary canons of human conduct." In his own mind, Hitler "was the Siegfried come to reawaken Germany to greatness, for whom morality, suffering and 'the litany of private virtues' were irrelevant." He saw himself as the agent of what Hegel would have called "the Will of the World Spirit."[11]

In her fiction, Welty calls to mind an American variation on such an idea—the concept of self-reliance. The great nineteenth-century American proponent of self-reliance, Ralph Waldo Emerson, believed that the divinity or oversoul incarnates itself in every man and that every man should therefore trust in his divine intuitions. As Robert Richardson notes, Emerson believed that "the divine manifests itself in the human, much as the Hegelians say spirit manifests itself in matter." Of course, Emerson believed that such a philosophy becomes false when "divine nature is attributed to one or two persons, denied to all the rest, and 'denied with fury.'"[12] Moreover, Emerson's concept of union with the divine often involved a mystic dissolution of self into a greater whole. Nevertheless, in passages that seem to glorify unqualified individual autonomy, America's very own Emerson inadvertently set forth the rationale for a self-concept like Hitler's or like that of Welty's Jamie Lockhart, Billy Floyd, Aaron Burr, James Murrell, Lorenzo Dow, John James Audubon, or even Miss Sabina.

In *The Robber Bridegroom*, Welty uses legendary history to depict the destructive nature of self-glorification. The nineteenth-century Trace where the novella is set was a moral wilderness; its outlaws, including Joseph Hare, Samuel Mason, and Little Harp, were thieves and murderers. Similarly, Jamie Lockhart, the affable hero of Welty's tale, is also a thief whose dirk is "not unstained with blood" (*RB*, 112). And he rapes Rosamond, though she would have given herself freely had he granted her that opportunity. He insists upon the preeminence of self; he acts to please himself and feels no guilt about his actions. "'Guilt is a burden-

11. Welty, "What Stevenson Started," *New Republic*, 5 January 1953, 8; Otto D. Tolischus, "Portrait of a Revolutionary," *New York Times Magazine*, 19 May 1940, 21; Alan Bullock, *Hitler: A Study in Tyranny* (New York: Harper and Row, 1962), 384, 385, 383.

12. Robert Richardson, *Emerson: The Mind on Fire* (Berkeley: University of California Press, 1995), 289.

some thing to carry about in the heart,' said Jamie. 'I would never bother with it'" (*RB*, 27). He sounds like Emerson proclaiming, "Absolve you to yourself, and you shall have the suffrage of the world." His is a sort of Emersonian self-worship run amok. Indeed, Little Harp in *The Robber Bridegroom*, as Michael Kreyling has noted, is the dark side of Jamie's self-reliance and links Jamie to the evil fairy tale robber bridegroom of the story's title. Harp drugs and then throws himself upon an Indian girl, killing her; he violates this girl just as clearly as Jamie has violated Rosamond. And Jamie is not pleased by the sight of Harp's activity; he finds it abhorrent. In fact, he finds his own egotism abhorrent at this point in the tale, and the bandit Harp is an emblem for that egotism. When Welty and her friend John Robinson were working together in late 1948 on a *Robber Bridegroom* screenplay, Robinson suggested that Harp's scene with the Indian girl be cut, but Welty wanted to retain it. She wrote Robinson, "About the Indian girl scene, I'm not sure. I feel in one way that the murder or rape should stand—because in that scene we have detached Jamie from it, as hero, and yet all that bandit scene with girl who might have been Rosamond if she weren't herself really pertains to him and is the black half of his deeds—and is a reality of the times—and I feel that the actual horror should be given—simply and quickly, but no mistake—I feel that this element should be in it."[13] This "reality of the times," which also recalls the murder perpetrated by the Grimms' robber bridegroom, Welty links to Jamie's and to America's central concern with the autonomous individual.

Of course, the refusal to recognize the sanctity of other lives and the willingness to destroy those lives was not merely a reality of the American frontier. In her short story "At the Landing," Welty depicts the same landscape of *The Robber Bridegroom* one hundred years later. In this story the once booming river port of Rodney has become almost a ghost town, and the life of Jenny Lockhart is a record of losses as well. The river man Billy Floyd seems to promise love and renewal, but after he saves her from the flood, "he violated her and still he was

13. Ralph Waldo Emerson, "Self-Reliance," *Selections from Ralph Waldo Emerson*, ed. Stephen E. Whicher (Cambridge, Mass.: Riverside Press, 1957), 149; Kreyling, *Eudora Welty's Achievement of Order*, 46; Welty to John F. Robinson, Tuesday [December 1948], Welty Collection, MDAH.

without care or demand and as gay as if he were still clanging the bucket at the well" (*WN*, 200–1). Like Jamie Lockhart with Rosamund, Billy Floyd takes what Jenny would have given and feels no remorse. Unlike Jamie, however, Billy Floyd abandons Jenny, never to realize the nature of this violation. Still she follows after him, walking to the river. There a group of river men take her into a houseboat and rape her—they are Billy Floyd's doubles, and their sons seem destined to follow in their fathers' footsteps. The story concludes as the young boys symbolically reenact the rapes: They take "their turns throwing knives with a dull pit at the tree." The rapes by Little Harp and Jamie, by Billy Floyd and the other river men, seem in part to be a consequence of the American philosophy of self-reliance, "a taking freely of what was free" (*WN*, 214, 201), but in acting solely in self-interest, Welty asserts, the characters violate the sanctity of others. Such a theme is scarcely limited to the Natchez Trace country. In examining *The Robber Bridegroom* and "At the Landing," the reader may conclude that the dark side of American experience has its double in the Axis leaders of the 1930s and 1940s, who set themselves up as gods and viewed the sanctity of others as nonexistent.

Of course, it is tempting to find only a feminist statement in Welty's portraits of Jamie Lockhart and Billy Floyd. Anne Goodwyn Jones believes that at least three southern women writers—Katherine Anne Porter, Lillian Hellman, and Harriette Arnow—used "the representation of the Second World War as an occasion for reflection about the relationship of domestic, personal, gendered relationships to international military combat. Put differently, they looked for the origins of war in the construction of a particular type of manhood that feeds on war, that requires war for its own survival." But Jones's analysis does not really apply to Welty. In key ways the stance Jones describes is the obverse of Welty's—in Welty's fiction it is the representation of "domestic, personal, gendered relationships" that leads to reflection about the Second World War, and Welty does not find that violating the sanctity of others is limited to men or occurs only in gendered relationships. Violations of women are representative of violations more far reaching in nature.[14]

---

14. Anne Goodwyn Jones, "Every Woman Loves a Fascist: Writing World War II on the Southern Home Front," in *Remaking Dixie*, ed. Neil R. McMillen (Jackson: University Press of

In "First Love," the opening story in *The Wide Net*, for example, the character Aaron Burr, based upon the actual Burr, engages in a pattern of self-glorification and violation that is far removed from gender issues. In 1807 Burr, envisioning himself as the ruler of a vast new nation, launched a plot to bring about the secession of United States lands in the West and to take control of Spanish lands in the Southwest. He and his conspirator Harmon Blennerhassett, an Irishman who had emigrated to the United States with his niece/wife, began to make their way down the Mississippi River, only to have nine of their boats taken at the Bayou Pierre, north of Natchez, Mississippi. Burr was put under house arrest but was treated as the darling of society—his romance with Madeline Price began and ended in Natchez. He was eventually tried in a sort of grand jury proceeding, reportedly under the live oaks at Jefferson College, but no charges were brought. Nevertheless, federal troops planned to rearrest him, and Burr fled, in disguise and still hoping to bring off his conspiracy. All of these Natchez events are part of Welty's story "First Love."[15]

The key figure in the story, however, is one wholly of Welty's making—the young deaf-mute Joel Mayes, an orphan who comes under the sway of Aaron Burr. Through the perceptions of Mayes, Welty dramatizes the appeal of a would-be dictator for those whose lives are desolate. From the time he arrives in Natchez until the moment he encounters Burr, young Joel is scarcely alive. He resembles those "unsignalling passengers submissive and huddled, mere bundles

---

Mississippi, 1997), 112. Jones further argues that the concept of masculinity which led to war was a concept southern women both loved and hated (112). In *The Robber Bridegroom* and "At the Landing," both Rosamund and Jenny Lockhart might be seen as embracing such a doubled-edged attitude. But such an argument is not wholly convincing. Rosamund and Jenny tend to accept Jamie and Billy Floyd not because of the power they represent, but in spite of it. Billy Floyd's behavior quite literally makes Jenny sick, and Rosamund refuses to allow Jamie to be an all-powerful force in her life.

15. Numerous critics have discussed Welty's sources for the historical information in "First Love." See Victor H. Thompson, "Aaron Burr in Eudora Welty's 'First Love,'" *Notes on Mississippi Writers* 8 (Winter 1976): 75–81; Albert J. Devlin, *Eudora Welty's Chronicle* (Jackson: University Press of Mississippi, 1983), 41–79; John M. Warner, "Eudora Welty: The Artist in 'First Love.'" *Notes on Mississippi Writers* 9 (Fall 1976): 77–87. These scholars, however, have not considered the relationship between the historical elements in Welty's story and the moment in history at which she was writing.

of sticks" who travel the Mississippi River in the bitter winter cold. He keeps "always to himself," isolated by his inability to hear or speak. He refuses, for the most part, to confront the past because it involves the loss of his parents. Occasionally, he thinks "frugally, almost stonily, of that long time" (*WN*, 4, 5, 6), but his memories are controlled and seemingly unaffecting. In short, Joel lives almost wholly in and for the present moment, unwilling to recall the past, making no plans for the future.

This situation begins to change the moment Burr enters Joel's room at the inn. The "tense, yet gentle and easy motion" by which Burr removes his cloak is magical to Joel. It seems to him that the world has "been up to that night inanimate." But now Joel and his world become animate. And when Joel wakes the next morning, he wonders whether Burr and Blennerhassett "would take him each by the arm and drag him on further, through the leaves" (*WN*, 11, 12). The language here echoes the language used to describe Joel's stony memory of the day his parents were lost: "Arms bent on destination dragged him forward through the sharp bushes, and leaves came toward his face" (*WN*, 6). Joel's thoughts of the future draw him toward the past, and his memory "reached back and hung trembling over the very moment of terror in which he had become separated from his parents, and then it turned and started in the opposite direction, and it would have discerned some shape, but he would not let it, of the future" (*WN*, 12–13). Though he refuses to speculate about the direction in which Burr might take him, Joel's love goes out to Burr, and if he does not see Burr each evening, he has "a strange feeling of being deserted and lost, not quite like anything he [has] ever felt in his life" (*WN*, 17). But, of course, this feeling of "being deserted and lost" is very much like something Joel has felt before— the loss of his parents—and his ability to face that loss develops as a direct response to Burr and Burr's dreams for the future. Burr, Joel believes, has "no awareness whatever of the present" (*WN*, 16). The great man's thoughts are only of conquests ahead. And this distorted, though typically American, view of time paradoxically helps Joel to understand time's continuity. As Joel comes to feel that he too has a future, that he can follow Burr "wherever it was that he meant to go" (*WN*, 16), then Joel can more easily deal with his past. When Mrs. Blennerhassett's playing of the violin prompts Burr to think of the country he plans to establish, Joel thinks of his mother and the story she had told him long ago in Virginia. Here, as he reacts to Burr's futurism, Joel begins to realize that the idea of a future presupposes a past. Because of Burr, Joel gains access to the past and to a holistic sense of time.

But though Burr has this positive effect on Joel, Joel means nothing to Burr. When Burr and Blennerhassett first enter Joel's room at the inn, they do so without knocking, and Joel feels a "violation." As they continue to use Joel's room as a place for conspiracy, he realizes that "they had learned somehow of his presence, and that it had not stopped them. Somehow that appalled him. . . . They were aware that if it were only before him, they could talk forever in his room" (*WN*, 11, 15). But Joel finds himself able to rationalize these violations: "Then he put it that they accepted him. One night, in his first realization of this, his defect seemed to him a kind of hospitality." The "dominion promised in [Burr's] gentlest glance" is seductive to Joel, but even Joel recognizes that there is "no kindness" in Burr's face and that Burr and Blennerhassett pay "no more attention to him than they paid the presence of the firelight" (*WN*, 15, 16, 17). Burr, in quest of dominion, will use Joel's room and accept the food Joel serves, but Joel holds no importance for him. His focus is upon dominion. His concern is for self, and the future he proposes would be enslaving to Joel. His optimism opens the past for Joel, but his plans for the future include no provisions for Joel's development. The appeal of this demagogue is powerful to Joel, but the appeal is as misleading as those fascist appeals being made in Europe even as Welty was writing her story.

In "A Still Moment" the Natchez Trace, in its historical backgrounds as well as its physical appearance, yet again provides the stimulus for Welty's imagination. Historically, the story relies on very specific facts about the nineteenth-century Trace and three men who traveled it—Lorenzo Dow, John Murrell, and John James Audubon. Dow was an itinerant Methodist evangelist, and Welty incorporates many details of his fanatical life into her story. Dow's relationship with his wife, his ingenious escapes from the Indians, the Spanish race horse that he rode—all of this is factual information. John (renamed James by Welty) Murrell was also a real person, a horrible outlaw along the Trace. The letters "H. T." were branded on his thumb, labeling him a horse thief, but horse theft was the least of his crimes. This murderer also organized the so-called Mystic Confederacy. His plan was to stage a great slave rebellion in the Southwest, and during the panic it created, he hoped to loot plantations and whole towns and to establish himself as ruler of a pirate kingdom. Audubon, the ornithologist and author of *The Birds of America*, was a man of mysterious origins; rumor had it that he was the son of the lost Dauphin. Welty uses actual quotations from Audubon's journals and accurately depicts Audubon's method of painting. Audubon typically shot the birds he painted; he stuffed them and posed them before beginning work.[16]

Reading about John Murrell may well have called to Welty's mind images of contemporary fascist leaders. Like Hitler, Welty's Murrell sees himself as "an instrument in the hands of a power" (*WN*, 78). Murrell seeks to penetrate the "mystery of being" not only by observing men at the moment of their transition from being to death but also by establishing his own significance as the man in control. Murrell's Mystic Confederacy is designed to bring him the kind of power and adulation Hitler craved and that Leni Riefenstahl photographed in *Triumph of the Will*. When Murrell first sees the white heron of the story, "he looked at the bird with the whole plan of the Mystic Rebellion darting from him as if in rays of the bright reflected light, and he stood looking proudly, leader as he was bound to become of the slaves, the brigands and outcasts of the entire Natchez country, with plans, dates, maps burning like a brand into his brain, and he saw himself proudly in a moment of prophecy going down rank after rank of successively bowing slaves to unroll and flaunt an awesome great picture of the Devil colored on a banner" (*WN*, 86–87). Of course, the appearance of the snowy heron temporarily deflects Murrell from this vision and brings him a momentary sense of union with the natural world and with his two companions, but ultimately he returns to his obsessive quest for preeminence. His destructive and egomaniacal essence endures, and he clearly evokes in a distanced manner

---

16. Victor Thompson, Albert Devlin, and Peggy Prenshaw have discussed Welty's use of Audubon's journals, Dow's autobiography, Coates' *Outlaw Years*, and Virgil Stewart's memories of Murrell (*The History of Virgil A. Stewart*). See Victor H. Thompson, "The Natchez Trace in Eudora Welty's 'A Still Moment,'" *Southern Literary Journal* 6, no. 1 (1973): 59–69; Devlin, *Eudora Welty's Chronicle*, 41–80; Devlin, "From Horse to Heron: A Source for Eudora Welty," *Notes on Mississippi Writers* 10, no. 2 (1977): 62–69; Prenshaw, "A Study of Setting in the Fiction of Eudora Welty," 233–40; Prenshaw, "Coates' *The Outlaw Years* and Welty's 'A Still Moment,'" *Notes on Modern American Literature* 2, no. 2 (1978): Item 17.

the horror Welty felt as she read contemporary accounts or recalled newsreels of fascist leaders in Europe.

Welty depicts neither of Murrell's chance companions as having his patholog-ical drive for power, but she does show that they are like Murrell in their single-minded obsessions and in experiencing the brief transcendental moment in which these obsessions fade away. Dow is so focused upon his own role in saving souls that his momentary sense of union with the natural world proves threaten-ing for him. Before the bird appears, he sees himself as an instrument of God's will, the man called by God to save others. At times he seems almost to equate himself with God: "I must have souls! And souls I must have!" is his cry. And when the heron does appears, Dow gives "the bird a triumphant look, such as a man may bestow upon his own vision." The sight of the feeding bird, however, momentarily suspends this focus upon himself as God's instrument. And once the bird has been killed, Dow finds his faith in God and self shaken: "Its beauty had been greater than he could account for" (*WN*, 73, 86, 93).

Finally, even Audubon, who alone of the three sees the heron for itself rather than imposing an image upon it, acts to control the beautiful bird and assumes that "surely he alone had appreciated" the sight of it (*WN*, 92). After sharing in a moment of union with nature and his companions, he kills the bird so that he can paint it. He kills it even though he acknowledges that "the best he could make would be, after it was apart from his hand, a dead thing and not a live thing, never the essence, only a sum of parts" (*WN*, 92). His killing of the bird for the purposes of art thus destroys the still moment in which he, Murrell, and Dow respond as one; he acts to reassert the single, separate self.

In an August 1941 letter to Diarmuid Russell, Welty described her own still moment of mystic union:

> Every evening when the sun is going down and it is cool enough to water the garden, and it is all quiet except for the locusts in great waves of sound, and I stand still in one place for a long time putting water on the plants, I feel some-thing new—that is all I can say—as if my will went out of me, as if I had a stubbornness and it was melting. I had not meant to shut out any feeling that wanted to enter. —It is a real shock, because I had no idea that there had been in my life any rigidity or refusal of anything so profound, but the sensation is

one of letting in for the first time what I believed I had already felt—in fact suffered from—a sensitivity to all that was near or around.

Russell responded, "I think I understand the feeling you speak about. It is really a curious melting of the personality into nature and I think every now and again it happens to all people who like the outdoors even if they are the grossest of human beings. Emerson in his essay on the OVERSOUL tried to speak about it and I think Wordsworth when he wrote the poem about 'A being whose dwelling of the light of setting suns Etc.' also had experienced the same curious sensation." Welty grants this moment of transcendence, this moment of becoming a sort of transparent eyeball, to her three characters, one of whom is, to use Russell's words, "the grossest of human beings." And she suggests that the obsessions of the three have heretofore blocked such moments of transcendence. She might also have sensed that such self-absorption typified, to use Russell's words, the ways in which "people and governments all over the world refused to see and have even denied the existence of a world spirit."[17]

Welty's focus upon the way her characters exercise power is finally crucial to a story less centrally grounded in Mississippi history but equally distant from the ostensible world of international relations. In "Asphodel" issues of power are depicted in a narrowly circumscribed realm. "Asphodel" is set in the late nineteenth century near the ruins of a house reminiscent of Mississippi's Windsor ruins. In "Asphodel," three "old maids" recall the life of Miss Sabina, the woman who has ruled their town and who has just died. Miss Sabina, they recall, found herself married to Mr. Don McInnis solely because her father believed it was time she married. According to Cora, "She was no longer young for suitors; she was instructed to submit" (*WN*, 99). And submit she did until her three children met tragic deaths and until she discovered her husband to be unfaithful and until her father had died. But then Sabina became dominant and dominating, driving her husband from the house and dictating behavior to the town. Cora reports that "her power reached over the whole population—white and

17. Welty to Diarmuid Russell, 28 August 1941; Russell to Welty, 29 August 1941, 26 December 1941; these letters (restricted papers, Welty Collection, MDAH) are cited by Kreyling, *Author and Agent*, 78–79, 79, 81.

black, men and women, children, idiots, and animals—even strangers. Her law was laid over us, her riches were distributed upon us. . . . And we stood in fear of her, old and young and like ourselves" (*WN*, 105). Sabina's self-assertion denies anyone else the right to be an individual. Having originally been denied self-determination, Miss Sabina seizes power and exercises it as inappropriately as it had been exercised by men. The feminist issue is clear; so too may be its tangential application to the international scene in the early 1940s and to the rise of fascist dictators.

Just as she opposed individuals imposing their will upon others, Welty also endorsed social and cultural diversity. Such diversity, quite obviously, was anathema in Hitler's Germany. Writing between 1940 and 1942, of course, Welty could not have known about the German death camps, but she would have known a good deal about Hitler's systematic efforts to disenfranchise and discriminate against Jews. From the time Hitler came to power in 1933 until the war commenced, the *New York Times*, Welty's favorite newspaper, was filled with stories of German anti-Semitism, and the *Jackson Daily Clarion-Ledger*, Welty's hometown newspaper, ran similar though less extensive stories. In March 1933, for example, both papers covered the Nazi dismissal of Jewish doctors, judges, and attorneys from their positions; both covered the abuse of Jewish citizens and tourists; and both covered the 55,000-person Madison Square Garden interfaith demonstration against Nazi policy. In 1935, both the *Times* and the *Daily Clarion-Ledger* reported on the promulgation of the Nuremberg Laws that banned marriage or sexual relations among Jews and non-Jews and denied other civil rights to Jews. And in 1938, the *Times* and the local paper covered and denounced the deadly violence of Kristallnacht.[18] Because of extensive press coverage, Welty was aware of the human rights violations in Europe, and she hated these violations.

Jones believes that works by southern women writers of the 1940s had "little to do with racism" so evident in Germany. Instead, she argues that their works focused upon the "complicated and risky project of critiquing American manhood while supporting the boys in battle."[19] Not so with Welty. Though Welty's

18. See *New York Times* and *Jackson Daily Clarion-Ledger* issues of March 28, 1933, September 16, 1935, and November 11, 1938.

19. Jones, "Every Woman Loves a Fascist," 115, 111.

fiction of the early forties does not deal explicitly with German policy, it does deal with other incarnations of racism: Most especially, it confronts white settlers' displacement of the Native American, their annihilation of entire Indian tribes, and their self-serving rationalizations for this course of action. In her essay "Some Notes on River Country," Welty discusses the Natchez nation, which had been destroyed in Mississippi in the eighteenth century. Nowhere does Welty idealize the Natchez, yet everywhere she treats them with respect. She writes that the Natchez "were proud and cruel, gentle-mannered and ironic, handsome, extremely tall, intellectual, elegant, pacific and ruthless." Welty tells us that the "Natchez never spoke except one at a time; no one was ever interrupted or contradicted; a visitor was always allowed the opening speech, and that after a rest in silence of fifteen or twenty minutes, to allow him to get his breath and collect his thoughts." Though the Natchez practiced sacrifice among themselves, they were a peaceful people until betrayed by the French; then they massacred many Frenchmen at Fort Rosalie in Natchez. The French in return "one day, in a massacre for a massacre, slew or sent into slavery at Santo Domingo every one" of the Natchez (*ES*, 293, 295, 294).

In *The Robber Bridegroom* Welty postpones the demise of the Natchez in order to question the definitions of *savage* and *civilized* that we have inherited from the nineteenth century. Daniel Singal discusses the very different sorts of definitions eighteenth-century and Victorian societies placed upon these terms. In the eighteenth century, he argues, "some ambivalence about savagery had been present . . . , but the balance had generally tipped toward savage virtues rather than defects. In America especially one finds late eighteenth-century figures like Benjamin Franklin, Thomas Jefferson, J. Hector St. John de Crevecoeur, John Bartram, and Philip Freneau avidly celebrating the untutored emotions of the American Indian in contrast to Old World oversophistication." But Victorians placed "everything they most valued under the heading of 'civilization,' while consigning the many things they loathed to the netherworld of 'savagery.' To the first they assigned all that was moral, pure, rational, advanced, and prosperous; to the second category went all that was backward, animalistic, irrational, and poor." Singal further notes that people of color inevitably were placed in category two. *The Robber Bridegroom*, set in nineteenth-century America, denies the validity of this nineteenth-century definition while also qualifying the idealized eighteenth-century view. As Welty repeatedly uses the term *savage,* whether in speaking as narrator or in writing dialogue for her characters, the term itself becomes more positive than negative. The Indian society is a cohesive one—Little Harp's murder of an Indian maiden will be punished by the tribe to which she belonged. The white settlers, on the other hand, see themselves individualistically; Salome proclaims, "No one is to have power over me! . . . No man, and none of the elements! I am by myself in the world" (*RB,* 160–1). In *The Robber Bridegroom,* only the Indians know what it means to be part of a community. And Welty's nineteenth-century tribe also knows that the natural world should be revered. Kreyling notes that "the Indians inhabit the enchanted forest of the novella in a mysterious way that contrasts sharply with the noisy intrusion of the pioneers. . . . The Indians enjoy an organic union with the place, appearing and dissolving in the surrounding forest, to the eyes of the pioneers, as if Indian nature were not restricted merely to the human but partook of the animal and the vegetable as well. White men never spy the Indians first; they see them only after the Indians have chosen to be seen, when escape from a 'reckoning' is impossible."[20] Clearly, the Indians' religion is the source of their organic union with the natural world: "The sun asks worship" (*RB,* 161), the tribe's chief tells Salome, but the self-reliant Salome reveres only herself and presumes to command the sun.

Though the Indians go on to put Salome to death, they know that their community, their worship of nature, and their opposition to the Salomes of the world are ultimately doomed. As Clement tells Jamie, "The Indians know their time has come. . . . They are sure of the future growing smaller always, and that lets them be infinitely gay and cruel" (*RB,* 21). The Indians who live harmoniously together and with nature are victims of nineteenth-century individualism and progress, and victimization has prompted their self-transformation into instruments of terror. For Welty, therefore, the nineteenth-century's negative use of the word *savage* is untenable. As Clement Musgrove observes, "The savages have only come the sooner to their end; we will come to ours too. Why have I

20. Daniel J. Singal, *The War Within: From Victorian to Modernist Thought in the South, 1919–1945* (Chapel Hill: University of North Carolina Press, 1982), 26, 27; Kreyling, *Eudora Welty's Achievement of Order,* 38.

built my house, and added to it? The planter will go after the hunter, and the merchant after the planter, all having their day" (*RB*, 161). Through Clement, Welty here refuses to see change as improvement; she refuses to equate social and moral evolution. Instead, she suggests that the term *savage* should be free of the negative value judgments conventionally attached to it and that assumptions of racial superiority should be abandoned. Such a sentiment is certainly an appropriate one to express in the face of the Nazi anti-Semitic propaganda that was being spewed forth as Welty was writing her novel.

Definitions of savagery are not Welty's concern in "The Winds," but the virtue of diversity certainly is in this most autobiographical story of her young career. In "The Winds" Welty drew upon her own experiences and emotions to shape her story, to describe her beginnings as a writer, and to set forth the private values that the Axis powers had challenged on an international scope. The distinguished novelist Reynolds Price, Welty's close friend, has written that "by the time a potential novelist begins to read, most of the encounters and relations about which he will write have passed, are history and lie in the mind pure as diamond, unyielding to one's long education, waiting only to assert their power, to challenge one's life and all one has learned to a battle which is the battle of understanding against mystery, in which victory can only be a work of art—an act of temporary understanding, temporary order or, if not so much, a celebration of mystery itself."[21] The encounters and relations of which Price writes, of course, need not directly enter a writer's fiction; their appearance may be more oblique. But in Welty's story "The Winds," two childhood experiences assert their power and result in a remarkable work of art. Remembered experiences and emotions glow with the light of imagination and become metaphors for the mature writer's most profound contemporary concerns. And as Welty the writer discovered that her own past furnished appropriate metaphors for her fiction, her protagonist discovers through the spiraling process of memory a passion for the "wild and beloved and estranged" life of the artist, a life that thrives on diversity and eschews class-conscious judgments (*WN*, 139).

Young Josie, the protagonist of "The Winds," lives in a house much like the

---

21. Reynolds Price, "The Thing Itself," in *A Common Room* (New York: Atheneum, 1987), 12–3.

Welty house on North Congress Street in Jackson, and the storm with which the story begins derives from a storm Welty herself survived. As she wrote her story, Welty remembered the tension this storm occasioned between her parents: Her mother, who as a girl in West Virginia had loved a storm, thought it foolish to rouse the children in the middle of the night; her father, who was always a cautious individual, thought it a necessary precaution. Welty also remembered thinking that the nighttime sounds of the storm were made by revelers outside her house. Josie's memories during the storm are Welty's own: Daisy the cow; the surprise appearance of an organ grinder; the Princess bicycle; the children in the disreputable house across the street; the picture of a young girl in the May Festival; walks through Smith Park; a man who cries, "The time flies, the time flies!"; rides in the pony cart; the teacher running to catch snowflakes on her cape—all are the more than twenty-year-old memories that Welty transformed through the metaphor of plot.[22] In the story, these memories become emblems; images of order, security, convention, routine—the orderly house and the protective father—are set against images of change, adventure, risk, imagination, and passion—the disorderly double house and its inhabitants, the bicycle, the statue of a dragon in the park, Old Biddy Felix. And the storm transforms Josie's apprehension of her secure home just as her summertime experiences transform her from a contented child who cherishes a stable environment into a girl who longs for all that is "wild and beloved and estranged" (WN, 139). The "good strong house" that keeps the family safe seems a strange place during the storm. An empty bed rolls around on its own, Will's Tinker-Toy tower collapses, the stairway seems to sway as the family descends it, petals spontaneously shatter from roses in a bowl, lightning stamps the pattern of the father's dressing gown on the living room walls. Everything seems subject to change, and the storm itself signals a change of season. Like "First Love," "The Winds" takes place in a season of change. Welty, writing in the season of change that we call World War II, deals in her story with the individual change that Josie herself experiences.

22. The biographical information contained in this discussion of "The Winds" comes not only from a personal interview with Welty (14 November 1986), but also from *One Writer's Beginnings*, editor Patti Carr Black's *Eudora* (Jackson: Mississippi Department of Archives and History, 1984), and restricted family photographs at the Welty Collection, MDAH.

In addition to drawing upon her own experience with a tornado, Welty has drawn upon her family's outing to the Redpath Chautauqua. The Chautauqua came to Jackson each year, and every day and night for a week it provided the city with lectures and musical entertainment. One night, like Josie, a youthful Welty saw a women's trio perform. Though the performance did not occur on the night of the storm, Welty has arranged for this conjunction in the story so that the Chautauqua may further develop the pattern of change in Josie. The lady cornetist of the fictional trio has come "from far away" and seems to have "the long times of the world" about her. Her eyelids seem "to whir and yet to remain motionless, like the wings of a hummingbird," and her breaths are "fearful" (*WN*, 137). The exotic and the unusual call out to Josie; she longs for experiences that are richer than those her small town can provide. The cornetist sounds a metaphorical clarion call, and Josie longs to follow after her, to know the kind of passion that inspires her playing. The young Eudora Welty who heard the cornetist play may or may not have had the response young Josie feels, but the thirty-two-year-old Welty who wrote "The Winds" certainly recognized the meaning implicit in her youthful experience and would live out its promise. She was following her passion in writing stories like "The Winds." And when at age seventy-five, she wrote not autobiographical fiction but the autobiography *One Writer's Beginnings*, Welty would conclude the book by saying, "As you have seen, I am a writer who came of a sheltered life. A sheltered life can be a daring life as well. For all serious daring starts from within" (*OWB*, 104).

It is significant, of course, that Welty found in this memory of a female cornetist the symbol of the passion that brought her to fiction. Feminist theory would certainly seize upon this fact. Susan Stanford Friedman, for instance, contends that men's autobiographies have focused upon individualism while women's autobiographies tend to stress a "sense of shared identity with other women," "the central role collective consciousness of self plays in the lives of women." In some respects, Welty's autobiographical story tends to validate Friedman's contention. Young Josie finds her deepest passion when she encounters the female cornetist and when she looks across the street at the big girl Cornella. But, writing in the shadow of a war justified by theories of racial superiority, Welty had a far more inclusive purpose than theories of female solidarity can suggest. Josie is not so concerned with defining and confining her identity through a collective consciousness as she is with expanding her experience. She seeks an imaginative identification with as many individuals, male or female, as she can encompass: "Cornella, sweet summertime, the little black monkey, poor Biddy Felix, the lady with the horn whose lips were parted? Had they after all asked something of her? There, outside, was all that was wild and beloved and estranged, and all that would beckon and leave her, and all that was beautiful. She wanted to follow, and by some metamorphosis she would take them in—all—every one" (*WN*, 139). Josie, in fact, sounds very much like Eudora Welty, who in 1979 at the age of seventy wrote, "I never doubted . . . that imagining yourself into other people's lives is exactly what writing fiction is," and who went on to add that "the emotions, in which all of us are alike involved for life, differ more in degree than in kind." Writing fiction, in short, is the antithesis of the fascist spirit. To write fiction is to imagine yourself into other lives, not to denigrate and dismiss the humanity of others. It is no coincidence that, according to Alan Bullock, Hitler's library "contained not a single classic of literature."[23]

In recalling two incidents from her childhood and turning them into fiction, Welty not only described the importance of opening one's self to others, she also relied fully upon her most treasured source as a writer and began to use what would become one of her most valuable fictional techniques—memory. And Welty in her story stresses the living, changing nature of memory, not a fixed or authorized version of the past.

In an early version of "The Winds" written before the war in Europe had begun, Welty had not yet made memory a central concern. "Beautiful Ohio," which Welty dated as a 1936 story, begins as a very young Celia and her parents leave home for the evening's Chautauqua concert—Celia's first evening out. When Celia's father lifts her onto the streetcar that will take her family to the concert, Celia senses that the evening holds special promise. And something out of the ordinary does occur for Celia—she hears a lady trumpeter play, and the

---

23. Susan Stanford Friedman, "Women's Autobiographical Selves: Theory and Practice," in *The Private Self*, ed. Shari Benstock (Chapel Hill: University of North Carolina Press, 1988), 44, 56; Eudora Welty, "Looking Back at the First Story," *Georgia Review* 33 (1979): 755; Bullock, 398.

trumpet playing calls Celia away from home and away to a life of independent questing. For the first time in her life Celia feels separate from her parents, an entity unto herself. Celia's mother comes in to tell her good night, and Celia begins to cry. "Were you lonely here in the dark by yourself?" her mother asks, but Celia can only say no: "It was as though she wanted to be lonely and could not. Something had come to stay."[24]

This same trip to the Chautauqua is, as we have seen, a crucial event in "The Winds," but in the later story this event becomes part of Josie's past, the past she recalls during the equinoctial storm. In writing "The Winds," Welty made the present action of "Beautiful Ohio" part of the new story's past, a past Josie recalls in bits and pieces and in a purely associative fashion. As a result, "The Winds" deals with memory as surely as it does with the importance of passion, imagination, and risk-taking. As Welty has written in *One Writer's Beginnings*, "It is our inward journey that leads us through time—forward, or back, seldom in a straight line, most often spiraling. As we discover, we remember; remembering, we discover" (102). This is certainly the case with Josie. She has not realized the significance of events as they have occurred. They take on meaning for her only in retrospect—the night of the storm seems "slowly to be waking something that slept longer than Josie had slept" (*WN*, 119). This ten- or twelve-year-old girl discovers the most intimate facts about herself only by remembering the Chautauqua concert and placing it in the context of other events in her young life. Such is not possibly the case with the much younger Celia in "Beautiful Ohio," and in Welty's transformation of that early story we see her vision and technique unite; the narrative structure of "The Winds," emerging from the process of memory that prompted Welty to write, allows the reader to participate in Josie's inward journey through time to a meaningful past. Josie discovers that knowledge and understanding of the past is not fixed, but is subject to the living moment. In a small and private fashion, Welty's story thus denies the view of history that supported fascism. Bullock points out that Hitler's view of history was "rigid and inflexible," and he adds that "Hitler's was a closed mind, violently rejecting any alternative view, refusing to criticize or allow others to criticize his assumptions. He read and listened, not to learn but to acquire informa-

24. Eudora Welty, "Beautiful Ohio," Welty Collection, MDAH.

tion and find additional support for prejudices and opinions already fixed in his mind."[25] This is not the view Welty sets forth in "The Winds." Though this story was not written for the purpose of contradicting the current Nazi notion of history, it does. Writing in early 1941, Welty espouses the values she cherished, values that were literally under siege.

The evolving nature of memory is also a concern in "Asphodel," the story Welty wrote after "The Winds." The history of Miss Sabina has become a set piece for the story's three old ladies to tell to each other, and they see the past as fixed and unchanging. When Cora begins to tell the tale, "the lips of the others moved with hers" (*WN*, 98). And when Phoebe begins to speak, the story seems even more clearly detached from life: "When the story was taken up again, it was in Phoebe's delicate and gentle way, for its narrative was only part of memory now, and its beginning and ending might seem mingled and freed in the blue air of the hill" (*WN*, 100). This narrative of the past is free from contingency because it has become fixed in memory and is not subject to new insights or discoveries. Both its beginning and ending are known and are therefore free to be mingled, but nothing unexpected will emerge in the telling. And when the ladies finish the story, Welty explicitly tells us that they have turned the past into an object, that for them the past is not vulnerable to the present moment: "Here in the bright sun where the three old maids sat beside their little feast, Miss Sabina's was an old story, closed and complete. In some intoxication of the time and the place, they recited it and came to the end" (*WN*, 109).

All of this changes, however, when Mr. Don McInnis appears "buck-naked" before them. They flee, but not without looking back over their shoulders at this man who is "as rude and golden as a lion" (*WN*, 110, 109). This encounter with Mr. Don at Asphodel unsettles the ladies' view of the past. Is he really alive? How will his continuing existence fit into the story they thought was closed? Have they only seen a vine? Have they had too much blackberry cordial? After this encounter, the three "old maids" no longer speak in unison. Their voices are disparate. Irene speculates that Miss Sabina would despise them for their flight. Cora thinks of reporting Don McInnis to the law. But the shyest, most repressed member of the trio has perhaps the most interesting response. Phoebe

25. Bullock, 398.

laughs: "Her voice was soft, and she seemed to be still in a tender dream and an unconscious celebration—as though the picnic were not already set rudely in the past, but were the enduring and intoxicating present, still the phenomenon, the golden day" (*WN*, 113). For Phoebe the past is now alive. She knows what Laurel Hand discovers in *The Optimist's Daughter*: As long as memory is "vulnerable to the living moment, it lives for us, and while it lives, and while we are able, we can give it up its due" (*OD*, 179). "Asphodel" thus tells us a good deal about Eudora Welty's attitude toward the past and its significance. For Welty, memory provides a stay against our losses to time, but only an evolving memory can make the past vital and alive; any attempt to hold the past within fixed boundaries leaves it dead and apart from us. A lost past, a past dead and apart, was one threat the war in Europe posed as Welty wrote her story in April 1941, and that threat would become more intense to Welty as the war expanded to include the United States.

*The Robber Bridegroom* and *The Wide Net* thus mark a distinct shift in Welty's writing career: They mark her explicit turn to the past as the source of inspiration for fiction, her shifting understanding of the past in the light of her wartime experience, and her implicit look at the war-torn present in the light of past events and legends. *The Robber Bridegroom* and *The Wide Net* were prompted by memory, memory as recorded in history or as recalled by an individual, but memory is more than a starting point here. Memory "takes on the strength of an instinct of survival and acquires the power of an art." It provides Welty with the emotional distance from which to confront "a terrible time" and with the plots and characters by which to dramatize the values she hoped would emerge victorious.

IV

## "The Treasure Most Dearly Regarded"
Memory and Imagination in *Delta Wedding*

By the fall of 1942, Eudora Welty had written all of the stories to be published in *The Wide Net* (1943), but afterward, for more than a year, she did not write fiction. Worry about the nature of war, the course of the war, the dangers into which friends and family had been or would be placed—all these things distracted Welty from creative pursuits. As a result, she busied herself instead with work for the war effort, with gardening, with the writing of "Some Notes on River Country" for *Harper's Bazaar*, and with reviewing for the *New York Times*. When she finally was able to return to fiction, she returned haltingly at first but ultimately found that "The Delta Cousins," begun as a short story, was the impetus toward the novel *Delta Wedding*, a novel that would encompass more and more details from Mississippi's past, from stories John Robinson had brought to her attention, and from her own memories of childhood. Welty once again relied on the past as she had in *The Robber Bridegroom* and *The Wide Net*, and again her look backward drew criticism. Critics felt her first novel was essentially escapist in nature. Its nostalgic portrait of the 1923 Mississippi Delta, they claimed, ignored the ugly realities that plagued the contemporary South. A review in *Time* magazine even labeled *Delta Wedding* a "Cloud-Cuckoo Symphony."[1]

Since the novel's publication in 1946, Welty readers have typically recognized that the charges of nostalgia are wrong-headed, but few have realized how closely, if obliquely, tied to contemporary issues *Delta Wedding* actually is. Albert Devlin is a notable exception. He writes that because the novel "was written in wartime and published in 1946," it involves a "probing for a humane order." Indeed, writing in the midst of war profoundly governed the sort of novel Welty would produce and the sort of order she would implicitly seek. By late 1943 when Welty began work on "The Delta Cousins," the threat of an Axis victory had diminished, but the threat of spiritual devastation in the wake of war remained full blown. This threat was still of preeminent concern when Welty completed the novel in September 1945. Not able to address directly this worry, Welty was able to "translate" her concern into what she later called "domestic or other dimensions of my writing"[2]; therefore, though the events of *Delta Wedding* are set in the past, the issues it investigates were of great importance in Welty's present. In the novel Welty explores the importance of courageously confronting the imminence of death and loss, of recognizing the urgency that life's transience brings to our lives, of discovering the continuity of love and the humanity of others, and of perceiving life's beauty despite its many horrors. Surely these traits are ones she must have felt to be endangered by totalitarian regimes during the war, and surely these traits are the ones she desperately hoped would survive the war years.

The story of *Delta Wedding*'s composition has been perceptively recounted by both Michael Kreyling and Albert Devlin, but Kreyling and Devlin are primarily concerned with aesthetic issues, not with the novel's connection to the political and social context from which it emerged.[3] That connection is deep and strong,

---

1. "Cloud-Cuckoo Symphony," *Time* 47 (22 April 1946): 104, 106, 108.
2. Albert Devlin, "The Making of *Delta Wedding*," in *Biographies of Books*, ed. James Barbour and Tom Quick (Columbia: University of Missouri Press, 1996), 227; Ruas, 66.
3. Kreyling, *Eudora Welty's Achievement of Order*, 55–76; Devlin, "The Making of *Delta Wedding*," 226–61.

as a comprehensive look at Welty's life and work between 1943 and 1946 helps to reveal.

Of course, two reviews Welty wrote in 1942–43 in lieu of writing fiction might be taken as a sign that she embraced a respite from the war-torn present. It is true that in reviewing novels about the pre-World War II South, Welty declined to level the charges of escapism that later would be directed at *Delta Wedding*. She accepted these books on their own terms, but she did not retreat from criticizing or commending the values they conveyed. Welty firmly believed that values particularly relevant in the 1940s could and should be integral to books about the past. In a review of *But You'll Be Back* by Marguerite Steedman, for instance, Welty praises Steedman's ability to re-create the surface of southern life, but objects to the novel's lack of passion: "Her thesis that no little town need die is laudable and full of interest, but the mind and heart and spirit of the town that would prove this thesis and rise above it are not examined. A glimpse of the town's real core of feeling and a timid hint of imagination are in the last chapter or so, but much more could have been made of the town's story and its overtones of medieval pride and joy in its work." Steedman, Welty argues, does not embody the values of small-town life in her story's plot, and it is those values Welty expects the author to be passionately committed to: "The author herself has not been emotionally affected by her ethical ideas, one feels. She is sure of them, often enthusiastic, sometimes sentimental, but not possessed."

In her review of *Sweet Beulah Land* by Bernice Kelly Harris, Welty praises Harris for providing a wide-ranging portrait of "a section of river plantation country in North Carolina," a section whose "inhabitants include river gentry, sharecroppers and Negroes, and their in-betweens." And Welty particularly praises Harris for her openness to diversity, for her lack of judgmental class consciousness. Welty believes that Harris is "completely at ease in every mansion, cottage, or shack" and that Harris "never preaches in any social-study manner."[4] In reviewing these novels of the South, Welty may have been looking ahead to the story and later novel she would write about a plantation region in Mississippi and its wide range of characters, but she may also have been anticipating the

4. Eudora Welty, *A Writer's Eye: Collected Book Reviews*, ed. Pearl Amelia McHaney (Jackson: University Press of Mississippi, 1994), 5, 6, 7.

sort of passionate ethical statement she would embed in her plot and the sort of acceptance of diversity for which her novel would call—a statement and an acceptance that might provide a vision for a meaningful postwar existence.

Certainly by summer 1943, Welty was feeling impatient with her inability to write fiction and was perhaps contemplating a fictional world like Steedman's and Harris's. But as fall arrived, she had been unable to create such a world. She wrote to Katherine Anne Porter, "For myself, I haven't written anything—in a year at least—except for a little article that was commissioned (Harper's B.) and I had to. I hope some day to be able to start again. It's not lack of concentration, but concentration on other things, and things I can't help—a form of indulgence in the long run maybe—if you can call dwelling on the warfront an indulgence." To the war Welty attributed her year-long fictional silence, but her anxieties about the war would ease, though not disappear, in the last few months of 1943. As she told Porter, "My friend John [Robinson] who was in the invasion and battle of Sicily came out of it all right, with nothing worse than a little fever they all got from bites got sleeping in haystacks etc., and a week in hospital— and is now doing something confidential for the British in Africa. . . . My little brothers are both still in this country at this writing." The comfort Welty drew from the current safety of those she loved and the catharsis she experienced in the aftermath of Robinson's first danger seem ultimately to have freed her to write again. She must also have taken heart from Robinson's posting to North Africa and from the humorous anecdotes he felt able to tell. The very fact that Robinson chose to report on his comically annoying French landlady in Africa—the woman who had requested that he "please swallow up nothing in the bedroom and bathroom and also to not sit on the bed"—marked his well-being and helped to move Welty herself toward new fiction with a comic vision.[5] Not surprisingly, when Welty did write fiction again, she wrote about a world John Robinson had shown her.

During the thirties, Robinson had taken Welty to visit his family homes, homes upon which *Delta Wedding*'s Shellmound and The Grove would be

5. Welty to Porter, [October 1943], Katherine Anne Porter Papers, Special Collections, University of Maryland Libraries. John Robinson turned the incident mentioned here into a story titled "Room in Algiers" (*New Yorker* 22 [19 October 1946]: 89–95).

based, and had introduced her to the distinctive ambiance of the Mississippi Delta. Sometime in October 1943, Welty began writing "The Delta Cousins," a story drawing upon what Robinson had taught her of the Delta and a story that would eventually become the novel *Delta Wedding*. On November 5, 1943, immediately upon completing this story, Welty mailed it to Robinson, in Africa.[6] Perhaps she sought to send a piece of home to Robinson who could not come home himself.

The story must have delighted Robinson with its descriptions of typical Mississippi Delta settings and characters. It opens with nine-year-old Laura Kimball making a train journey like ones Robinson had often made, a journey from Jackson to see her Shelton cousins who live in the Delta, cousins much like Robinson's own. The story then goes on to detail Laura's love for Uncle Raymond, the visit she and cousins Cindy and India make to Parthenia's house and to the store, the adventure India and Laura share when they go the house that would be called Marmion in *Delta Wedding*, the hostile behavior of Maurine toward Laura, the experience Laura has making mayonnaise with Aunt Mim, and the Sheltons' picnic on the banks of the Sunflower River.

Yet however much "The Delta Cousins" owes to John Robinson, the story also draws heavily upon Welty's memories of her own childhood and college years. The games Laura and her cousins play, the party favors they receive, the movies they have seen, the books Laura reads, Laura's love of bottles and boxes—all these aspects of her 1943 story Welty drew from memories of childhood. And memories of her college years in Columbus, Mississippi, at the Mississippi State College for Women (1925–27), also played a role for Welty. The train on which Laura rides is like the one Welty took from Artesia to Columbus as a college student, and one significant location in the story is based upon a Columbus landmark Welty had often visited, a deserted antebellum home called Waverley. This house served as a model for the bee man's house in "The Delta Cousins" and eventually for Marmion in *Delta Wedding*.

Recalling details from such a distance seems to have helped Welty view actual events in the metaphoric and transforming light of the imagination. Welty has written that "without the act of human understanding . . . experience is the

6. "The Delta Cousins," Welty Collection, MDAH.

worst kind of emptiness; it is obliteration, black or prismatic. . . . Before there is meaning, there has to occur some personal act of vision. And it is this that is continuously projected as the novelist writes, and again as we, each to ourselves, read" (*ES*, 136–7). Recalling the long ago seems to have made a "personal act of vision" possible for Eudora Welty as it has for many writers, including her friend Elizabeth Bowen. Indeed, Bowen has noted that "remote memories, already distorted by the imagination, are the most useful" ones for a writer of fiction to use in constructing a scene.[7] Not surprisingly, then, Welty calls her memory "the treasure most dearly regarded by me, in my life and in my work as a writer" (*OWB*, 104). The present world may be too intractable, too much itself, to be manipulated by the writer, but the past is not. In turning to the past for material, therefore, Welty was not denying the significance of present events, but was discovering strategies to convey the import of those events. Indeed, she has written that "the events in our lives happen in a sequence in time, but in their significance to ourselves they find their own order, a timetable not necessarily— perhaps not possibly—chronological" (*OWB*, 68–69).

If the passing of time encourages a metaphoric use of memory, a metaphoric sensibility seems to summon a long-held memory from its place in the unconscious. The mathematician Jules Poincare, for instance, believed that his theories had their origins in an aesthetic impulse. And according to Rollo May, an aesthetic impulse "is why the mathematicians and physicists talk about the 'elegance' of a theory. The utility is subsumed as part of the character of being beautiful. The harmony of an internal form, the inner consistency of a theory, the character of beauty that touches one's sensibilities—these are significant factors determining why a given idea emerges."[8] With Welty, then, we can speculate that the harmony between her past experiences and her worries of the 1940s, the ways in which a particular place or event from her own past could define the characters she was just now creating in "The Delta Cousins," enabled Welty's thematic investigation of time and change, of love and death, to emerge. Moreover, discovering connections between her past and her work in the present, as

7. Elizabeth Bowen, "Notes on Writing a Novel," in *The Mulberry Tree*, ed. Hermione Lee (San Diego, New York, London: Harcourt Brace Jovanovich, 1986), 40.
8. Rollo May, *The Courage to Create* (New York: Norton, 1975), 68.

she had not been able to do for more than a year, must have been reassuring to Welty as she continued to anticipate the traumatic changes World War II would inevitably bring about—some things at least promised to endure.

Reassuring or not, it was months before Welty would begin to revise "The Delta Cousins." Shortly after Welty finished the story in late 1943, Diarmuid Russell and *Harper's Bazaar* fiction editor Mary Lou Aswell suggested strategies for revision. Welty adopted none. Instead, for four months she wrote no fiction. Then in the spring of 1944 Welty began work on "A Sketching Trip" and mailed it to Russell by early May. In "A Sketching Trip," Welty once again turned to her distant past to find her story's subject. As a child of five or six, Welty had joined her mother and brother Edward in a retreat from the summer heat of Jackson. They spent two or three weeks in residence at a small establishment twenty or so miles southwest of Jackson; this establishment, called Hubbard's Wells, offered room and board, a number of wells with mineral waters thought to cure a variety of ailments, and weekend dances with music provided by Eddie Stiles. This very real place becomes Fergusson's Wells in Welty's story, and Delia Farrar, the story's adult protagonist, returns on a sketching trip to this spot she had visited as a young girl in the company of her mother. She also returns to visit the nearby haunted house, the ruins of an early-nineteenth-century house based upon an actual house that had belonged to someone in John Robinson's family. This is all the story has in common with actuality; the subsequent plot is Welty's invention. That plot deals with betrayal and loss and desolation, and it deals with the nature of memory. Delia recalls a childhood tour of the haunted house led by an "old maid" who fancies herself an artist, and she recalls the lurid story the old woman has told about the house, the story of a husband discovering his wife and her lover, murdering his wife, and then dying himself even as he kills the lover in a duel. Delia further recalls that a similar, though somewhat ludicrous, incident was part of her childhood stay at Fergusson's Wells. Mr. Fergusson had discovered his wife's infidelity and, in the midst of festivities for all guests, had shot at Mr. Torrance, her unlikely looking lover, with a rabbit gun. The young Delia and all the other guests had then abandoned Fergusson's Wells, but on her return years later Delia discovers that Mr. Fergusson, now a drunk, still lives at the wells and that he had not killed Mr. Torrance after all. Instead, Mr. Torrance and Mrs. Fergusson have set up housekeeping a mere forty miles down the road. The story's first words are "Violence! Violence!" and this is a story about the destructive violence called forth by betrayal. It is also a story about hope for renewal. When Delia returns to the haunted house, she sees that "it rose taller than any happenings or any times that forever beset the beauty itself of life. It was no part of shelter now, it was the survivor of shelter, an entity, glowing, erect, and a fiery color, the ancient color of a phoenix."[9] On a domestic scale, this story concerns the very issues and the very values that concerned Welty about the international scene of 1944—violence, betrayal, and the survival of "the beauty itself of life"—and these issues would prove central, if less melodramatic, in *Delta Wedding*.

A week after sending Russell this story, Welty went to New York and on June 1 began working at the *New York Times Book Review*. At the *Times*, she later recalled, were the rather hostile Lester Markel and an even more hostile colleague who refused to work in the same room with a woman. But such negative experiences were few, and Welty relished her May-to-October stay in the city. Robert Van Gelder proved to be a wonderful boss, Welty's copyediting and writing for the *Review* were sources of fulfillment, and the theaters and galleries of New York delighted her as they always had. Welty was particularly amused by a Mae West production of *Catherine Was Great*. Before this play opened at a theater within sight of her office, Welty occasionally managed to watch rehearsals. There she saw West, as Catherine the Great, inspect her identically clad troops, singling out one young man for special notice: "You're new here, aren't you," West inquired as she looked him over, up and down. More than fifty years after these events, Welty continued to repeat Mae West's line with great relish and enjoyment. Welty's fabled sense of humor was thoroughly engaged during her New York stint, and it seems especially appropriate that Welty reviewed S. J. Perelman's *Crazy Like a Fox* while she was on the staff of the book review. Humor had not been killed by war, and Welty's revitalized sense of humor signaled that she once again possessed the aesthetic distance required for a major achievement in fiction.

Good times notwithstanding, Welty remained concerned with the war. Operation Overlord had been launched in June, and by September 1 victory in Eu-

---

9. Eudora Welty, "A Sketching Trip," *Atlantic Monthly* 175 (June 1945): 62, 70.

rope seemed to be in the offing. In the summer and fall of 1944, Welty's reviews of books about war displayed both confidence in victory and distress at the continuing casualties. Writing under the name Michael Ravenna, Welty reviewed George Biddle's book *Artist at War* for the 16 July *Book Review*. Biddle had gone to Africa and then Italy with U.S. troops for the express purpose of providing "a pictorial record of the war." In her review, Welty deems Biddle's record both admirable and inadequate. She feels that his sketches "fail in immediate impact" because, unlike the drawings of Goya, they show the "aftermath of disaster" rather than "disaster in the act." Goya, Welty writes, "often showed human beings at the moment they met death, but at that moment they were supremely alive, aware—the very passion of his feeling for war's horror seemed to dictate this moment to him for its translation into art." Biddle, Welty suggests, seems not to recognize the intimate connection of life and death. However, Welty does praise the sense of humor in the text Biddle wrote to complement his drawings: "He has an eye out for the absurdities that make life even on the front bearable from one minute to the next." And Welty offers high praise for the nature of the project itself. The idea of trying to show people at home something real and concrete about the individual soldier at war, Welty contends, "is an interesting and hopeful example of a new, a human and subjective attitude of a country toward war, that may be a sign in itself that we can never tolerate another one."[10] Welty's comments about the Biddle book are, of course, very relevant to the sort of story she had written in "The Delta Cousins" and to the sort of changes she would make in transforming it into a novel. Her focus upon loss and upon the importance of facing "death on its way" would grow as her manuscript did. So too would her focus upon the urgency that death brings to our lives, her focus upon the importance of humor, and her focus upon "a human and subjective attitude" toward her subject.

By mid-October 1944, Welty had returned to Jackson, her internship at the *New York Times Book Review* at an end. Russell viewed Welty's departure from New York with ambivalence. He wrote to say that she would be missed, but added, "Its [sic] probably not a bad thing that you went for you'd never do any work up here and you write too well for us to accept that very happily." Back in

---

10. Welty, *A Writer's Eye*, 33, 34, 35, 36.

Jackson, Welty had decided that a visit to John Robinson's cousins in Webb, Mississippi, might spur her revisions to "The Delta Cousins." Russell wrote to encourage this visit, saying "I hope you can manage to visit the people in the Delta because I am looking forward so eagerly to see what the story becomes." That visit didn't occur for several months. But in February 1945, Russell wrote to Welty about her imminent trip to the Delta:

> I'll be curious to know how your visit to the Delta turns out. I think it will produce something inside your head, perhaps not anything that you ever thought of. But the place is ancient in its way and historied and somthing [sic] of that is bound to affect you and if you can see old journals with accounts of the day to day life you will be moved. I don't really care if it results or not in rework of the story, though that is the ostensible reason. But I am sure that a dip into the past of the South will have some effect—even if it only means that you start dressing in crinolines.[11]

The trip did indeed have a profound effect; Welty read the nineteenth-century diaries of Nancy McDougall Robinson and found the impetus for turning "The Delta Cousins" into *Delta Wedding*. Those diaries told of a young bride coming to the 1832 Mississippi Delta and eventually facing isolation, yellow fever, war, and loss. Nancy Robinson's struggles and her ability to cope with the ravages of time and change struck Eudora Welty, who was herself confronting the devastation wrought by the war, who was only now learning the full horror of Hitler's Final Solution, and who knew that a changed world lay ahead. Welty would remove her characters in *Delta Wedding* from the mind-boggling difficulties of 1945, but by setting her story in 1923 and by granting her Fairchild characters an ancestor like Nancy Robinson, Welty placed the Fairchilds in line for the changes of the Great Depression and World War II and made Nancy Robinson a model for the way they might eventually be able to cope with change. If Welty could not turn the horrors of Hitler's Germany into fiction, her novel would stress the importance of facing life's terrors directly, of understanding the mean-

11. Russell to Welty, 19 October 1944, 31 October 1944, 14 February 1945, restricted papers, Welty Collection, MDAH.

ing of one's own experience. The diaries show that sort of ability, an ability Welty finds lacking in most of her novel's characters.

Even as Welty was revising and expanding "The Delta Cousins" in the light of her visit to the Delta and her discovery of Nancy Robinson's diaries, she continued to write reviews. Of particular interest is her May 1945 review of William Sansom's *Fireman Flower*. In this review, Welty centers her commentary upon the volume's title story about a fireman attempting to save London buildings from the fires caused by bombings. At the end of this story, she tells us, "Fireman Flower is consumed inwardly by a vision of love—a quiet love for all he sees and knows through the greater vision of the world."[12] Writing this review even as she was writing *Delta Wedding*, Welty recognized in Sansom the very values that she would place at the heart of her novel. As *Delta Wedding*, though not "The Delta Cousins," closes, a love of the beautiful and the continuity of love promise to sustain young Laura McRaven.

On May 8, 1945, V-E Day was celebrated, and by mid-June Welty was roughly halfway through the writing of *Delta Wedding*. When victory over Japan was achieved in August, Welty was well into the second half of her novel, and by September 11 the entire manuscript was in Diarmuid Russell's hands. Fostered by the growing assurance of victory in war and by the survival of ones near and dear, Welty had completed the novel. She had found her inspiration in the need to communicate with a beloved friend, the emergence of personal memories from the unconscious, the careful reading of books she had been hired to review, and the need to define sustaining values in the face of devastation and social upheaval.

The transformation of "The Delta Cousins" into *Delta Wedding* is the record of Welty's growing emphasis upon the very values that she hoped would survive and triumph over the world Hitler envisioned. That transformation sharpens and deepens Welty's stress upon the significance of love in the face of time's inexorable movement, upon the need to face life's dangers courageously, upon the reality of beauty despite the horrors of experience, and upon the importance of granting each individual his humanity—all themes that had been central to Wel-

12. Welty, *A Writer's Eye*, 67.

ty's reviews of the Biddle and Sansom wartime books. In particular, Welty's revisions and additions to actual settings, to historical contexts, and to the development of peripheral characters serve to develop ideas only touched upon in her short story.

A key setting in "The Delta Cousins," for instance, takes its source in Eudora Welty's own experience, but becomes increasingly emblematic in the process of revision. During her two years at the Mississippi State College for Women, Welty and her classmates would occasionally hike out into the country, take the ferry across the Tombigbee River, and visit Waverley, a once grand plantation home that had become derelict. Almost twenty years after first entering this house, first seeing its double stairway ascending to a cupola with sixteen windows, and first standing beneath the massive chandelier that hung suspended from the top of the cupola, Welty chose to use Waverley as a model for the bee man's house in "The Delta Cousins" and eventually for Marmion in *Delta Wedding*.

In 1943, when in her mind's eye she journeyed back to days as a student as MSCW, Welty remembered Waverley in great detail. She recalled that the ferry man who had brought her across the river to the derelict house was also a bee man, that the gardens approaching the house were filled with boxwood, that the large octagon-shaped foyer of the house was topped by a cupola, that a double stairway in the foyer led to three tiers of galleries, and that a chandelier hanging from the cupola had once been lighted by gas manufactured from the plantation's own pine knots. The house still contained some furnishings, most notably a piano with mother-of-pearl keys, but its only inhabitants were dirt daubers and wasps, wrens and sparrows, chimney swifts, bats, and woodpeckers. Waverley's desolation, Welty remembered, seemed symbolized by the dead goldfinch she saw on the house steps during one of her visits. As she recalled these details, moreover, Welty knew that they, lit by the light of imagination, defined her deepest concerns. In "The Delta Cousins," when Laura and her cousin India come to the bee man's house, a dead finch on the house steps and the chandelier "like a pendulum that wants to swing in a clock but no one starts it" seem ominous and suggest the finality of death. But the truly sinister threat to the young girls' innocence lies not in such images of time's power, but in the bee man. As the girls return to his boat, he touches "his trousers and a little old fish seemed to come out."[13] The two cousins never realize what they have seen, but the visit to the house has been a potential sexual initiation as well as a potential initiation into the power of time itself.

These suggestions persist, are more subtly developed, and are closely tied to episode after episode in *Delta Wedding*. In the novel, the threat is not one of violation, as it had been in the story and in earlier stories like "At the Landing." In the novel, Laura and her cousin Roy Fairchild (not India, as in the story) must confront the intensity that the looming presence of death brings to life and love, the very intensity Welty had discussed in her review of George Biddle's *Artist at War*. The short story is only peripherally concerned with the power of time. Not so with the novel. In the novel, it is life's transience that most members of the Fairchild family refuse to face, and it is this aspect of reality that young Laura McRaven encounters when she and Roy come alone to Marmion. But suggestions of danger and death do not wholly define the experience Laura and Roy have at Marmion. The very chandelier that is like a stopped pendulum to Laura has seemed "like the stamen in the lily down-hanging" (*DW*, 122) to her older cousin Dabney. Dabney thinks of the house, or the chandelier at least, in sexual terms. And Roy and Laura's experience at Marmion reiterates those terms. The house's tower around which the adventurous Roy runs and the delicate piano that Laura plays seem to embody the union of masculine and feminine that the forthcoming marriage of Troy and Dabney, an event that plays no role in the story, will bring to the house. From the tower Roy can see "the whole creation," while inside the house Laura focuses her attention on the beautiful piano, "looking small as a fairy instrument" (*DW*, 176). Thus, when the old black woman Aunt Studney, a character based upon an actual woman Welty had heard of during visits to the Delta, a character who appears in the novel though not the story, and one who has entered Marmion with Roy and Laura, sounds "a cry high and threatening like the first note of a song at a ceremony, a wedding or a funeral" (*DW*, 176), she captures the double spirit of the house and the nature of the initiation that Laura undergoes there. Chandelier, tower, and piano—Welty has recognized a harmony between these elements of an actual place and the evolving concerns of her novel, and she has transformed the house and its furnishings

13. Welty, "The Delta Cousins," 24, 26.

into metaphor. Death, she suggests, is the source of life's urgency, of the need to cherish love and marriage and procreation. Writing as World War II moved toward its close, Welty reasserted the value of love that war's destruction had made so evident in other contexts.

The use of an actual place to define or confine the novel's concerns, of course, may involve a tension within a writer, a tension between the free flights of imagination and the restraining forces of memory, or between the demands of thematic development and the demands of verisimilitude, or between the desire to use invented details that will seem credible in a story and the desire to describe a very real locale in an accurate fashion. And tension itself seems to characterize all sorts of creative endeavors. According to John Briggs, psychiatrist Albert Rothenberg believes that "polarities and oppositional elements are pervasive in creative thinking," and Briggs adds that for creative individuals, "contradictory feelings are experienced not as mere conflict or ambivalence, but as possibilities, potentials, mystery, openness." Briggs's assertion well describes not only the way that seemingly contradictory images converge in *Delta Wedding* but also the way that possibility and potential arise for Welty from a polarity between the real world and her story's needs. Her metaphoric concept of place, in fact, embodies a possibility or potential for harmony. As Rothenberg has written, "a metaphor is a unity referring simultaneously to disparate aspects of experience." That sort of unity was missing in "The Delta Cousins," for as her agent Diarmuid Russell noted, "every individual section seems good and yet as a whole it doesn't quite have the effect it ought to have." And as Mary Lou Aswell later added, the bee man episode was not "integral" to the story.[14] Marmion, however, is an integral part of *Delta Wedding*. In this setting, past and present, memory and vision, are harmoniously united, as are images of love and death, and all converge to develop Welty's most central concerns and values.

But a particular memory cannot always provide the writer with appropriate

14. Briggs, 93, 110; Albert Rothenberg, "The Process of Janusian Thinking in Creativity," in *The Creativity Question*, ed. Albert Rothenberg and Carl Hausman (Durham: Duke University Press, 1976), 317; Russell to Welty, 10 November 1943, restricted papers, Welty Collection, MDAH, and as cited by Kreyling, *Author and Agent*, 103; Aswell to Welty, 16 December 1943, enclosed in Russell letter to Welty 21 December 1943, restricted papers, Welty Collection, MDAH.

imagery, and when it cannot, the polarity between reality and fiction must be resolved in another way. Robert Penn Warren discusses the writer's reliance on memories that emerge from the unconscious mind, and he argues that the ability to break free from such memories is crucial to creativity. A "creative reverie," Warren asserts, does not deny "the needs of the unconscious," but "it gives new contexts to the images arising from the unconscious and criticizes projections of it, and in that process 'liberates.'"[15] Welty makes much the same assertion when she states that "the writer must accurately choose, combine, superimpose upon, blot out, shake up, alter the outside world for one absolute purpose, the good of his story. To do this, he is always seeing double, two pictures at once in his frame, his and the world's" (*ES*, 124–5). In "The Delta Cousins," Welty has chosen aspects from Waverley for inclusion and exclusion, but in *Delta Wedding* she has more thoroughly altered that setting and combined it with other settings for the good of her story. And whether Welty selects elements from the outside world or invents details in order to establish her own world, she is working "in a state of constant and subtle and unfooled reference between the two." Indeed, Welty believes this state of conscious and "unfooled reference" is at the heart of any writer's achievement. And she knows that "at the moment of the writer's highest awareness of, and responsiveness to, the 'real' world, his imagination's choice (and miles away it may be from actuality) comes closest to being infallible for his purpose" (*ES*, 125).

In *Delta Wedding*, as in "The Delta Cousins," Welty locates Marmion, alias Waverley, literally "miles away" from actuality. (A story or novel about so distinctive a region as the Delta can hardly have one of its major locales one hundred miles to the east, in Columbus.) Yet in developing her novel's most crucial themes, Welty needed a landscape described in more detail than her story had permitted. Thus, the novel's first view of Marmion occurs when Dabney, who is scarcely mentioned in "The Delta Cousins," who is not a bride-to-be in that story, and who does not visit the bee man's house, comes alone on horseback to look across the Yazoo River, not the Tombigbee, at the "magnificent temple-like, castle-like house" (*DW*, 122). The location of the house on the Yazoo River and

15. Robert Penn Warren, "A Poem of Pure Imagination: An Experiment in Reading," in *Selected Essays* (New York: Random House, 1958), 288.

near a Delta swamp is integral to the thematic development of the novel. When Dabney rides away from Marmion, for example, she seizes "a last chance to look" at the river's backwater "before her wedding," and she sees the swamp in a rather suggestive light. She dismounts from her horse, parts "thronged vines of wild grapes, thick as legs," and looks at snakes in the bayou and at "vines and the cypress roots" growing in the water "more thickly than any roots should grow, gray and red" some of which "moved and floated like hair." Dabney then ponders a whirlpool: "And the whirlpool itself—could you doubt it? doubt all the stories since childhood of people white and black who had been drowned there, people that were dared to swim in this place, and of boats that would venture to the center of the pool and begin to go around and everybody fall out and go to the bottom, the boat to disappear? A beginning of vertigo seized her, until she felt herself leaning, leaning toward the whirlpool" (DW, 123). Dabney never describes this experience to anyone, not even to her future husband, though she, as Louise Westling has noted, clearly associates the tangled vines and the dangerous whirlpool with the mysteries of sex and marriage. And just as clearly, Dabney associates the whirlpool with the dissolution of self and the inescapable mortality which she must face to enter adulthood. Life and death are linked in her perceptions of the Delta landscape just as Welty had thought they should be linked in illustrations demonstrating the reality of a soldier's existence.

When Laura and her cousin Roy visit Marmion, the landscape surrounding the house becomes even more complexly emblematic. As we have already seen, Welty uses elements drawn from Waverley to associate the house with death as well as love, and when Roy throws Laura into the Yazoo River, not the Sunflower River of "The Delta Cousins," these concepts reappear: "As though Aunt Studney's sack had opened after all, like a whale's mouth, Laura opening her eyes head down saw its insides all around her—dark water and fearful fishes" (DW, 178). Laura, whose only previous swim has been in Jackson's Pythian Castle with the protection of water wings, is immersed in the Yazoo, literally the River of Death, which is now linked to Studney's sack. Roy believes her mysterious sack is the place his mother "gets all her babies," while Studney's home beyond the Deadening makes her seem an emblem of mortality.[16] In "The Delta

16. The argument I advance in this paragraph appears in a different context in my 1986

Cousins" Laura undergoes no such immersion, and the metaphorical Studney is nowhere in evidence. In the novel, however, both Studney's sack and the Delta's Yazoo River bring Laura an awareness of life's most fundamental mysteries, of its transience, and of the consequent urgency to love.

In expanding her story into a novel, Welty, even as she transformed the environs of Waverley, thus added descriptions of the swamps and rivers that had survived the Delta's metamorphosis from wilderness to plantation country. Dabney gazing into the whirlpool and Laura immersed in the River of Death encounter the frontiers of their own experience, the wilderness of their own emotional lives. The untamed physical world Welty describes is a psychological landscape as well. These descriptions, however, spring not from Welty's intuitive reliance upon archetypal concepts, but upon her very conscious decision to read and use the at times mundane, at times exciting, and always concrete diaries of Nancy McDougall Robinson, John Robinson's great-grandmother. Welty read the diaries over a year after she had completed her short story. Indeed, Welty's agent Diarmuid Russell wrote to her on Valentine's Day in 1945, predicting that the as yet unread diaries would have a powerful effect upon her.[17] Russell's remarks were prophetic, for Welty's venture into the journals led to her transformation of "The Delta Cousins" in both overt and oblique ways.

The diarist, Nancy Robinson, came to the Delta as a young bride in 1832, and her journals reveal just how much a frontier region nineteenth-century Mississippi was. Her first Delta home, Robinson writes, was a house made of "sticks and mud like a dove's nest" where she lived "more than 150 miles from any near relative in the wild woods of an indian nation, a stranger and unknown sitting in a low roofed cabbin [sic] by a little fire, nothing to be heard (that is cheerful) save the shrill note of the skylark the loud shriek of the night owl or the tinkling

---

article "The Metaphor of Race in Eudora Welty's Fiction" and in my 1988 book *The Welty Collection*. In 1980, Carol Moore discussed the significance of Aunt Studney's sack at some length and in similar terms ("Aunt Studney's Sack," *Southern Review*, n.s. 16 [1980]:591–6). Her discussion of the bees that emerge from the sack and of their symbolic import is of particular interest, though Louise Westling persuasively takes exception to Moore's conclusions (*Sacred Groves and Ravaged Gardens* [Athens: University of Georgia Press, 1985], 89–90).

17. Russell to Welty, 14 February 1945, restricted papers, Welty Collection, MDAH.

of a distant bell."[18] Robinson goes on to describe the bears her husband and later sons killed in the wilderness, the visits from plantation to plantation that family members made or received, the yellow fever epidemics that threatened the Delta population, her efforts to nurse both blacks and whites afflicted by fever, the devastating effects of the Civil War, the arrival of a federal steamboat on the bayou, and the 1869 conflict between her son and a business associate, a conflict that resulted in the associate shooting at her son Douglas, and in Douglas returning fire and killing his assailant.

In "The Delta Cousins," Welty makes no attempt to re-create a sense of the Delta past and makes little attempt to re-create the untamed Delta landscape. But in *Delta Wedding* the diaries have clearly inspired the Fairchild family history that Welty presents, the dark waters into which Laura has plunged, and the bayou landscape that Dabney encounters before her marriage. The frontier in *Delta Wedding* embodies that world that the Fairchilds typically attempt to repress, the world of mystery and the unknown, and the frontier persists in the land that planters have yet to bring under their control and into cultivation. The Fairchilds, of course, pay homage to their frontier past, hanging portraits of their ancestors, consulting the old cookbooks and diaries, but in doing so they fail to discover anything that is profoundly relevant to their lives. When Tempe sees the firearms displayed in the Fairchild living room, she sighs with distress and along with India looks for a moral: "There was Somebody's gun—he had killed twelve bears every Saturday with it. And Somebody's pistol in the lady's workbox; he had killed a man with it in self-defense at Cotton Gin Port, and of the deed itself he had never brought himself to say a word; he had sent the pistol ahead of him by two Indian bearers to his wife, who had put in it this box and held her peace, a lesson to girls" (*DW*, 98).[19] Both Tempe and India ignore the powerful and complex questions the firearms might evoke and arrive at a motto that neither can live by—that women should quietly accept the actions of their men.

18. Nancy McDougall Robinson, Diary 1832, Mississippi Department of Archives and History, Jackson, n.pag.

19. There is actually a town named Cotton Gin Port in the Columbus, Mississippi, vicinity.

Dabney and George, however, are not guilty of simplistic and comic distortions. They seem to feel what their ancestors felt and to revere the mysterious heroism of those who confronted the Delta wilderness. Dabney gazes at the portrait in which Mary Shannon has circles under her eyes, "for that was the year the yellow fever was worst and she had nursed so many of her people, besides her family and neighbors; and two hunters, strangers, had died in her arms" (*DW*, 41). Here, as Welty enlarges upon Nancy Robinson's experiences with yellow fever and superimposes the appearance of Eudora Carden Andrews, Welty's own grandmother, upon the fictional Mary Shannon, the relevance of the past is clear (*OWB*, 49). Dabney, anticipating her own marriage and the challenges it may involve, recognizes the heroism of her great-grandmother, who married, left her parents and friends, and came to the unsettled Delta: "How sure and how alone she looked, the eyes so tired. What if you lived in a house all alone and away from everybody with no one but your husband" (*DW*, 41). Like Dabney, George reveres those who can face the unknown with courage and serenity. Robbie believes that for George, "old stories, family stories, Mississippi stories, were the same as very holy or very passionate, if stories could be those things. He looked out at the world, at her, sometimes, with that essence of the remote, proud, over-innocent Fairchild look that she suspected, as if an old story had taken hold of him—entered his flesh. And she did not know the story" (*DW*, 191). George, like Dabney, grants family stories their meaning, a meaning that embraces rather than denies mystery; as a result, the past is not prismatic to uncle or niece. These two individuals recognize the courage with which their ancestors confronted isolation, death, the unknown, the courage with which they faced those realities rather than retreating from them. Writing in 1945 to readers of the forties, Welty clearly relied upon dramatic irony: She and her readers knew that neither George, Dabney, nor any of the Fairchilds would be able to remain in the relatively secure world of 1923. They would have to face a severe economic depression and a world war; the courage of their ancestors would have to become their own if they were to lead meaningful lives.

Although Welty relied upon Nancy McDougall Robinson in creating these Fairchild ancestors, she felt free to create her own history for the house she renames Marmion. The actual house, Waverley, was constructed by Colonel George Hampton Young, probably in 1852. During the Civil War, Confederate officers, including General Nathan Bedford Forrest on at least one occasion, met there. The mansion was abandoned in 1913 when Young's last surviving son died. A Delta house near Greenwood would be unlikely to have such a history, and Welty uses none of this information in "The Delta Cousins" or in *Delta Wedding*. In "The Delta Cousins," Welty provides no history for the house; its origins are wholly mysterious and no Shelton seems ever to have owned it. But in *Delta Wedding*, she tells us that Marmion—Welty, like the owners of Waverley, found a name for her house in the works of Sir Walter Scott—was built in 1890 by James Fairchild, father of Denis, Battle, George, Tempe, Jim Allen, Primrose, and Annie Laurie, and abandoned in the same year after James Fairchild was killed in a duel. As the novel begins, we learn that it is to be the home of Dabney and Troy once they are married. And one day Laura may live at Marmion, for it is her rightful inheritance from her mother. Laura's inheritance from her dead mother, however, consists not only of this property, but also of the ability to accept the complex terms of human existence. Appropriately, then, Welty establishes one as the symbol of the other. In the novel, though not the story, Annie Laurie, who left the Delta in order to marry Laura's father, has inherited Marmion, and Marmion therefore should one day be Laura's. As Carol Moore and Peggy Prenshaw have noted, when Annie Laurie makes her young daughter a doll and names the doll Marmion, she looks forward to the legacy that will be Laura's.[20] The doll is aptly linked to the house, for Annie Laurie will bequeath a knowledge of love and death to Laura—the love she has given her daughter, the love implicit in her making of the doll, but also death, her own death. Ellen believes that Uncle George is the only Fairchild who sees "death on its way" (*DW*, 188), but she is wrong. Nine-year-old Laura shares this perception. Laura will be able to live in Marmion because she can appreciate its history of loss and its return to life during the tenure of Troy and Dabney.

The fictional history of Marmion is perfectly appropriate for a novel located in the slow-to-be-developed lands of the Delta interior.[21] More importantly, it

20. Waverley, Subject File, Mississippi Department of Archives and History, Jackson; Moore, 591–6; Peggy W. Prenshaw, "Woman's World, Man's Place,"in *Eudora Welty: A Form of Thanks*, ed. Louis Dollarhide and Ann J. Abadie (Jackson: University Press of Mississippi, 1979), 51.

21. The Mississippi Department of Archives and History reports that "The 4,000,000 rich acres in the interior of the Mississippi Delta were sparsely settled before 1880 because of flood-

focuses attention on the empowering nature of Laura's dual inheritance, not on the sterile memories of a lost cause; it suggests the possibility of renewal, not merely the reality of desolation. And as Welty wisely invents a family history for the house, she also fortuitously discovers in her own experience the metaphor of the doll. Welty's memory of her own mother making a stocking doll one rainy day, gratifying her daughter's wish almost as soon as it was expressed, becomes in *Delta Wedding* an emblem of a mother's love and the promise of love's continuity. And that promise enables Laura to embrace her Fairchild aunts and uncles and cousins and to see the beauty in the world around her. At the novel's close, "One great golden star [goes] through the night falling," to be followed by another. And Laura joyously responds to this beauty, holding out both arms "to the radiant night" (*DW*, 247). Here again Welty must "choose, combine, superimpose upon, blot out, shakeup, alter the outside world" to serve the purposes of her story. Here again the success of her story has emerged from the tension between the demands of memory and the demands of the story and from the writer's ability to know when those demands coincide and when they do not. And here again Welty asserts the power of love's continuity and of life's beauty despite the pain of loss, a domestic version of the power she describes in her review of William Sansom's World War II stories, the only power capable of redeeming a war-torn world.

Redemption of that world, Welty further suggests in her novel, lies in granting each individual his humanity, and Welty revised "The Delta Cousins" in order to focus on this very issue. In "The Delta Cousins," Parthenia is an amusing figure. Suspected by Ellen of taking her garnet pin, Parthenia effectively fends off Dip's tentative inquiries about the pin and relishes the attention her drawer leg hat commands. The scene is an amusing but somewhat stereotypical one. Not so in the novel. In *Delta Wedding*, Welty grants Partheny her humanity as most of her white characters do not. The plantation-owning Fairchilds deal

---

ing from the Mississippi River and its many tributaries" ("The New Cotton Kingdom," Exhibition text, Old Capitol Museum, Jackson, Mississippi). In the novel, the nineteenth-century Fairchilds live at the Grove, "a cypress house on brick pillars" (*DW*, 37), until Marmion is built in 1890, and they return to the Grove when tragedy seems to taint that house. The early house on pillars would have been, before 1880, far better suited to the landscape of the Delta interior and far more feasible to construct there.

with their servants in a congenial fashion, white and black children play together, and Ellen Fairchild sees to the health and well-being of black servants.
But these surface relationships mask a very deep separation. When the black ma-
triarch Partheny is subject to spells of mindlessness, for instance, the Fairchilds
are sympathetic, but they never see the tragic import of the spells. Partheny,
whose seizures resemble those experienced by Jackson midwife Ida M'Toy, describes her latest spell to Ellen Fairchild: "I were mindless, Miss Ellen. I were
out of my house. I were looking in de river. I were standing on Yazoo bridge wid
dis foot lifted. I were mindless, didn't know my name or name of my sons. Hand
stop me. Mr. Troy Flavin he were by my side, gallopin' on de bridge. He laugh
at me good—old Partheny! Don't you jump in dat river, make good white folks
fish you out! No, sir, I ain't goin' to do dat! Guides me home" (*DW*, 78). Partheny's "mindlessness" takes a particularly appalling form—she loses all sense of
her identity. Mindlessness for Aunt Shannon Fairchild takes the form of senility,
not of blackouts; she is able to "talk conversationally with Uncle Denis and
Aunt Rowena and Great-Uncle George, who had all died no telling how long
ago, that she thought were at the table with her" (*DW*, 13). The white woman
retreats into the past. Partheny doesn't know her own name or the names of her
sons. She recalls no past. In fact, Partheny scarcely has a past of her own. Her
life has been focused upon the Fairchilds. Her contact with the family has been
close and affectionate; she attended Ellen Fairchild at the birth of her daughter
Shelley, was the nurse to several of Ellen's children, and assists in the final prepa-
rations for Dabney's wedding to Troy Flavin; Ellen Fairchild, similarly, has min-
istered to the ailing Partheny, provided her with Shellmound Plantation's old
wicker furniture, and refused to criticize Partheny's appropriation of insignificant Fairchild possessions. But no other family members even think about Partheny except as she plays a role in family activities. They take her for granted,
never questioning that her life should be devoted to them, never realizing that
she had been denied a separate past of her own. Though they are more sensitive
than Troy, the overseer who laughs as he stops Partheny from jumping into the
Yazoo River, the Fairchilds' empathy for their servants is limited. There is no
indication that Welty intended this implicit indictment of racism to serve as a
commentary upon wartime issues. Nevertheless, writing in 1945 as Nazi anti-
Semitic and racist atrocities were becoming widely known, Welty portrays the

attitudes that along with greater economic opportunity had led many black Mississippians to emigrate northward during the war years and that ironically failed to match the nobility of the American crusade again Nazism. At the same time, her characterization of Partheny conveys the hope that those attitudes may yet change.

We can thus learn much about one writer's imagination by studying the origins of "The Delta Cousins" and *Delta Wedding*. The reliance upon distant memories, the impetus to metaphoric thought that distance in time can provide, the intuitive recognition that a remembered place can define issues and values crucial to the present moment, a tension between the power of memory and the demands of fiction—these elements all characterize Eudora Welty's creative process and are crucial to the achievement of *Delta Wedding*. More crucial perhaps are the values that emerge from this process, values that Welty believed must answer the challenges posed by World War II. Implicit in Eudora Welty's *Delta Wedding* is an affirmation of faith that William Faulkner would later explicitly make: It is the writer's privilege, Faulkner wrote, "to help man endure by lifting his heart, by reminding him of the courage and honor and hope and pride and compassion and pity and sacrifice which have been the glory of his past."[22] In *Delta Wedding* Eudora Welty surely prefigured Faulkner's Nobel Prize address and proved herself deserving of that very honor.

22. William Faulkner, "William Faulkner's Speech of Acceptance upon the Award of the Nobel Prize for Literature," in *The Faulkner Reader* (New York: Random House, 1954), 4.

V

# "When Our Separate Journeys Converge"

*The Golden Apples*

*A Curtain of Green*, Eudora Welty's first book of stories, grew primarily from the excited recognition that her imagination was "as dearly matched to the world as its secret sharer" and that her daily encounters with Mississippi could be the subjects of stories. Of course, she occasionally turned to the past in writing these early stories, but more typically she discovered her subjects in the present. Quite the reverse was true for the more mature writer of *Delta Wedding*. Prompted by an ongoing friendship with John Robinson, Welty drew upon her personal past and the past of Robinson's family in writing her first novel. A somewhat different sort of inspiration led to Welty's next and perhaps finest book; unlike Welty's earlier books, *The Golden Apples* takes its origins in a thoroughgoing convergence of past and present as certainly as it also shows a convergence between story and novel and between mythic, literary, and personal sources.[1] Though in *The Robber Bridegroom*, *The Wide Net*, and *Delta Wedding*

1. Because there exists an extensive body of research upon Welty's use of mythic and literary sources, my focus here will be upon Welty's use of Mississippi experiences in creating *The Golden Apples*. For examples of other approaches, see Rebecca Mark's *The Dragon's Blood* (Jack-

Welty uses the past to comment upon the present, in *The Golden Apples* she allows her past and present experiences to comment upon each other. Here Welty has transformed contemporary experiences into stories and found that those contemporary stories prompt memories of the past, which in turn inspire other stories. Moreover, the stories themselves converge in terms of plot and characterization as stories in *A Curtain of Green* and *The Wide Net* did not. Confluence then is the term that best describes Welty's creative process in *The Golden Apples*.

Between 1945, when she completed *Delta Wedding*, and 1949, when she published *The Golden Apples*, Welty's life was one of many changes, and writing on the edge of change seems to have prompted the convergence of past and present for Welty. As historian Ray Skates has argued, "The Second World War was a watershed for Mississippi, a convenient and readily identifiable era, before which there was basic historical continuity for a century, but after which nothing ever again was quite the same." Skates goes on to write that after 1945, "revolutions occurred in agriculture, industry, demography, income, and, most important of all, race—revolutions that brought an end to sharecropping and Jim Crowism, to the hegemony of King Cotton, to Mississippi's isolation from the nation."[2] In many ways, *The Golden Apples* addresses prewar stability and from its postwar perspective questions the assumptions that undergirded that stability; in particular, Welty is concerned with Mississippi small towns, with their traditional virtues and limitations, and with their slowly evolving nature. She is also very concerned with race, with the white Mississippian's belief in white supremacy, and with the consequences of that belief for both whites and blacks. Beyond addressing these public issues, however, Welty also focuses on private locations of change. Prompted by a moment of decision in her own life, Welty's stories investigate the roles that women have been expected to play in southern society, they investigate the nature of relationships between men and women, and they

son: University Press of Mississippi,1994); Thomas McHaney's "Eudora Welty and the Multitudinous Golden Apples," *Mississippi Quarterly* 26 (Fall 1973): 589–624; Franklin D. Carson's "'The Song of Wandering Aengus': Allusions in Eudora Welty's *The Golden Apples*," *Notes on Mississippi Writers* 6 (Spring 1973): 14–7; and Patricia Yaeger's "'Because a Fire Was in My Head': Eudora Welty and the Dialogic Imagination" in *Welty: A Life in Literature*, ed. Albert J. Devlin (Jackson: University Press of Mississippi, 1987), 139–67.

2. John Ray Skates, *Mississippi: A History* (New York: Norton, 1979), 150, 154.

explore the possibilities for women to lead independent, fulfilling lives in the postwar world. Past and present comment upon each other in *The Golden Apples*; the virtues and the shackles of tradition, the possibilities and the dangers of the contemporary South, converge in this book of interlocking stories.

In August 1945 as the Second World War came to its conclusion, Eudora Welty was completing her first novel, with merely fine turning revisions lying ahead of its publication in 1946. Though the horror of the atomic bomb appalled Welty, a sense of relief must have been hers now that the tense war years were at last over, now that her friends and brothers would be returning home, and now that her own career seemed so promising. That relief, however, was soon to be qualified by a sense that the ideals of the war had failed to transform the political realities at home, that desperate problems remained to be solved abroad, and that those she loved had been sadly changed by the war. Change—change that was desperately needed and slow to come, change that involved tragic loss, change that required hard decisions—was the keynote of Welty's life from 1945 to 1949 and would provide the central issues in her fiction.

Certainly, Welty felt that Mississippi must move beyond the provincial outlook that had long separated the state from national and international communities and must move beyond the racism that separated Mississippi citizens from each other. In this spirit, on December 20, 1945, Welty wrote to the *Jackson Clarion-Ledger*, complaining about the paper's coverage of Gerald L. K. Smith's recent visit. While in Jackson, Smith, who had been a devout disciple of Huey Long, proclaimed himself opposed not only to "Stalinism" but also to "Internationalism and other forms of alienism" and sought to expand his Nationalist movement in the South. Knowing that Smith was, to use the words of Walter Goodman, "the country's noisiest anti-Semite," a man who had praised Hitler, blamed Jews for the Great Depression and World War II, and denied the reality of the Holocaust, Welty was offended by the *Clarion-Ledger's* non-judgmental coverage of Smith's speech. Recognizing the legacy of Nazism and the spirit that would eventually fuel McCarthyism, Welty asked the editor, "Isn't there anybody ready with words for telling Smith that that smells to heaven to us, that we don't want him, won't let him try organizing any of his fascistic doings in our borders, and to get out and stay out of Mississippi?" She went on to ask, "Is there still nothing we can do to atone for our apathy and our blindness or our closed minds, by maintaining some kind of vigilance in keeping Gerald Smith away?" Then Welty concluded her letter by denouncing Smith's ideological pals: "We will get Bilbo and Rankin out when their time, election time, comes, God willing."[3] In her hometown newspaper, the usually circumspect Welty thus made a forceful and impassioned political statement, a statement for openness, tolerance, freedom of speech and of belief, the very values she had championed in her wartime fiction and would continue to champion in her stories of the late forties. In rejecting Smith, Senator Theodore Bilbo, and U. S. Representative John Rankin, Welty denounced the isolationism, anti-Semitism and racism that were their staples, recognized that the defeat of Nazism had not destroyed the hatreds it represented, and called for change.

Well might Welty have called for the defeat of Bilbo and Rankin. Indeed, both represented values that were anathema to her. Elected to the United States Senate in 1934, Bilbo sought "to send blacks 'back to Africa,' opposed anti-lynching and anti–poll tax bills, and spent much of his energy preaching race hatred and white supremacy." In a stump speech during his 1946 campaign, Bilbo was in rare form: "Do not let a single nigger vote. If you let a few register and vote this year, next year there will be twice as many, and the first thing you know the whole thing will be out of hand." Attitudes like Bilbo's were especially shocking in the wake of a war ostensibly fought against Nazi Aryanism. And Welty must have been especially appalled to see the effect of these attitudes upon returning black soldiers, who might be beaten for continuing to wear their military uniforms and who certainly were expected to merge without complaint back into a Jim Crow society. Equally repugnant to Welty were the policies of Congressman Rankin. Rankin, who served in the House of Representatives from 1921–52, was a rabble-rousing member of the House Un-American Activities Committee. Caustically anti-Semitic, Rankin taunted his Jewish colleagues in the House, equating them with Communists. In addition, he sought to block

3. "Bilbo and Rankin Get Blessings of Former Huey Long Chieftain," *Jackson Clarion-Ledger*, 20 December 1945; Walter Goodman, *The Committee* (New York: Farrar, Straus, and Giroux, 1968), 181; Eudora Welty, "Voice of the People," *Jackson Clarion-Ledger*, 28 December 1945.

Chinese immigration into the United States, and he opposed any political measures that might move black Americans toward equality. When the American Red Cross sought to cease labeling blood as "black" or "white," Rankin exploded; this idea, he contended, was put forth by the "crackpots, the Communists and parlor pinks . . . to mongrelize the nation."[4] Welty must have cringed at such comments, comments that denied the validity of the American war effort. Her public call for the defeat of Bilbo and Rankin is testimony to her extreme disgust with their values.

Welty's support of President Truman in the election of 1948 was similarly a rejection of southern separatism and an embracing of tolerance and openness. Truman, Welty felt, was the "nearest to liberal choice" in the election, and she rejoiced in his victory. She might have regretted that Truman attacked racial prejudice not merely on idealistic grounds but also on opportunistic ones, seeking "to gain black votes in the North."[5] But her approval of Truman's liberal positions indicates that she wholeheartedly approved his 1947 appointment of the Committee on Civil Rights and his 1948 order integrating the American military. Unfortunately, Welty's support of Truman left her in a distinct minority at home; the likes of Bilbo and Rankin continued to carry the day. When the States' Rights Party (otherwise known as the Dixiecrat Party) was formed to defy Truman's liberal agenda, Mississippians were centrally involved. Mississippi Governor Fielding Wright was a key leader in establishing the new party, he then ran for vice-president on the Dixiecrat ticket, and the States' Rights Party carried Mississippi in 1948.

Beyond her concern with the close-minded nature of much Mississippi life, Welty was also troubled by the economic suffering being faced in the postwar years by citizens of Europe. The need to face this crisis prompted Welty to con-

4. Loewen and Sallis, 239; Theodore Bilbo, as cited by Loewen and Sallis, 239; Neil McMillen, "Fighting for What We Didn't Have: How Mississippi's Black Veterans Remember World War II," in *Remaking Dixie: The Impact of World War II on the American South*, ed. Neil McMillen (Jackson: University Press of Mississippi, 1997), 98–99; John Rankin, cited in *Dictionary of American Biography*, s.v. "Rankin, John."

5. Welty to Robinson, Friday [November 1948], Welty Collection, MDAH; Charles P. Roland, *The Improbable Era: The South Since World War II*, rev. ed. (Lexington: University of Kentucky Press, 1976), 31.

sider a European trip: Early in 1948, Welty wrote to Katherine Anne Porter, saying, "The world seems so awful and I want to see that, having always wanted to see it when it seemed beautiful." Surely Welty had been moved by George C. Marshall's plan for European renewal. In his June 5, 1947, address at Harvard University, an address that inaugurated the Marshall Plan, Marshall had called for an American foreign policy directed "against hunger, poverty, desperation and chaos," all of which were particularly rampant in postwar Germany. Ten million houses in Germany had been destroyed or severely damaged; there were shortages of those things most needed by industry—"of machinery, of raw materials, and especially of fuel and power"; transportation systems were crippled; inflation was tremendously high, food was tremendously short, and millions of homeless Germans wandered the country. Welty was both moved by this suffering and unsure how to respond appropriately to it. She told Porter that she had "gotten a lot of letters from Germans—couldn't help but wonder what you would say to some certain ones—and what you've said to those you must have gotten—I send food and clothes, but the answers trouble me."[6] Welty's comment is enigmatic, but it seems that, in humanitarian fashion, she had attempted to help destitute Germans regardless of their loyalties during the war, that she wondered what Porter, given her negative view of the German character, might say about that policy, and that Welty was herself bothered by the prospect of aiding those who likely had supported Hitler. The international scene, now free from armed conflict, continued to trouble Welty. Her impulse toward openness and sympathy for anyone's suffering was countered by her horror at the Nazi war machine and the Nazi concentration camp atrocities. For Welty there was no simple, right or wrong choice. Like Virgie Rainey in her story "The Wanderers," Welty knew that all things were double.

Such doubleness also characterized Welty's attitudes toward the social mores of life in small town Mississippi, mores that seemed increasingly oppressive and absurd in the wake of World War II. In fact, Welty's friend Hubert Creekmore

6. Welty to Porter, 25 January [1948], Papers of Katherine Anne Porter, Special Collections, University of Maryland Libraries; George C. Marshall, as cited by Richard Mayne, *The Recovery of Europe, 1945–1973*, rev. ed. (Garden City, New York: Anchor Press, 1973), 128; Mayne, 37–44.

returned from service in World War II to write a novel denigrating life in the small southern town, but Welty's own view would prove less extreme. In *The Welcome*, Creekmore attacks the class-conscious nature of the small southern town, the lack of a cultural life there, and most especially the conventional roles played by women. Early in the novel, a young married woman named Doris Furlow criticizes the unmarried Isabel Lang for "all those peculiar habits she's got—smoking on the street, reading deep books, painting naked figures, wearing pants around town." According to Doris, her husband "would never like a woman who thought *thoughts*. No man would, as far as I can tell. They want a pretty, sweet woman they can admire—and worship."[7] Creekmore thus suggests that women have perversely made themselves into creatures they believe men desire, creatures without minds or passions, and in his portrait of Isabel Lang he calls for change. He calls for women to use their intellect and to free themselves from repression. Nevertheless, Creekmore suggests that without a man, even a woman like Isabel Lang is incomplete. He sees no possibility for women to lead vital and fulfilling independent lives. In the course of *The Golden Apples*, Welty would investigate these very issues, issues she must have discussed with Creekmore. Welty would suggest that though the conventions of small town life can be constricting, the advantages of that life are many. Though she would agree that women may be complicit in their own subordination and silencing, she would not, as Creekmore did, ignore male power as the more primary source. And she would end her interlocking collection of stories with an affirmation of the separate independent life as a viable option for women.

Although Creekmore is quite discerning in his discussion of the roles played by women in southern society, he avoids explicitly confronting the cracks that World War II would bring to Mississippi's conventional facade. He sets *The Welcome* in 1936, not in the postwar South. The stories of *The Golden Apples*, on the contrary, are variously set between 1905 or so and the late 1940s. Having the stories range over this time period clearly indicates Welty's interest in both the ruling conventions and the incipient changes in her home state. The decline of a rural farming population and the growth of an urban and rural nonfarming population is one such change. Between 1900 and 1950, Welty's hometown of

7. Hubert Creekmore, *The Welcome* (New York: Appleton-Century-Crofts, 1948), 9.

Jackson had grown from almost 8,000 residents to more than 100,000; between 1940 and 1950 Jackson had grown from 62,107 to 100,261. Along with this shift in population came improved transportation. Dirt roads and mule-drawn wagons slowly gave way to paved highways and automobiles. As dirt roads vanished, so too did some still untouched Mississippi forests. As Nollie Hickman reports, "World War II brought high prices for timber products. The number of mills increased from 1,409 in 1940 to 1,996 in 1946. The production of lumber increased from 1,481,000,000 board feet to 1,851,539,000 in 1942." In the 1950s, tree planting and improved land management helped timber growth to exceed the amount harvested in most of Mississippi, but in the Delta and northeast Mississippi, there continued to be a decline in forest acreage.[8] In "The Wanderers," Welty depicts just these changes and confronts their social implications.

Distressed as she was by the political and social situation in Mississippi and by the suffering so prevalent internationally, Welty found her personal situation also unsettled and changing. In December 1945, John Robinson was home from the war but in poor health and poor spirits. In January 1946, Welty wrote Diarmuid Russell that John "has been a little low in his mind," and perhaps as a result Welty was a bit low in her own. "I feel nervous and bad," she told Russell, "really not like any way I ever felt before—don't know what I can do about it but maybe the weather will help if it gets nice and either warm or sunny." By February, Welty could tell Russell, "I feel a little better in my mind most of the time now," but her worries were not over.[9] Though she had been able to write both "The Whole World Knows" and "Golden Apples" (later retitled "June Recital") by mid-October, those stories do not confront the effects of war upon those who served and upon those to whom they returned. Set respectively during the Depression and around 1920, they avoid dealing with World War II. Such

8. John N. Burrus, "Urbanization in Mississippi, 1890–1970," in *A History of Mississippi*, ed. Richard Aubrey McLemore, vol. 2, p. 352; Thomas D. Clark, "Changes in Transportation," in *A History of Mississippi*, vol. 2, p. 297–9; Nollie W. Hickman, "Mississippi Forests," in *A History of Mississippi*, vol. 2, pp. 227, 228–9.

9. Welty to Russell, n.d. [January 1946], 3 January [1946], n.d. [Feb. 1946], restricted papers, Welty Collection, MDAH.

issues were too close to Welty. But her new stories did reflect the darkness of her mind-set in 1946.

December 1946 promised better times for Welty. She traveled to San Francisco to visit Robinson, who was residing there, trying to earn a living and establish himself as a writer. Her planned two-week stay became almost a four-month sojourn, much of which was happy. Michael Kreyling writes that "Welty liked everything about San Francisco—the company she had found in John Robinson's friends, the sunsets, the fog, the ocean, even the batty landladies she encountered in her quest for a cheap apartment or furnished room," but perhaps Kreyling overstates the case. Welty's ability to take pleasure in this new setting was limited by her continued worries about Robinson. She wrote again to Russell that Robinson was depressed and expressed concerned about the consequences if his attempt at a writing career proved unsuccessful. She might also have been worrying about her future with Robinson, about the possibility of marriage, about the prospects for happiness in marriage. Welty never discussed with interviewers the nature of her relationship with Robinson, but it had long been a close one: their 1937 car journey to Mexico, Welty's visit to Lt. John Robinson in St. Petersburg, Florida, the affection and worry for him expressed in Welty's wartime letters to Katherine Anne Porter, and her lengthy 1946–47 stay near him in San Francisco all suggest that theirs was a serious relationship. But stories that both she and Robinson wrote while in San Francisco are about conflicted men in failing relationships. In "'. . . All this Juice and All this Joy,'" Robinson's protagonist seems like a male version of the typist in T. S. Eliot's *The Waste Land*; a seduction scene prompts Tom to think only "'So that's that' . . . It seemed to be the end of a long journey and why he had set out on it was not so clear to him." And in Welty's "Music from Spain," marriage seems a trap to the protagonist, then named Francis Dowdie, and Dowdie finds himself drawn toward another man, a Spanish guitarist.[10]

10. Kreyling, *Author and Agent*, 122–3; Kreyling in *Author and Agent* also notes that Welty's visit to San Francisco was intended "to test a relationship that had survived one long crisis—the war—and was faced with a second: two writers sharing the same career" (121); Welty to Porter, 11 November [1942], 23 November 1943, Katherine Anne Porter Papers, Special Collections University of Maryland Libraries; John Fraiser Robinson, "'. . . All this Juice and All this Joy,'" *Horizon* 18 (November 1948): 347.

At the end of March 1947, Welty headed back to Jackson, her future with Robinson still in question. She would remain only a short time at home, leaving again in July to speak at the Northwest Pacific Writers' Conference in Seattle. And as soon as her speaking commitment was finished, Welty would move on to San Francisco for another extended stay near Robinson. Her ten weeks in California were productive ones; here she would complete "Moon Lake" and "A Shower of Gold," and here she would realize that her stories, save "Music from Spain," were interlocking in nature. But on November 1, when Welty left to visit the Grand Canyon and return home, her satisfactions were more professional than personal. As she wrote Katherine Anne Porter, probably in January 1948, "I never fell for San Francisco as people are supposed to do. Moments I thought it beautiful—those brown hills and the blue water, and maybe—surely—it was my fault that it never gave me much elation—I was troubled a little in my life, and when the fog came down it seemed to *close in*. Sometimes even that was beautiful—it was so fantastic—and often, of course, the sea was beautiful, the sunsets out there magnificent—the moon on the sea down under the cliffs, at another part of the coast—I'll be so eager to know how you find it there."[11] Here Welty looked back on her two sojourns in San Francisco somewhat ruefully. Being "troubled a little in [her] life," Welty felt had colored her view of San Francisco, but she attempted not to prejudice Porter against the city.

The trouble Welty experienced seems likely to have been trouble in her relationship with Robinson. Perhaps she and Robinson both were beginning to realize that he needed a man, not a woman, to share his life. It is tempting to conclude that their Jackson friend Hubert Creekmore had predicted the opposite realization in his novel *The Welcome*. In that 1948 novel, Creekmore describes the return of Don Mason to his southern home long after Jim Furlow has rejected him. Mason at last finds a fulfilling relationship with Isabel Lang, an intelligent, self-reliant, and unconventional woman, and himself rejects Furlow. Yet whether or not Creekmore saw the marriage of Mason and Lang as prefiguring the union of Robinson and Welty, that union would not materialize.

After her second trip to San Francisco, Welty would remain John Robinson's

11. Welty to Porter, n.d. [January 1948], Katherine Anne Porter Papers, Special Collections, University of Maryland Libraries.

close friend, though never again would the two spend such an extended time together. In the first months of 1948, Welty would at least twice visit Robinson in Delisle, Mississippi, where he had moved, and would join him on a trip to Oxford, Mississippi, where she met William Faulkner. But Welty would spend the summer of 1948 in New York City, far from Delisle or Oxford. In New York, Welty had many good times and turned her hand to a new sort of writing. She and Hildegarde Dolson worked diligently to write a theatrical revue, each contributing separately authored sketches. Welty's pieces are lively and amusing: In "The New York Times," a character claims that the Sunday paper is as heavy as a "half-grown child," at which point a half-grown child falls from the paper; in "Hormones!" the contemporary sexual explanation for all behavior is the subject of song; in "Yes, Dear," modern reliance on machines is the subject of satire, while in "Fifty-Seventh Street Rag," individuals who frequent art galleries are caricaturized; in "What's Happened to Waltzes Like This?" and "Choo-Choo Boat," Welty turns almost nostalgically to her childhood; and in "Bye-Bye Brevoort," she parodies the proper old ladies who lived in the defunct Brevoort residential hotel.[12] In writing these comic sketches, Welty drew upon past and present experiences, focused upon moments of change or transition in contemporary life, and had a rather good time in the process.

When Welty returned to Jackson, she continued on an even keel and seemed content with her life. Certainly, her correspondence with Russell indicates as much. And the story she wrote upon returning may well reflect this change in mood from her San Francisco days. "The Hummingbirds" (later titled "The Wanderers") closes with Virgie Rainey, still unmarried at forty-something, leaving home and listening to the "magical percussion" of a Mississippi rainfall and hearing "through falling rain the running of the horse and bear, the stroke of the leopard, the dragon's crusty slither, and the glimmer and the trumpet of the

---

12. Eudora Welty, sketches from "What Year Is This?" Welty Collection, MDAH. According to Peggy W. Prenshaw, "Bye-Bye Brevoort" helped Welty discover the central theme of *The Golden Apples*: "What is preserved and celebrated and mocked with comic humor in the skit is a story of a domicile that yields to its inevitable end. In the fiction, too, which invokes tragic and heroic as well as comic strains, Welty gives an elegiac account of a passing Morgana life" ("Sex and Wreckage in the Parlor: Welty's 'Bye-Bye Brevoort,'" *Southern Quarterly* 33 [Winter/Spring 1995]: 115).

swan" (*GA*, 244). Virgie moves beyond the confines of her life in Morgana, Mississippi, beyond the insistence that she must marry, and into a freedom and self-knowledge signaled by her transcendent vision.

In late 1948 and early 1949, Welty seemed to have a similar freedom and self-knowledge, though she still had some hope for a shared life with Robinson. She would attempt to help Robinson by working with him on a screenplay of *The Robber Bridegroom*, but that work was done primarily by correspondence between Jackson and Delisle. In the spring, she would visit him briefly on the Gulf Coast, and in August would again travel with him to Oxford, Mississippi, where they would go sailing with William Faulkner. And during her year abroad, 1949–50, Welty would see a good bit of Robinson in France and Italy. When she returned home, however, Robinson remained in Italy, where he would settle into a lifelong relationship with a man, and future visits between Robinson and Welty, though warm, would be infrequent. The romantic attachment that had lasted through the war would not ultimately endure; the friendship would. And her stories written between 1946 and 1949 would typically explore the nature of relationships between men and women, the possibilities for fulfillment, and the hope that an independent life could be a fulfilling one as well.

Writing in the postwar years of 1946–1949, Welty was poised on the edge of change, change she could either see coming or felt must come. Change in the rural nature of her home state, change in attitudes that had existed since the Civil War, change in the roles open to women, and change in her personal life were all in the offing, and Welty's new book of stories would look both at what had once been and at what might lie ahead.

A book of seven interrelated short stories set primarily in the fictional town of Morgana, somewhere between Jackson and Vicksburg, *The Golden Apples* traces the life of Morgana from the turn of the century until the late 1940s. When Welty began writing the stories that would constitute this book, however, she had no plan to connect them. The stories were variously set in towns like Sabina and Battle Hill, and the characters of one story did not appear in other stories. Midway through the composition process, however, Welty realized that these stories belonged together, that the characters of one story might be younger or older versions of the characters in other stories, and she decided to create a book that was neither novel nor story collection. We still have no generic name for the closely linked book of stories that Welty produced.

"The Whole World Knows," the fifth story in *The Golden Apples*, focuses upon the adult lives of Jinny Love Stark and Ran MacLain, two characters we see as children in the early stories of the volume. Nevertheless, Welty began "The Whole World Knows" in August of 1946, before she had even conceived of the stories that would eventually surround it. In 1946 Welty often traveled to Vicksburg with friends; during this forty-five mile journey, they would drive through Bolton and past the site of the Champion's Hill Civil War battle—the landscape described throughout *The Golden Apples*.[13] In Vicksburg they would picnic overlooking the Mississippi River, or like Ran MacLain, take the water taxi out to a floating saloon. Here then Welty's imagination was sparked, as it had been in *A Curtain of Green*, by contemporary experiences. The story Welty wrote just after she had completed this one, however, drew upon her distant memories of childhood. "June Recital," the second story of *The Golden Apples*, previously titled "Golden Apples," is set in post–World War I Mississippi, and describes the lives of Cassie Morrison, her brother Loch, and Cassie's classmate Virgie Rainey. The experiences of these children and the nature of the town in which they live sprang quite directly from Welty's memories of small-town Jackson and the piano recitals in which she participated. In the process of writing these two stories, Welty thus alternately took her inspiration from the present and the past, a pattern she continued to follow in composing the seven stories of *The Golden Apples*.

In the spring of 1947 Welty completed "Music from Spain," a story written in San Francisco and based on her extended stay there. When Welty left San Francisco for home, however, her thoughts turned from the present to the past, and she conceived of the story "Moon Lake." In the fall of 1947 after she returned to San Francisco, Welty would write "Shower of Gold," another story drawing upon Mississippi's past, and in the process she would realize that "The Whole World Knows," "Golden Apples," "Moon Lake," and "Shower of Gold"

---

13. Seven miles from Bolton, Mississippi, lies Raymond, a small courthouse town that is clearly the model for MacLain Courthouse in "The Wanderers," the concluding story of *The Golden Apples*.

were really dealing with a common cast of characters. It was not until she returned to Mississippi that Welty knew "Music from Spain" belonged with the other stories—the character she had called Francis Dowdie, she now knew, was the brother of Ran MacLain from "The Whole World Knows." She wrote to Russell, "I should have foreseen [that "Music from Spain"] would be part of the others, because what worried me about the leading character in all the work I'd done was his lack of any taproot."[14] Welty then went on to complete "Sir Rabbit" six months before writing "The Hummingbirds" (to be renamed "The Wanderers") in September of 1948. That story, appropriately enough, would draw on both Welty's past and present in bringing the collection to a close. And just as Welty's past and her present had converged in the volume's final story, so too had all the collection's stories converged to provide the history of a small town called Morgana, Mississippi.

"The Whole World Knows," the first of *The Golden Apples* stories to be written, is set in Depression-era Mississippi and is dark in mood. It draws not upon the past, however, but upon Welty's contemporary discontent with the South, the discontent she had expressed with Mississippi politicians like Bilbo and Rankin, and upon her need for the cultural tonic of a city, a need she would indulge during two long stays in San Francisco. Still, the story also draws upon Welty's rather pleasant contemporary experiences in Mississippi. Welty had all her life gone to Vicksburg for high-spirited picnics or evenings out. On the eve of one such trip to Vicksburg, for example, Welty watched in amusement as a friend pulled a small pair of scissors from her purse and cut the hair over her forehead into bangs—a spontaneous decision much like the one Jinny Love Stark MacLain makes in "The Whole World Knows." Moreover, both croquet and bridge were common entertainments at the Welty home as they are at the Starks. Such details were part of recent fond memories for Welty, but in her *Harper's Bazaar* story, these very details establish Ran MacLain's sense that life in Sabina, Mississippi, is barren indeed. The dual impetus for her story suggests much about the doubleness of Eudora Welty's imagination, but that imagination was not simply double. Public issues prompted her to write about the private lives

14. Welty to Russell, 28 February 1948, restricted papers, Welty Collection, MDAH, and as cited by Kreyling, *Author and Agent* 141.

of her characters; personal experiences she transformed into a plot distanced from self. Moreover, Welty uses Ran MacLain to voice her discontent with the narrowness of southern life, but Ran's self-indulgence and self-pity are quite sinister and undercut the credibility of his indictment of the South. Conversely, Welty drew upon her pleasant contemporary experiences not to further undercut Ran's criticism of Sabina, Mississippi, but to suggest the constriction of small-town southern life. Writing in 1946 and knowing that the southern small town was on the wane, Welty sets her story in the thirties, when that way of life seemed more stable, and asks herself whether it should or should not endure. She comes to no clear answer.

Very soon after concluding "The Whole World Knows," Welty was working on a story to be called "Golden Apples." She eventually revised and lengthened the story during the spring of 1947 and published it in *Harper's Bazaar* in September 1947. Like "The Whole World Knows," "Golden Apples" sprang from Welty's saturation in the landscape west of Jackson and may also have sprung in part from the discontent that sparked the earlier story, from that contemporary mood; however, it took its subject not from the present but from the rather distant past. Her own affectionate memories of childhood provided much of the substance of "Golden Apples" and at the same time complicated the themes she had used her contemporary experiences to embody. In "Golden Apples," set sometime around 1920, Welty recalls small-town Jackson. She recalls her piano teacher, who "swatted my hands at the keyboard with a fly-swatter if I made a mistake; and when she wrote 'Practice' on my page of sheet music she made her 'P' as Miss Eckhart did—a cat's face with a long tail." She recalls that the piano recitals held every June provided "a fair model for Miss Eckhart's" (*OWB*, 100). She recalls that the lady who made and sold ice cream was known as "Mrs. Ice Cream McNair," and she calls one of her characters "Mrs. Ice Cream Rainey." She draws upon her own childhood memories of a bout with malaria in order to describe Loch Morrison's illness. She uses memories of the first airplane to appear over Jackson, of her father's telescope, of her own childhood temper tantrums, of a livery stable that became a theater where rats ran over your feet, and of a movie house sign extolling the "Typhoons of Alaskan Breezes" produced by its fan. The list could go on and on. Clearly, then, Welty's memories of childhood in Jackson allowed her to create the town of Battle Hill, a town that seems both more attractive and more threatening than the Sabina of "The Whole World Knows."

"The Whole World Knows" and "Golden Apples" thus depict different eras of Mississippi history and draw upon different periods in Eudora Welty's experience, but regarded as a pair, they represent the converging of past and present upon a central concern—the nature of small-town life as it had long existed in the South, even though its very nature was threatened by postwar development. Community in these stories—whether Sabina, Battle Hill, or the Morgana they eventually became—is a source of identity and coherence for its citizens, but it is also a source of oppression and restriction. It is "a definer and confiner" of its citizens just as it is "a definer and confiner" for Welty the writer. As Welty told an interviewer, place helped her to "identify, to recognize and explain"[15]; in *The Golden Apples* the small town provides Welty with focus and structure and order, even as it serves as the thematic center of her stories. Convergence could not be more complete.

In "The Whole World Knows," Sabina lies in the midst of Mississippi cotton fields, fields that represent not beauty and fecundity but monotony. Ran MacLain repeatedly calls attention to that fact: As the 1947 *Harper's Bazaar* version of the story opens, Ran leaves his job at the Sabina Bank and stands "looking out at a cotton field across the way until the whiteness nearly put me to sleep." And the monotony of the view is evident in all aspects of life in Sabina, Mississippi. Maideen Summers is "at first the only stranger—then finally not much of one." The only entertainments of a summer evening are bridge and croquet. The only suitors that Jinny MacLain has had to choose from are Ran and Lonnie Dugan. Sabina is also a place where there is no privacy. Miss Callie Hudson comes into the bank and offers intimate advice in a public way. And everyone in town knows the details of everyone else's life. Ran imagines Maideen observing that "you can't get away in Sabina. Away from anything." But perhaps the most difficult aspect of life in Sabina is the veneer of politeness that covers and obscures the most heart-felt emotions. Only when he imagines beating Lonnie Dugan to a bloody pulp or when he imagines firing bullet after bullet into his wife's breast does Ran break through this veneer. There are no shared acts of

15. Kuehl, 87.

imagination in Sabina. In "A Piece of News," Ruby and Clyde know a rare moment of communication when they jointly imagine that Clyde has murdered Ruby, but in "The Whole World Knows," Ran cannot communicate, even momentarily, with anyone. "Sabina," he observes, "had held in my soul to constriction."[16]

He longs for more—for love, for intensity, for the exotic and unusual—and he hopes to find them when he brings Maideen Summers to Vicksburg. Vicksburg, that important nineteenth-century port on the Mississippi River, continued to be a more cosmopolitan, less restrictive place than the towns of the Mississippi interior. Mississippi River towns, in general, were wide-open places. Despite prohibition, for instance, liquor flowed as freely through Vicksburg as the Mississippi River flowed past it. Vicksburg thus seems to offer Ran the freedom to feel that Sabina has denied him. But ultimately Ran can find no release, even in Vicksburg. The blacks who come out to a floating saloon on the river disappear "in the colored barge at the other end, in single file, as if they were sentenced to it." These black revelers live in the segregated South, and even dissipation seems to be part of a judicial sentence; Ran is similarly trapped, though by less institutionalized forces. Ran and Maideen see, as Eudora Welty herself once saw in this very location at the time she was writing "The Whole World Knows," two men with fighting cocks come out to the barge—the license of Vicksburg has a sordid side. And when Ran and Maideen spend the night in a tourist court, what Ran might call seduction may in fact be the rape of a Sabina woman. Ran longs both for freedom and for connection, but he finds neither. The Vicksburg Civil War battlefield, where Welty had often been on happy family picnics, provides an appropriately grim image for his experience: "We drove a long way. All among the statues in the dark park, the repeating stances, the stone rifles again and again on lost hills, the spiral-staired and condemned towers."[17] Ran's desire for meaning and passion and rich experience has been defeated, and he has victimized both Maideen and himself. East and West are in his eyes as he sits on the barge in Vicksburg, but Sabina alone will finally occupy his vision.

16. Eudora Welty, "The Whole World Knows," *Harper's Bazaar*, March 1947, 198, 198, 199, 336.

17. Ibid., 336, 337.

Welty's vision is far more encompassing. She has drawn upon her experiences, forced those experiences to double back upon themselves, and created a very ambivalent portrait of home. Ran's perceptions are more selective ones: He fails to see the beauty of the rich land or the humor in the peculiarities and provincialities of his home. In a vastly more important failure, though he tries, he cannot justify his violation of Maideen through a recitation about the town's oppressive nature. In addition, Ran fails to appreciate that in some ways the town is a rather tolerant place. Miss Callie Hudson is willing to accept that a "thing of the flesh" can endanger any marriage and to urge forgiveness within the marriage. The unfaithful Jinny is not ostracized in the community and neither is the equally wayward Ran. In Welty's Sabina, as in other southern communities, unexpected behavior is tolerated, especially within class boundaries. James W. Silver's comments about white attitudes toward race during the "period from the depression of the 1930's through World War II and its aftermath" seem also to describe white attitudes toward all sorts of unconventional beliefs and behaviors, whether they be moral, social, or political. According to Silver, "When there is no effective challenge to the code, a mild toleration of dissent is evident, provided the non-conformist is tactful and does not go far."[18] When Welty wrote to the *Clarion-Ledger* to protest the mindless conformity championed by Gerald L. K. Smith, she proclaimed that most *Clarion-Ledger* readers shared her abhorrence of Smith's ideas. She did not label all her fellow Jacksonians as reactionaries, nor did she fear a backlash against herself, and she was right not to do so. In "The Whole World Knows," similarly, Welty drew upon her quite natural discontent, but Ran MacLain's despair is not her own. And even Ran's vision of home is somewhat paradoxical. Though he imagines beating Lonnie Dugan and imagines shooting Jinny, he soon recognizes that he has chosen not to act. Though he longs to escape to Vicksburg, he misses the Sabina card game he has left behind, and he escapes with Maideen, who is herself a younger version of Jinny and the home tie.

The ambivalence that Welty displays toward the traditional small town of Sabina in "The Whole World Knows" points toward a more fully developed am-

---

18. Ibid., 332; James W. Silver, *Mississippi: The Closed Society* (New York: Harcourt, Brace and World, 1966), 6.

bivalence in her next story, "Golden Apples." Writing about Battle Hill, Mississippi, she suggests that implicit in the advantages of small town life are its disadvantages: The small town that encourages the imaginative life of children and accepts eccentrics does so only within the bounds of convention; the small town that provides a secure environment and avoids the depersonalization of the city is also a world without privacy and a world that chooses to ignore the inevitable threats posed by time and evil; the world in which nature is close at hand is also a world in which educational and occupational opportunity is radically limited. Welty well knew the doubleness of small-town life as she had encountered it in small-town Jackson, and she conveys that doubleness in "Golden Apples."

The small community is perhaps most attractive for the life it offers children. In small towns, if not because of small towns, as Welty observed in her autobiography *One Writer's Beginnings*, children seem to have a vital life of the imagination. Listening to adults tell stories about themselves, their families, or their neighbors, going to the movies, being read to or reading to themselves, children may find that their imaginations flourish. Among Welty's friends in small-town Jackson was a distinguished crew of individuals who would become fiction writers, poets, and composers. In "Golden Apples," Battle Hill may not have produced such a line-up, but its children are quite sensitive and imaginative. Loch's parents have clearly read to him, for he imagines that a world of fairy tales, of wild men and giants and talking horses, lies in the deserted house next door. And when he describes the porch roof of that house, with its banisters gone, hanging "like a cliff in a serial at the Bijou," he anticipates Welty's later assertion that "all children in those small-town, unhurried days had a vast inner life going on in the movies" (*OWB*, 36). Virgie Rainey, of course, is full of imagination, as is evident in her brief teen-age career accompanying the silent movies on the piano:

> Virgie sat nightly at the foot of the screen, ready for all that happened at the Bijou and keeping pace with it. Nothing proved too much for her or ever got too far ahead. When the dam broke everywhere at once, or when Nazimova cut off both feet with a saber rather than face shame with Sinji, Virgie was instantly playing *Kamennoi Ostrow*. . . . Some evenings, she would lean back in her chair

and let a whole forest fire burn in dead silence on the screen, and then when the sweethearts had found each other, she would switch on her light with a loud click and start up with creeping, minor runs—perhaps "Anitra's Dance." But that was the way Virgie was and had to be.

The way Virgie is and has to be is imaginative, whether she is being ironic or passionate. At age thirteen, playing Beethoven's "Fantasia on the Ruins of Athens" as her recital piece, Virgie becomes so totally involved in the music that, when she finishes and stands for her bow, she is "wet and stained as if she had been stabbed in the heart, and a delirious and enviable sweat ran down from her forehead and cheeks and she licked it in with her tongue." This is the moment at which Sally (to be called Cassie in later versions of the story) finds Virgie the most wonderful, and the conventional Sally is herself sensitive and imaginative. It is Sally who knows the myths of Perseus, Cassiopeia, and Circe, it is Sally who knows Yeats's "Song of the Wandering Aengus" by heart and at a younger age than Welty herself came to know it, and it is Sally who recognizes the relevance of the poem to life in Battle Hill. Sally intuitively knows that the quests upon which Loch, Virgie, and Miss Eckhart embark may be glorious but are also doomed. Aengus claims that he will "pluck till times and times are done / The silver apples of the moon / The golden apples of the sun." But like the alchemist who sought to combine silver and gold into the perfect and most precious metal, Aengus seeks the impossible. No one can have the silver and the gold, no one can catch the glimmering girl, no individual can establish a perfect relationship with another. The beauty of the poem's lines suggests the glory of Aengus's quest, but the logic of those lines portends failure. Similarly, the quests that Miss Eckhart and Virgie have pursued and will pursue may be "wonderful," to use Sally's word, but Sally implicitly knows that these two wanderers are "human beings at large, roaming in the face of the earth," that their faces may be "radiant," but they will always be "unappeased."[19] Adults in Battle Hill may try to shelter themselves from such knowledge, but they have encouraged their children to read the fairy tales, myths, and literature that convey it.

19. Eudora Welty, "Golden Apples," *Harper's Bazaar*, September 1947, 217, 302, 311, 320; W. B. Yeats, "The Song of the Wandering Aengus," in *The Poems*, ed. Richard J. Finneran (New York: Macmillan, 1983), 60.

Just as "Golden Apples" suggests that the small town can encourage the imaginations of its children, it suggests that the small town encourages the kind of personal relationships that are often missing from the life of a city. In her Harvard lectures, though not in *One Writer's Beginnings*, which was based upon those lectures, Welty described life on North Congress Street in Jackson, Mississippi, much as she describes life in Battle Hill:

> They spoke to you, the ice man climbing off his wagon with your 25-pound or 50-pound cake of ice in his tongs, the delivery man bringing your groceries from the market, the postman who came to the door, not only speaking but blowing his whistle if you had a letter.
>
> There were knife-grinders, jacks-of-all trades, the monkey-man cranking his organ with his monkey on a leash holding his cup for pennies, there was the blackberry lady and the watermelon man, all with their calls.
>
> "Milk, milk,
> Buttermilk,
> New Potatoes, snap beans, green peas
> And buttermilk."

This song might be Fate Rainey's song:

> "Milk, milk,
> Buttermilk.
> Fresh Dewberries and—
> Buttermilk." (*GA*, 22)

Having milk brought down your street and announced by song makes the world in which you live seem a rather gentle, hospitable one. So too does the thought that Fate Rainey's milk becomes the ice cream his wife makes and sells at the community "speakings." More profoundly important, family life is typically cohesive in a community like Battle Hill. Loch, who longs for freedom, rues this cohesiveness, but knows it even when his parents put a newspaper over their lamp to shade him out of their conversation. His experience is the experience of Eudora Welty, who describes just such a scene in her autobiography and concludes, "What I felt was not that I was excluded from them but that I was included, in—and because of—what I could hear of their voices and what I could see of their faces in the cone of yellow light under the brown-scorched shade" (*OWB*, 21). There is a similar cohesiveness in households throughout the community, as is evident in the community-wide preparation for the June recital. And the Raineys' support of their daughter transcends the general enthusiasm. As a father, Fate Rainey defies custom to attend the June recital, but attend he does. And as a mother, Katie relishes Virgie's recital performance and astonishes Sally when she proclaims, "Oh! I wish Virgie had a sister!"[20]

Finally, the small town offers its citizens a closeness to nature that the expansive, well lit, paved city cannot. Eudora Welty grew up feeling that closeness to nature; she writes that her father kept "a telescope with brass extensions, to find the moon and the Big Dipper after supper in our front yard, and to keep appointments with eclipses" (*OWB*, 3). Welty later adds, "The night sky over my childhood Jackson was velvety black. I could see the full constellations in it and call their names; when I could read, I knew their myths" (*OWB*, 10). The fictional Sally also knows the constellations, and her father's telescope, like the Weltys', emerges from the library table "for eclipses of the moon." Not only the natural world above but the natural world all around captured Welty's attention, and she has granted her interest in the natural world to Loch. He is aware of the magnolia blossoms glittering "like lights in the dense tree" and filling the house with an "extra deep" smell; he watches the thrush's nest. And most of all he waits for the figs to ripen: "When they cracked open their pink and golden flesh would show, and golden bubbles of juice would be there, to touch your tongue to."[21] The natural world that Sally and Loch cherish is much more accessible to them because they live in Battle Hill just as it was more accessible to Welty because her home was in one of the nation's least populous states.

This is not to say the community we see in "Golden Apples" is in any sense ideal. In 1946 and 1947, as she worked on "Golden Apples," Welty was intensely aware of the oppressive power of social convention, and she joins that contemporary awareness to her distant memories in creating the story. In the

---

20. Welty, Massey Lecture I, 34, Welty Collection, MDAH; Welty, "Golden Apples," *Harper's Bazaar*, 286, 311.

21. Welty, "Golden Apples," *Harper's Bazaar*, 286.

forties, oppressiveness must have been a common topic of conversation among her friends. Lehman Engel had been taunted in Jackson because he was Jewish and because he was a boy who played the piano. In his 1950 story "The Inspector," John Robinson depicted rural life as barren and desolate. And Hubert Creekmore would be especially acerbic in his comments about small-town Mississippi. In "Golden Apples," Welty expresses similar reservations about the oppressive power of convention and the plight of the imaginative artist amid oppression. As a native of Jackson, as the daughter of one of its leading businessmen, as a product of the Jackson schools, Welty never knew the kind of exclusion that the fictional pianist Miss Eckhart experiences in Battle Hill, but Welty nevertheless drew upon her own experiences in creating Miss Eckhart. In *One Writer's Beginnings*, Welty writes,

> As I looked longer and longer for the origins of this passionate and strange character, at last I realized that Miss Eckhart came from me. There wasn't any resemblance in her outward identity: I am not musical, not a teacher, nor foreign in birth; not humorless or ridiculed or missing out in love; nor have I yet let the world around me slip from my recognition. But none of that counts. What counts is only what lies at the solitary core. She derived from what I already knew for myself, even felt I had always known. What I have put into her is my passion for my own life work, my own art. Exposing yourself to risk is a truth Miss Eckhart and I had in common. What animates and possesses me is what drives Miss Eckhart, the love of her art and the love of giving it, the desire to give it until there is no more left. (*OWB*, 101)

Miss Eckhart's passion for her work animates her, and that passion might have been accepted in Battle Hill, as Welty's passion for her work was accepted in Jackson, had Miss Eckhart been part of the community in some distinctive way. Young Missie Spights knows very well why the community cannot accept Miss Lotte Elisabeth Eckhart: "Missie Spights said that if Miss Eckhart had allowed herself to be called by her first name, then she would have been like other ladies. Or if Miss Eckhart had belonged to a church that had ever been heard of, and the ladies would have had somewhere to invite her to belong . . . Or if she had been married to anybody at all, just any horrible old man." In Battle Hill, Mississippi, women, even young girls, expect other women to assume conventional identities or to accept exclusion from the group. And a woman like Miss Eckhart, an outsider who forces her neighbors to confront the power of time and the reality of evil, is certainly not going to be tolerated. The inexorable movement of time that Miss Eckhart's metronome represents is an abomination to the town: "It *was* an infernal machine; Sally's mother said it was that. . . . 'Mercy, you have to keep moving, with that infernal machine. I want a song to *dip*.'" Sally's mother scorns the metronome and values music that "dips," that seems to retard the passage of time. She does not want to "keep moving," to recognize time's urgency. When Mr. Sissum drowns and that urgency is brutally apparent, Miss Eckhart moves to the edge of his grave and nods her head "the way she nodded at pupils to bring up their rhythm, helping out the metronome." But the community fails to understand her actions, and "some ladies stopped their little girls from learning any more music." The community fears Miss Eckhart because she seems to accept the unusual, the extraordinary, the terrifying aspects of life and does not try to hide from them. When a "crazy nigger" jumps out from behind a hedge and rapes her, she does not decide to leave town. She considers one thing, even a racial and sexual assault that strikes at the heart of white southern taboos, not so much more terrifying than another and goes on about her business, much to the town's consternation. She is able to confront life's terrors as the citizens of Morgana are typically unwilling to do. Her brilliant playing of a classical composition signifies as much. As Miss Eckhart plays, Sally realizes "What Miss Eckhart might have told them a long time ago was that there was more than the ear could bear to hear or the eye to see, even in her."[22]

Nevertheless, though ultimate realities may be ignored, the eyes do see too much and the ears hear too much in many a small town. Though a village may be a hospitable place where business transactions can be conducted in a personal fashion, the village does thrive upon gossip and has little respect for privacy. Welty recalls the prevalence of gossip in the Jackson of her youth, describing a neighbor who was an accomplished storyteller and a sewing woman who carried stories of her clients from household to household (*OWB*, 13–14). There is a

22. Ibid., 306, 298, 301, 301, 302; Louis Rubin advances this view of the metronome and of Morgana. See *The Faraway Country: Writers of the Modern South* (Seattle: University of Washington Press, 1963), 131–54.

similar lack of privacy in the fictional Battle Hill. When the ladies of the town see Virgie and her sailor come out of the deserted house, Miss Billie Texas Spights calls after her, "He went the other way, Virgie! . . . Don't you wish you could run fast?" Miss Jefferson Moody then intercedes, "Hush, Billie Texas. . . . As if her mother didn't have enough on her, just burying her son." The community knows the most intimate concerns of the Rainey family and even draws some pleasure from Virgie's dalliance. They do not condemn her, but they do invade her privacy. In the same way, community members deny Miss Eckhart her privacy. Not only does Mr. Wiley Harvey "tell anybody that cared to ask him what Miss Eckhart telephoned him to send from the butcher block, and how she questioned her bills, too," but other community members go on to speculate that Miss Eckhart's treatment of her mother has been abusive, even criminal. After Miss Eckhart is put out of her house, "stories began to be told of what she had really done to her old mother. People said the old mother had been in pain for years, and nobody knew. What kind of pain they did not say. But they said during the War, when Miss Eckhart lost pupils and they did not have very much to eat, she would give her mother paregoric to make sure she slept all night and not wake the neighborhood with noise or complaint, or maybe still more pupils would be taken away. Some people said Miss Eckhart killed her mother with opium."[23] Such speculations might never occur in a large city; there an individual can choose to be anonymous. Not in a small town.

Finally, the small community cannot provide cultural and intellectual opportunities for its citizens. The closeness to nature that comes with village life also means there will probably be no concert halls, no universities, no theaters, no book stores—institutions upon which Eudora Welty herself depended. As a student Welty lived in New York for more than a year, she spent a good bit of 1944 working at the *New York Times*, and she spent several months in 1946 and 1947 living in San Francisco. She enjoyed the advantages of city life, but in Battle Hill, Mississippi, her characters find little opportunity and little encouragement for travel. The community literally confines its citizens, especially its women. Loch and Sally's mother is "absorbed" into a group of ladies who are off to play Rook; no other social activity seems available to ladies, and intellectual activities

23. Welty, "Golden Apples," *Harper's Bazaar*, 318, 318, 305, 305.

seem non-existent. Sally knows that "stretching ahead of her, as far as she could see, were those yellow Schirmer books: all the rest of her life." She will be Battle Hill's piano teacher; no other career is possible. Though Sally believes that upon leaving high school Virgie has entered "the world of power and emotion," there are no powerful career opportunities for Virgie in Battle Hill.[24] Both her sex and her social class limit her. A woman and the daughter of the milk man, she can play piano at the movie house or clerk in a store or be a secretary; nothing more. The employment prospects for men, though somewhat brighter, are also limited. Grocery store owner, publisher of a small town weekly newspaper, milk man, traveling salesman, shoe store clerk—these are the professions of men in the story. Viewed from this perspective, the small town seems an isolating and confining, not a life-enhancing, environment.

In "The Whole World Knows" and "Golden Apples," Eudora Welty thus uses her present and past experiences to investigate the nature of small town life, a way of life that in 1946 might have seemed to be fading in importance, and the convergence of present and past upon this central issue results in a vision that is simultaneously critical and affirmative. This sort of duality within convergence, Frank Barron argues, typifies the works of creative individuals. Barron writes that "creation goes hand in hand with destruction. . . . The strife between opposites is an important source of energy for an evolving new synthesis." Eudora Welty's creative process adds credence to Barron's assertion. Working on the *Norton Book of Friendship*, Welty repeatedly asked her collaborator to include works expressing the opposite of friendship. She wanted, for instance, "I do not like thee Dr. Fell" to be included. And such a habit of mind is clearly evident in "The Whole World Knows" and in "Golden Apples," but it is most intensely evident in the piano recital around which the second story revolves. For Miss Eckhart the recital is the highest gesture of her imagination, one in which she pulls together diverse talents and abilities into a performance. And after the recital, when refreshments are served, Sally thinks Miss Eckhart looks like Circe "on the fourth-grade wall, feeding her swine." Like Circe, she seems a commanding and magical presence. The Battle Hill adults do not share this perception; the June recital is a ritual the community claims as its own, and during the

24. Ibid., 305, 302.

recital, community members see Miss Eckhart not as Circe but as part of their community structure. When Miss Eckhart calls upon the town's mothers to make special dresses, to provide seating and an extra piano for the recital, to assist with a reception, the mothers fully understand these requirements. The recital is an emblem of order and predictability to them, and it marks the cyclical passing of time. For the townspeople, time is not linear and its passing is not a record of loss. Time moves, they sense, in a circular and recurring fashion, and the recital occupies a key point on that circle. Miss Eckhart, they feel, comes alive when she is part of this community ritual: "That blushing, special sensitivity sprang up every year at the proper time, like a flower of the season, like the Surprise Lilies in Miss Callie's yard, the pink bells that came up with no leaves, and overnight. Miss Eckhart stirred here and there, utterly carried away by the things that at other times interested her least—dresses and sashes, manners and bows. It was strange and exciting. With recital night over, the sensitivity too would be over and gone. But then all trials would be ended. The limitless part of vacation would truly have come."[25] Though Miss Eckhart lacks the ties of family or place or faith that would link her to Battle Hill, she is inextricably tied to the community and is an accepted part of it during the recital ritual. Within the bounds of the recital, Miss Eckhart's eccentricity is easily tolerated. In the June recital, then, the individual and the community, the free play of imagination and the restrictive power of convention converge.

Having investigated the nature of small-town life in both "The Whole World Knows" and "Golden Apples," Welty herself left the relatively small city of Jackson for an extended stay in San Francisco. And in San Francisco, she wrote of the populous city around her. The images and allusions in Welty's story "Music from Spain" largely emerge from her 1946–47 sojourn on the West Coast. There she went to show after show by Danny Kaye, came to view Pierre Monteux as the nation's preeminent symphony conductor, heard Segovia play the guitar, and roamed about the city, observing its people and sights. Yet despite the delights of city life, Welty found that the urban environment also had its own serious limitations.

25. Frank Barron, "Putting Creativity to Work," in *The Nature of Creativity*, ed. Robert J. Sternberg (Cambridge and New York: Cambridge University Press, 1988), 81; Welty, "Golden Apples," *Harper's Bazaar*, 311, 307.

In "Music from Spain," Welty sets the cosmopolitan nature of city life in opposition to its impersonality, sets its diversity against its tawdry commercialism, and finds that individual freedom and meaningful relationships are as difficult to achieve in the city as in the small town. In "The Flower and the Rock," the earliest extant version of the story ultimately to be named "Music from Spain," Francis Dowdie slaps his wife and walks out of the house on his way to work. At a jobbing butcher's, he has "to stand aside while without warning red and white beeves were sent across the sidewalk on hokks [sic] out of a big van. They were moving across, all right, and a tramp leaned on a cane to watch, leering at each one of the carcasses as though it were some haughty and demanding woman he kept catching like that. His red eye rolled Dowdie's way. Ladies were sometimes let by, but not men." There is no civility here—the beeves come rolling in Dowdie's path without warning from anyone—and the tramp seems to think that women are as dead as the carcasses he and Dowdie watch. Immediately, Dowdie decides that he cannot go to work, that he will deny the deadness of his own life, that he will spend the day roaming through the city. But the city offers scant hope of meaning to him. Market Street has "now become the street of trusses, pads, braces, false bosoms, false teeth and glass eyes."[26]

Of course, San Francisco has attractions that Battle Hill or Sabina, Mississippi, cannot match. The population is more diverse and more intriguing than could ever be found in the small southern town. On the street, Dowdie and the Spaniard he has saved from being hit by a taxi stand by an unusual woman:

> There was such strange beauty about her that he did not realize for a few moments that she was birth-marked and would be considered disfigured. She was, he thought, a Negress or Polynesian, and marked as a butterfly is, over her visible skin. Curves, scrolls, dark brown on light brown, were beautifully placed on her face, as if by design, with pools about the eyes, at the nape of the neck, at the wrists, and about her legs too, like faun spots, visible through her stockings. She was dressed in humble brown, but her hat was an exotic one, with two curving narrow feathers, one dark and one green, turned one downward and one upward about her head.

26. Eudora Welty, "The Flower and the Rock," Welty Collection, MDAH, 4, 5.

Dowdie sees a woman far more exotic than any Ran MacLain would have encountered in Mississippi; Ran goes to Vicksburg with a white girl from the rural South, not with a butterfly-marked African American or Polynesian woman. And Dowdie clearly feels himself attracted to this woman of color, an attraction a southern man would be unwilling to admit, though the history of the South is marked by many such attractions. Later when Dowdie and the Spaniard take the streetcar, they encounter other blacks, blacks who do not play out the ritual of submission expected in the southern small town: "The conductor was a big fat Negro woman who yelled out all the street names with joy. 'Divisadero! I say Divisadero!' At the Courtesy Barber Shop and from the fancy-fronted, engraved looking steep houses with all the paint gone, the conductor's friends hollered at her as they went by. Leaning and swinging out of the car, she called back, 'Off at two A.M.! See you at the Cat!'" This woman's vibrance and openness typify the city; she is not like the African Americans who in "The Whole World Knows" frequent the segregated bar on the river barge: "They were sulphur yellow all over, thickly coated with cottonseed meal, and disappeared in the colored barge at the other end, in single file, as if they were sentenced to it."[27] These men work ghastly jobs in the cottonseed mill and take no pleasure in the release of drink; unlike the San Francisco streetcar conductor, they are like prisoners.

Just as the city accepts this sort of racial diversity, it offers artistic diversity as well. Dowdie has been to see artists ranging from Monteux to Danny Kaye. And the classical guitarist whom Dowdie saves on the day of the story has the evening before provided him with a pleasure he is loath to admit: "Dowdie was not, as a matter of fact, altogether carried away by the music—only when the man played very softly some unbearably rapid or subtle songs of his own country, so soft as to be almost without sound, only a beating on the air like a fast wing. Sometimes the sounds seemed shaken out, not struck, with the unearthly faint crash of a tambourine."[28] Dowdie seems transfixed by the Spaniard's "unbearably rapid or subtle songs," by the "unearthly" sound of the Spaniard's guitar. Though Dowdie claims not "to be altogether carried away," music seems to provide him with a transcendent experience.

27. Ibid., 12–3, 19–20; Welty, "The Whole World Knows," *Harper's Bazaar*, 336.
28. Welty, "The Flower and the Rock," 17.

Such experiences, however, do not solve the central problem with which Francis Dowdie must cope—the relationship with his wife. At breakfast he has slapped his wife, and during the rest of the day he seeks to cope with his guilt and to understand his act. As the day passes, Dowdie alternately chastises and justifies himself. At one point, Dowdie feels "all at once the secret tenderness toward himself that he might have felt toward a lover; for considering that he might have done a reprehensible thing, then he would himself need the gravest and tenderest handling." And he goes on to project both his self-love and his self-hatred onto the guitarist. As the day draws to a close, Dowdie tells the Spaniard, "You assaulted your wife. . . . You slapped her cheek, only." Then he adds, "But in your heart . . . in your heart—you could kill a thing if it would not be any more now for you." Shortly after delivering these lines, Dowdie thinks of killing the Spaniard, of pushing him from the cliffs to which they have walked. Instead, however, Dowdie clings "to him now, almost as if he had waited for him with longing, almost as if he loved him, had found a refuge. He could have caressed the side of his face with the great pores in the loose cheek." Dowdie seeks to find in himself the independence, the expressiveness of the Spaniard, but Dowdie does not really know himself. And as Welty told Charles Bunting in a discussion of *Losing Battles*, "Unless you are very real in yourself, you don't know what it means to support others or to join with them or to help them."[29] That is the reason he is unable to close the gap between himself and Emma, to deal with the guilt they both feel over the death of their daughter Fan, to express his love to her. That is the reason he is frustrated and lashes out. Without a secure sense of himself, he cannot establish a viable relationship. In the Spaniard he sees an image of the man he might be or might love, but ultimately he abandons the Spaniard.

Neither city nor small town can provide a sense of identity; the individual must create himself, wherever he lives, and in town or city the possibilities are double. The title, "The Flower and the Rock," the title Welty ultimately abandoned for "Music from Spain," expresses this duality. The title flower is a mariposa lily, which the Spaniard finds near the cliffs above the sea, an image of fertility in a rather desolate landscape. Moreover, the word *mariposa* literally means

29. Ibid., 22, 30, 30; Bunting, 49.

butterfly, evoking the story's earlier portrait of the butterfly-marked woman. The beauty, fragility, freedom of the butterfly and of the butterfly flower are available to Francis Dowdie. But the city offers a second option, the title rock. The cliffs in Golden Gate Park are a sort of waste land: "There were caves where the paths dropped to the sea, and the Spaniard now went on his own to inspect them. He let himself down the steep rocks, and hands on knees, peeped into the caves like a dentist into mouths. Rats ran up the bald surfaces." The caves seem like Eliot's "Dead mountain mouth of carious teeth" and promise spiritual emptiness and desolation.[30] Both flower and rock are to be discovered in San Francisco, but only the rock seems to represent Dowdie's future.

Almost a year after completing this version of "Music from Spain," Welty realized that Francis Dowdie should really be Eugene MacLain, the twin brother of Ran MacLain in "The Whole World Knows." She had already decided that Miss Eckhart's studio in "Golden Apples" would be a room rented from Ran's mother, Snowdie MacLain. Stories that converged in terms of theme and in which Welty's past and present experiences converged as source materials would now converge in an even more basic fashion. In revising her periodical stories for book publication, Welty inextricably linked through proximity and kinship the characters who had earlier populated Sabina, Battle Hill, and San Franciso. Morgana, Mississippi, was now their home town. Most notably, Welty tied "The Whole World Knows" to "June Recital" (her new name for "Golden Apples") and to "Music from Spain" through the creation of King MacLain, Ran and Eugene MacLain's father and the mysterious man who returns to witness Miss Eckhart's attempt at arson. King is the archetypal wanderer, the character who is never content but is always questing for a fuller, more intense existence. He is linked to Aengus, the Irish love god, and to Zeus. He marries Snowdie Hudson in defiance of community expectations, for Snowdie is an albino. But even a marriage made in defiance of community expectations is too confining for King.

The addition of King MacLain to "The Whole World Knows" transforms that story in a very profound way. The revised version of the story begins when

---

30. Welty, "The Flower and the Rock," 29; T.S. Eliot, *The Waste Land*, ed. Valerie Eliot (New York: Harcourt Brace Jovanovich, 1971), 144.

Ran addresses his father, saying "Father, I wish I could talk to you, wherever you are, right now" (*GA*, 139). That wish is reiterated throughout the story and helps to explain Ran's relationships with Maideen and with his wife Jinny. No longer does it seem that he, as Michael Kreyling believes, is engaged in a "ritual of revenge through sexual domination." Instead it seems that Ran wishes to live as intensely as his father, to defy convention as did his father, even as he feels drawn back to the community and his wife. Significantly, Maideen of the original story is a Sojourner in the revised version, and Mattie Will Sojourner in the story "Sir Rabbit" becomes one of King's conquests some years after she has sported with his fifteen-year-old twin sons. When Ran realizes this connection between his own present and the past he and his father share, he cries out, "The name Sojourner was laid on my head like the top teetering crown of a pile of things to remember. Not to forget, never to forget the name of Sojourner" (*GA*, 153). Peter Schmidt suggests that Ran "resents being forced to measure his exploits with the Sojourners against his father's."[31] But it seems more likely that Ran has realized that his exploits, like his father's, will involve betraying wife and lover. Ran is bothered by his community's sexual double standard, by even his mother's assertion that "*it's different from when it's the man*" (*GA*, 157). Ran nevertheless continues to emulate the mythic King MacLain, only finally to "ruin a country girl" and to suspect that the myth has deceived him. The possibility of rape seems less overt in this final version of the story than it did in the *Harper's Bazaar* version, but Ran's despair is even more intense. "Father," he asks as the story concludes, "What you went and found, was it better than this?" (*GA*, 160) Ran now doubts that his father did find anything better than life in Morgana, and in the concluding story of *The Golden Apples*, Ran chooses to cast his lot with Morgana and not to see himself as a sojourner who is always on the verge of moving on. In a sense then, the addition of King undercuts the intensity of Welty's attack upon the small town. With the introduction of this mythic wanderer, Welty suggests that escape is not necessarily an answer to the oppressiveness of the small town. She suggests that intellectual or emotional isolation may be more a function of character or of the human situation than it is of place.

In "June Recital," King MacLain replaces Mr. Demarest, who peddles "8-in-

---

31. Kreyling, *Eudora Welty's Achievement of Order*, 93; Schmidt, 77.

1 Song Conditioner for canary birds"[32]; a key figure for the entire collection of stories replaces an incidental one. King, identified by Loch as Mr. Voight, arrives in Morgana just in time to see Miss Eckhart's attempt to burn down the house he had once owned. As Old Man Moody and Mr. Fatty Bowles try to stop Miss Eckhart, King asks all three why they are trespassing and orders them out of the house. He seems oblivious to the fact that time has passed, that his children are adults, that his wife no longer lives in Morgana, and that this house is no longer his. Perhaps King's life has been so filled with frantic activity that he has been able to ignore the passing of time. While the townspeople have used routine and ritual to block out an awareness of time, King seems to have used constant motion and sexual domination. His return to Morgana, however, makes him very aware of the toll time has taken. Though he is inevitably amused by the slapstick comedy going on in his old house, though he watches the events as he would watch a "show," time's power will send him running once again. When Miss Eckhart shows him the metronome and says "See . . . See, Mr. MacLain" (*GA*, 75), he groans, denies having ever known her, and leaves Morgana. His wandering seems not so much an attempt to live fully in the face of time's power as it does an attempt to avoid confronting that power. Miss Eckhart has been more courageous, though she has been finally reduced to madness. In the concluding story of *The Golden Apples*, Virgie will ultimately realize that Miss Eckhart has given her a knowledge of time and a meaningful way of confronting it. King MacLain provides no such model. His life has been totally self-absorbed, a destructive and untenable declaration of his own supremacy. Why else would he have insisted, as Katie Rainey reports in the book's first story, that his own wife meet him in the woods rather than joining him in "a good goosefeather bed" (*GA*, 4)? Why else would he in "Sir Rabbit," the story immediately following "June Recital," have raped Mattie Will Sojourner, who was so eager to embrace him? But King ultimately is powerless in the face of time. As Mattie Will discovers when she later finds King asleep, he looks of no "more use than a heap of cane thrown up by the mill and left in the pit to dry" (*GA*, 96–7).

In the revised "Music from Spain," Eugene MacLain associates his father with Miss Eckhart and with the Spaniard, but not one of these three figures have

---

32. Welty, "Golden Apples," *Harper's Bazaar*, 313.

been or will be able to bring Eugene any saving knowledge. When Eugene takes the Spaniard to a fine restaurant, he imagines that the guitarist looks like "the framed Sibyl on the wall in his father's study," but then Eugene realizes that the picture actually hung in "old Miss Eckhart's 'studio'" (*GA*, 179). Eugene then thinks back to his days of piano lessons:

> He had even forgotten all about old Miss Eckhart in Mississippi, and the lessons he and not Ran had had on her piano, though perhaps it was natural that he should remember her now, within the aura of music. . . . Eugene seemed to hear the extending cadence of "The Stubborn Rocking Horse," a piece of his he always liked, and could play very well. He saw the window and the yard, with the very tree. The thousands of mimosa flowers, little puffs, blue at the base like flames, seemed not to hold quite steady in this heat and light. His "Stubborn Rocking Horse" was transformed into drops of light, plopping one, two, three, four, through sky and trees to earth, to lie there in the pattern opposite to the shade of the tree. He could feel his forehead bead with drops and the pleasure run like dripping juice through each plodding finger, at such an hour, on such a day, in such a place, Mississippi. (*GA*, 180)

Miss Eckhart has offered Eugene her knowledge of time and of art as a way of combating time, and Eugene momentarily recalls that Mississippi has brought him artistic moments of fulfillment. In the story's next paragraph, however, Eugene sees his wandering father and the Spaniard as more powerful symbols of the artist: "Eugene saw himself for a moment as the kneeling Man in the Wilderness in the engraving in his father's remnant geography book, who hacked once at the Traveler's Tree, opened his mouth, and the water came pouring in. What did Eugene MacLain really care about the life of an artist, or a foreigner, or a wanderer, all the same thing—to have it all brought upon him now? That engraving itself, he had once believed, represented his father, King MacLain, in the flesh, the one who had never seen him or wanted to see him" (*GA*, 180). Eugene here identifies himself with his father, whom he both hates and longs to emulate, and with the Spaniard, who is an artist, a foreigner, and a wanderer. The waters of life seem destined for the quester, not for one who accepts a confined and rooted existence, not for the boy in Miss Eckhart's Mississippi studio. And Eugene goes on to project his hopes for independence upon the fatherly

Spaniard, but his day with the Spaniard leads only back to a subordinate role in a loveless marriage. Projection has not helped Eugene to know himself; neither has flight from a small town in Mississippi to the cosmopolitan world of San Francisco. But granting her protagonist a Mississippi heritage has helped Welty to create a more complex and believable character and to allow her portraits of city and small-town life to comment upon each other.

Welty wrote "The Wanderers," the final story in *The Golden Apples*, after she realized that all the stories in this volume would be linked by recurring characters and settings, and she constructed this story with prominent appearances by King MacLain to draw together the connections established in earlier stories. Moreover, in drawing those connections together she also pulled together experiences from her present and her past. Most notably, in "The Wanderers" (originally titled "The Hummingbirds"), she turned to the present in describing the changing nature of Morgana, Mississippi, and to her own past in creating the episode in which an old woman brings Virgie Rainey a night-blooming cereus. The present and the past of the small town are embodied in incident and setting.

"The Wanderers" is a powerful story about transience, and Welty drew upon her contemporary Mississippi experience to dramatize the changing nature of her home state. Patterns of racial oppression, which have yet to be annihilated, were beginning the move toward radical change. In addition, the road building and the revived logging industries were very active ones in post–World War II Mississippi, and they would transform not only the state's economy but the nature of its communities. The dramatic nature of these changes was not fully evident when Welty wrote "The Wanderers" in 1948, but change was surely in the offing. Early in "The Wanderers," for instance, Welty calls our attention to the shifting nature of race relations. Miss Lizzie Stark is dismayed because her black maid Juba has been absent without leave and because Juba is less than deferential. Later in the story, it is Juba who dares to mention the torment that led to Mrs. Morrison's suicide, and it is an old black woman who shares Virgie Rainey's transcendent moment of freedom at the story's end.

The changing racial order does not bother Katie Rainey, but other social changes do. Miss Katie, who all her married life has sold produce from a roadside chair parked in the shade of a chinaberry tree, no longer wants to sit "near the trafficking" (*GA*, 204). She believes that now the road is traveled by "the wrong people": "They were all riding trucks, very fast or heavily loaded, and carrying blades and chains, to chop and haul the big trees to mill. They were not eaters of muscadines, and did not stop to pass words on the season and what grew." As a result, Katie stays away from the road, but "clear up where she was, she felt the world tremble; day and night the loggers went by, to and from Morgan's Woods" (*GA*, 213–14, 204). The world is trembling metaphorically as well as literally—the world Katie Rainey has known is disappearing. The natural world is being "depleted," leisurely conversation is on the wane, the MacLain house next door is literally gone, and the population of the town is no longer stable. Loch Morrison has left, first for service in World War II and then for a career in New York City; strangers are moving into town; and the Morrison's house has been cut up into rooms for "road workers and timber people." As a result, or so thinks Katie Rainey, a "lack of chivalry" now typifies Morgana (*GA*, 240, 205). The survival of the cohesive community, with its faults as well as its virtues, seems in doubt as Welty's telling references to contemporary developments make clear. Time and change are realities from which many Welty characters flee, but with which they all need to cope.

For Virgie Rainey, this need to cope involves her private as well as her communal life. The death of her mother is the most crucial change in her life, and she must come to terms with that death. Welty prepares us for Virgie's ultimate triumph by drawing upon an actual experience from the past. Early in the 1930s, Welty, Lehman Engel, Frank Lyell, and Hubert Creekmore had amused themselves by answering newspaper invitations to visit Jackson homes where a night-blooming cereus was expected to throw its annual blooms. On one such occasion, an old lady had warned them that the blooms would look like wrung chickens' necks in the morning. For Welty and her friends, these occasions were the source of much humor. Almost twenty years later, however, when Welty created "The Wanderers," she used the night-blooming cereus for a rather different purpose. Virgie, home alone late at night after her mother's funeral, is wakened by a "pre-emptory pounding on the porch floor." When she comes to the door, she sees "an old lady in a Mother Hubbard and clayed boots, holding out something white in a dark wrapping." That something is a "naked, luminous, complicated flower," a night-blooming cereus. The old lady tells Virgie, "It's for you. Keep it—won't do the dead no good. And tomorrow it'll look like a wrung chicken's neck. Look at it enduring the night" (*GA*, 235). When Virgie invites the old woman into the house, she declines and leaves, but her parting words haunt Virgie: "'You used to play the pi-anna in the picture show when you's little and I's young and in town, dear love,' she called turning away through the dark. 'Sorry about your mama: didn't suppose anybody make as pretty music as you *ever* have no trouble.—I thought you's the prettiest little thing ever was'" (*GA*, 236). The "naked, luminous, complicated flower" might well be an emblem of Virgie herself, vulnerable to the power of time. Virgie recognizes the flower's import and throws it into the weeds, but the next day she resolves to leave Morgana, to act in the face of time's urgency. Significantly, it is the old woman, a character still connected to Morgana and its citizens, who has brought Virgie to this decision. Virgie is not anonymous in Morgana, at least not yet. Still Virgie's decision to leave Morgana might be seen as a decision to follow in the wandering footsteps of King MacLain and to assert that wanderers need not always be men. Virgie's decision, however, is far more complex in nature.

In "The Wanderers," King, home from his ramblings and living with his wife in Morgana, is none too happy about being old and being settled. He tells Virgie about his past: "You know in those days I was able to make considerable trips off, and only had my glimpses of the people back here. . . . I'd come and I'd go again, only I ended up at the wrong end, wouldn't you say" (*GA*, 223). He then recalls presenting Katie Rainey with a large swivel chair, but not waiting to see her pleasure at receiving it: "Looked to her, I know, like I couldn't wait long enough to hear her pleasure. So bent, so bent I was on all I had to do, on what was ahead of me" (*GA*, 224). King has spent his life avoiding the community of Morgana and looking always for something more than it can offer, but in his old age he has found nothing to sustain him. At the funeral, he gives vent to his frustration. He makes "a hideous face at Virgie, like a silent yell. It was a yell at everything—including death, not leaving it out—and he did not mind taking his present animosity out on Virgie Rainey; indeed, he chose her" (*GA*, 227).

Virgie herself might be inclined to "yell at everything—including death." Virgie, in her forties, has long lived with and cared for her ailing mother; in the process, she has squandered her musical talent and her passion; she has worked as a secretary for Mr. Nesbitt, who expects gratitude, deference, and perhaps sexual favors from her; and she has engaged in a series of love affairs, each with a man less interesting than the previous one. But her spirit has not been broken. When her mother's death frees Virgie from home ties, she does not follow Jinny Love Stark's advice to marry and become part of conventional Morgana. She chooses not to to be corsetted in marriage as Missie Spights Littlejohn literally is; she chooses not to wear "the iron mask of the married lady" (*GA*, 218, 225) and become a female version of the seventeenth-century French prisoner who was held in the Bastille for forty years. Neither does she choose to follow simply in the footsteps of Jinny's father-in-law, King MacLain, fleeing connections to the past and the community and willfully asserting power at the expense of others. Instead, Virgie looks not only at what lies ahead, but also recognizes the continuity of time and the enduring values that have emerged from her years in Morgana. When she leaves Morgana and drives "the seven winding miles to MacLain," Virgie is looking backward as well as forward. She comes to realize that she had not hated Miss Eckhart but "had come near to loving" her (*GA*, 240, 243). It is Miss Eckhart, she realizes, who has taught her to see "things in their time" and to recognize the meaning in a picture of Perseus holding the head of the Medusa: "Cutting off the Medusa's head was the heroic act, perhaps, that made visible a horror in life, that was at once the horror in love, Virgie thought—the separateness" (*GA*, 243). Accepting that duality is essential, wherever one lives or travels and whether one is male or female; Virgie Rainey, poised to leave her Mississippi home, will leave without the false expectations and judgments that had characterized King MacLain's travels. No longer will she seek comfort in the arms of lovers who cannot understand her or in the monotony of a job that requires no thought from her. She will leave alone, in full knowledge of life's horrors as well as its glories, and the future for this independent woman (not married lady) seems rich in possibilities. Virgie promises to become an individual like Eudora Welty, whose ties to home were strong and enduring, but whose thoughts of marriage had waned, whose career had flourished, and whose travels had been and would continue to be wide-ranging and enriching.

In these stories that eventually became part of Welty's book *The Golden Apples*, we see evidence of a pattern which dominates that book. Welty's reliance upon the contemporary world in one story leads to a reliance upon the past in another, and past and present experiences converge upon a common theme. The social cohesiveness, the power of convention, the racism, the closeness to nature, the limited roles open to women, the isolation in location and attitude that had characterized Mississippi for generations, were beginning to break apart after World War II, when Welty wrote *The Golden Apples*, and the direction of Welty's personal life was also poised upon the edge of change. Not surprisingly, then, continuity and change prove to be the central foci of *The Golden Apples*, and Welty's fictional portrait of the evolving small town is simultaneously one of affirmation and oppression. Furthermore, Welty's towns of Sabina and Battle Hill converge in her creation of Morgana, Mississippi, a town in which Jinny Love Stark, Ran MacLain, Cassie (alias Sally) Morrison, Virgie Rainey, and Miss Eckhart all live and interact. This convergence of sources, ideas, characters and settings is Welty's mode for confining and defining, for bringing coherence and development, to what might have been a diverse collection of very good stories about separate, unrelated moments. As a result, *The Golden Apples* is a triumph of the imagination, perhaps the greatest triumph of Eudora Welty's distinguished career.

Eudora Welty working at home, ca. 1943
Courtesy Mary Alice Welty White and Elizabeth Welty Thompson

Eudora Welty and her mother, Chestina Andrews Welty, in
their garden, Jackson, Mississippi, mid-1950s
Courtesy Mary Alice Welty White and Elizabeth Welty Thompson

Welty in New York City during her 1944 internship at the
*New York Times Book Review*
Courtesy Mary Alice Welty White and Elizabeth Welty Thompson

Welty and friends in Italy, 1950: poet William Jay Smith, front; Mississippi natives
Dolly Wells and John Robinson, back
Courtesy Mary Alice Welty White and Elizabeth Welty Thompson

Diarmuid Russell, Welty's agent and friend, early 1940s
Courtesy Mary Alice Welty White and Elizabeth Welty Thompson

Eudora Welty and Katherine Anne Porter, Yaddo, 1941
Courtesy Mary Alice Welty White and Elizabeth Welty Thompson

Welty at Mississippi's Windsor Ruins, April 1954
Courtesy Mary Alice Welty White and Elizabeth Welty Thompson

Elizabeth Bowen and Reynolds Price at the Jackson, Mississippi, airport, New Year's 1970
Courtesy Mary Alice Welty White and Elizabeth Welty Thompson

**VI**

# Divergence

## Place and the Displaced in *The Bride of the Innisfallen*

The pattern of convergence established in *The Golden Apples* did not appear again in Eudora Welty's short fiction. In *The Bride of the Innisfallen*, her next and final book of stories, Welty's plots and settings are diverse; her joining of past and present experiences largely absent. Only one story in *The Bride of the Innisfallen* deals with the past, only two stories are set in a quasi-contemporary Mississippi, and no characters or settings recur to link story to story. In some ways Welty was returning to the diversity of her first book of stories, and like the stories in *A Curtain of Green*, her new stories sprang primarily from contemporary experiences, experiences which were as new and exciting to the writer who had now turned forty as her discovery of Mississippi itself had been twenty years earlier. Eudora Welty's imagination was sparked in the early 1950s by the experience of travel—travel by train, ship, and car to states and countries not her own—and stories based very closely upon her various journeys dominate *The Bride of the Innisfallen*. Moreover, in the process of inventing characters who, like herself, were literally in transit, Welty discovered the sort of thematic motif she had earlier found in *A Curtain of Green*. In her new stories, however, that motif concerns not only the power of imagination to effect communication and connection, but also the multiple ways individuals can live and create meaning for themselves without being rooted in place and time. In particular, Welty focuses upon the nature of women's identities as they exist apart from any defining place. Even in "The Burning," "Ladies in Spring," and "Kin," her Mississippi stories, characters hope for identities that lie beyond the conventions of southern life. And when the South is absent from her stories, Welty depicts travelers in a mythic landscape, in the no man's or no woman's land of a train or ship, or in exotic, non-southern lands that can neither define nor shield them.[1] In "Circe," "The Bride of the Innisfallen," "Going to Naples," and "No Place for You, My Love," characters are not like the Fairchilds of *Delta Wedding* (1946) or the families of Morgana in *The Golden Apples* (1949); they do not find their identities in the home place and they do not suspect people from "off." Yet despite the rather alien nature of place in these travel stories, the characters are more often contented than tormented. They are not destroyed as Jenny Lockhart is in "At the Landing"; they are not "roaming, like lost beasts," as Cassie Morrison believes Virgie Rainey and Miss Eckhart to be in "June Recital"; they are instead like displaced versions of Virgie Rainey at the end of "The Wanderers." They, at times even joyfully, embrace the unknown and unpredictable.

Certainly, Welty's increased sense of self-confidence as an independent woman and as a writer was a determining factor in the new patterns her stories would follow. And certainly, travel, for extended periods and to faraway lands, influenced her fiction in dramatic ways. Travel clearly served to confirm the sense of independence and contentment that Welty felt as a writer and as an individual and that she would make the central focus of *The Bride of the Innisfallen*. In *One Writer's Beginnings* (1984), Welty writes, "Through travel I first be-

---

1. In her book *Gothic Traditions and Narrative Techniques in the Fiction of Eudora Welty* (Baton Rouge: Louisiana State University Press, 1994), Ruth Weston discusses a rather different concept of the no man's land in Welty's fiction. For her comments on "Going to Naples" and "No Place for You, My Love," see pages 79–88 and 37–9. Julius Rowan Raper, on the other hand, ignores the concept of the no man's land in Welty's fiction and writes that Welty is "the writer who speaks with such sensitivity to the way place defines and shields character" ("Inventing Modern Southern Fiction: A Postmodern View," *Southern Literary Journal* 22 [Spring 1990]: 10).

came aware of the outside world; it was through travel that I found my own introspective way into becoming a part of it." And she immediately adds, "This is, of course, simply saying that the outside world is the vital component of my inner life" (*OWB*, 76). In making this assertion, Welty stresses the importance of observation and the passing of her "self-centered childhood." But travel is also tied to "the fierce independence" Welty attributes to herself (*OWB*, 60), for the traveler is one freed from the everyday demands of home life, the traveler is one who literally chooses his course.

To some extent the home she loved so much posed a threat to Welty's fierce need for freedom. By 1950 she had decided to find a retreat where she could write, a Mississippi place away from Jackson, from family and friends. In September and October, she wrote to Diarmuid Russell about efforts to buy land between Jackson and Vicksburg. Her attempts to purchase a house in the small town of Learned, Mississippi, however, were foiled because the locals were reluctant to see a single woman buying into their community, located about twenty-five miles southwest of Jackson. The quest for a room of her own continued, nevertheless, and in 1951, as Welty told Elizabeth Bowen, she was still seeking a place of her own.[2] Though Welty never managed to buy a home in the country, she had managed to live for a considerable time in San Francisco and New York City. But surely she found herself most free when a Guggenheim Fellowship sent her abroad for almost a year in 1949–50 and when she returned for a lengthy stay in England in 1951. Crossing the Atlantic, as many an American traveler knows, is in itself a liberating experience, and Welty moved about the European continent as her fancy directed her. She moved from Italy to Paris, back to the Mediterranean, onto Florence, then to England and Ireland, before returning to Italy to sail home. The next year found her in London and Dublin, at Bowen's Court and in Hythe.

The experience of traveling was an exhilarating one for Welty. The eighth day into her first voyage to Europe, Welty wrote to her agent Diarmuid Russell, saying that throughout the journey she had been "interested & amused." Upon ar-

---

2. Welty to Russell, 21 September [1950], 11 October 1950, n.d. [October or November 1950], restricted papers, Welty Collection, MDAH; Welty to Bowen, 6 December [1951], Bowen Collection, Harry Ransom Humanities Research Center, University of Texas at Austin.

rival in Genoa, she wrote again, proclaiming, "It was a grand experience, and for me I know it's the only way to travel that would be so interesting, Turistica with passengers of another country." A letter of December 3, 1949, describes the fun she has had with Aristide and Mary Mian and with Mary Lou (Aswell) and Fritz Peters and goes on to report on a trip to Montmartre and on hearing a music hall performance by Yves Montand. A letter of February 9, 1950, eagerly anticipates Mardi Gras in Nice, and on March 3, Welty wrote, "Florence is at present smiting me in the eye with so much at once that I just don't look except for a little a day." Equally pleasing were her companions in Florence—John Robinson and the poets William Jay Smith and Barbara Howes, but after a month in Florence, Welty left for England and Ireland. On her April 13, 1950, birthday, Welty wrote Russell to describe her enchantment with Dublin, and she was soon to be delighted by seeing Bowen's Court and by meeting its owner Elizabeth Bowen. In May, she wrote of her pleasure in Capri and in Assisi, and in June she wrote Russell of her sadness at leaving Europe. Her delight with England and Ireland was no less the following year. Especially pleasing was a two week sojourn at Bowen's Court. "We stay out till around 8—walking, going to Mallow (a lovely town!), riding up in the hills," Welty told Russell, and she also relished listening to Elizabeth Bowen and the artist Norah McGuinness spin their tales: "*Such stories* as those two told—these whole family stories unrolling—wonderful. (*Sort* of like Miss.)"[3]

Just over a year later, Welty found herself at home and at work on *The Ponder Heart*, a novella in which Edna Earle Ponder regales readers with a Mississippi family story, yet this portrait of southern provinciality, amusing and affectionate

3. Welty to Russell, n.d. [October 1949], [31 October 1949], 3 December [1949], 9 February [1950], 3 March [1950], [13 April 1950], 11 April [1951], restricted papers, Welty Collection, MDAH. The kind of happy independence Welty experienced as a European traveler was a natural extension of her experience as a writer. In composing the stories that would become *The Golden Apples*, Welty had resolved to follow her fancy (Kreyling, *Author and Agent*, 116). In doing so, she wrote a new sort of book, discovering connections between stories as she wrote them and resisting pressure to write a novel. She was not troubled by the sort of doubts that plagued her during the composition of *Delta Wedding*. The writer who had written *The Golden Apples* was already an independent voyager, and her independence was the source of great contentment. The writer who had just turned forty would, as she told me in a conversation of 7 December 1986, find her forties one of her happiest decades.

though it is, defines just the sort of confinement from which foreign travels had so happily freed Welty. Edna Earle discourages Uncle Daniel Ponder's trip to Lookout Mountain and Rock City Cave, telling him that neither "the top of a real high mountain or a cave in the cold dark ground" is the place for him. "Here's the place," she concludes (*PH*, 16). She cautions her traveling salesman–beau Mr. Stringer about the dangers of "straying too far from where you're known and all—having too wide a territory" (*PH*, 20). And Edna Earle concludes that her uncle "wouldn't dream of going to Memphis" to retrieve his wayward wife: "Uncle Daniel belongs in Clay, and by now he's smart enough to know it" (*PH*, 53). Edna Earle Ponder may keep her Uncle Daniel at home, but Eudora Welty, however engaging stories about the Edna Earle Ponders of Mississippi might be, had no intention of foregoing travel. *The Ponder Heart* was published in January 1954, and six months later Welty was on her way to an extended stay in Cambridge and London.

Welty's life in the early 1950s was thus far less focused upon the South than it had ever been, and her fiction of this period often moves away from the South as it draws upon her travel experiences. The shift away from a realistic, regional landscape is immediately evident in "Put Me in the Sky!"—later retitled "Circe"—the story Welty wrote before she wrote any of the other stories to be collected in *The Bride of the Innisfallen*. Having just completed *The Golden Apples*, an interrelated series of stories held together in part by a mythological frame of references, Welty found herself rereading *The Odyssey* and felt impelled to retell the mythological tale of Circe and Odysseus from a woman's perspective.[4] In "Put Me in the Sky!" Welty approaches head-on, rather than by allusion, the image of the witch goddess as presented by Homer or later by Keats and makes Circe more complex than the male texts had allowed. In this explicit rather than allusive use of myth and in her choice of a Mediterranean setting, Welty departs from the dominant pattern of her earlier works. Ultimately, Welty decided that her direct address of the archetypal Circe could be even more inclusively archetypal, and in the wake of her European travels and of a meeting with Elizabeth Bowen, she revised the periodical version of her story to ensure that

---

4. Welty to Russell, 26 August [1949], restricted papers, Welty Collection, MDAH.

the story's greatest emphasis would fall not upon a female version of myth but upon the unresolvable mystery at the heart of human identity, the mystery that distinguishes men and women from gods and goddesses, the mystery involved in the quest for independence and the battle against mortality.

In recasting a tale from Homer, Welty grants Circe a very secure sense of self. Circe is Welty's narrator. The goddess, who essentially is denied a voice by Homer, has the voice here. She opens the story by saying, "Needle in air, I stopped what I was making" (*BI*, 102). And she goes on to describe the interval during which Odysseus is part of her life. But during this interval, her concern is more about her own situation and the significance of women's work than it is about Odysseus. Circe's skill with the needle and in the kitchen, the glory of her garden, and the beauty of her household are all crucial to the identity of Welty's character, and she wants the recognition that is not forthcoming from Odysseus and his crew. "In the end," Welty's Circe complains, "it takes phenomenal neatness of housekeeping to put it through the heads of men that they are swine" (*BI*, 103). Though even Circe's literal transformation of the crew into swine fails to effect a change in attitudes, Welty's goddess is far more assertive and far more self-conscious than Homer's character. In *The Odyssey*, Circe has rather long speeches, but she is not the narrator. Moreover, her speeches seek to ascertain who Odysseus is, to ask why Odysseus refuses food and drink and to assure him that she plots no more harm, to invite all of Odysseus' company to her house, to offer her hospitality to that company, and to describe the journey to the underworld that lies in store for Odysseus.[5] Every speech she delivers focuses upon Odysseus; not once does she describe her own feelings. In Welty's story, however, Circe is more self-aware and self-possessed. She does not derive her identity from her man or her place but from her powers, and she believes that her island serves to sustain, not to define her.

Because Welty's Circe is confident of her power and values her own work, she does not see herself as one who must manipulate men. Unlike Homer's Circe, she does not see her sexual allure as a weapon. In the Greek epic, Hermes warns

5. For a related analysis, see Ann Romines, *The Home Plot: Women, Writing, and Domestic Ritual* (Amherst: University of Massachusetts Press, 1992), 3–5; Homer, *The Odyssey*, trans. E. V. Rieu (Baltimore: Penguin Books, 1946), 159–70.

Odysseus that he must accept Circe's sexual favors, but that he must also "make her swear a solemn oath by the blessed gods not to try on you any more of her tricks, or when she has you stripped she may rob you of your courage and your manhood."[6] This is not an issue in Welty's story; the relationship between Circe and Odysseus is a passionate one, not a manipulative one, at least on Circe's part. When Homer's Odysseus tells Circe that he wants to leave her, she responds in an easy-going, unemotional fashion. When Welty's Odysseus does the same, the goddess responds in a distraught, passionate fashion: "He gave me a pecking, recapitulating kiss, his black beard thrust at me like a shoe. I kissed it, his mouth, his wrist, his shoulder, I put my eyes to his eyes, through which I saw seas toss, and to the cabinet of his chest." And later she wanders alone in the night and feels herself "flung backward by my torment." "I believed," she adds, "that I lay in disgrace and my blood ran green, like the wand that breaks in two" (*BI*, 108, 109).

Such is the Circe Welty depicted in both the periodical and book publications of her story, but the two versions are not identical. When Welty revised "Put Me in the Sky!" she both sharpened her comments on issues of gender and shifted her focus from those issues to questions of independence and mortality. The original title "Put Me in the Sky!" seems to express Circe's desire to become a constellation, to be like Cassiopeia and beyond the passions of life among humans: "I looked at the sky. I envy and hate them up there. Cassiopeia can rest." This Circe feels no desire to identify with the traditional male role of quester, but Circe in the revised story contemplates the attraction of such an alternative for women. In the story's final version, the goddess asserts that she could have had "a ship too, if I were not tied to my island, as Cassiopeia must be to the sticks and stars of her chair" (*BI*, 111). The revised Circe, no matter how secure her identity and her power, believes that escape from "a world completed, full, closed upon itself" might have allowed her, in the words of Alain Robbe-Grillet, "to invent [her] own life."[7] Instead, of course, she must unceasingly enact her mythic role. The option of travel is not open to her as it was to Eudora Welty,

6. Homer, 163.
7. Eudora Welty, "Put Me in the Sky!" *Accent* 10 (1949): 9; Alain Robbe-Grillet, *For a New Novel: Essays on Fiction*, trans. Richard Howard (New York: Grove, 1965), 156.

who on her 1949 voyage to Italy passed the island fabled to be Circe's and who wandered happily about the Continent, England, and Ireland before revising this story.

Even though Circe momentarily desires to become a Welty-like wanderer and transcend the limited roles that have been available to her, she fails fully to understand the implications of wandering. She fails to understand that human beings are involved in quests against time as the gods need not be, that time is the force that compels humans to invent their own lives. And most of Welty's revisions to the earlier version of her story suggest how powerful time's effect is upon Odysseus and how oblivious the immortal goddess is to time. In the final version of the story, time seems to be at the root of the mortal mystery the revised Circe would give anything to penetrate. In addition, the final version of the story stresses that time is the impulse for the storytelling that so entrances Odysseus but is rejected by Circe even as she tells her own story. When Odysseus recounts the story of his journey from Troy, the revised Circe complains, "I didn't want his story, I wanted his secret" (*BI*, 105). No story can intrigue her; she feels no compulsion to leave a record of her existence, because her existence cannot be ended. "For whom is a story enough?" Welty's goddess asks herself and then answers her own question: "For the wanderers who will tell it—it's where they must find their strange felicity" (*BI*, 111). Finally, time's threat is a source of value for relationships—reunions among humans are cherished because time ensures that reunions will not always be possible. "Reunions, it seems," Circe observes, "are to be celebrated. (I have never had such a thing)" (*BI*, 106). When all times are one, as they inevitably are for immortals like Circe, there is no past to be recaptured and celebrated. As Circe says of herself, "It was as though I had no memory, to discover how early and late the cicadas drew long sighs like the playing out of all my silver shuttles" (*BI*, 108). Circe feels herself cut off from a world in which mortals urgently seek to create their own stories and in which relationships are defined in terms of each individual's unique memories.[8]

8. In her book *Daughter of the Swan: Love and Knowledge in Eudora Welty's Fiction* (Athens: University of Georgia Press, 1994), Gail Mortimer offers another interpretation of the mortal/immortal contrast in "Circe," writing that "the men's urgent experience of time . . . expresses a preoccupation much more characteristic of men than of women—certainly as it is depicted in most modernist fiction" (90).

If Welty's personal experience as an independent traveler appears obliquely in "Circe," such experience is overtly present in three others stories from *The Bride of the Innisfallen*—"The Bride of the Innisfallen," "No Place for You, My Love," and "Going to Naples." "The Bride of the Innisfallen" is the first of these travelogue stories to have been written, and in this story of travelers cut off from their homes, Welty drew extensively upon her 1951 journey from London to Ireland. Indeed, in a letter to Diarmuid Russell, Welty noted that most of the conversations in "The Bride of the Innisfallen" were "overheard ones—though not in the context of course."[9] And in a conversation with me, Welty recalled that the greyhounds, whose passage through the lounge of the ferry sounded like "tapping, as of drumming fingernails" (*BI*, 77), were actual parts of her experience, as were most of the story's details. Here Welty transcribes an experience more directly than she had typically done before—no longer does a mere bit of conversation or the isolated event spark a story that significantly diverges from actuality. Here Welty reports on an overnight journey in extensive detail, though she never brings herself explicitly into the story. Her decision to transcribe this experience may have been the result of a meeting with Elizabeth Bowen, a meeting that was the purpose of her journey. Welty wrote "The Bride of the Innisfallen" while in residence at Bowen's Court, and her description of the boat-train's arrival in Cork is very much like the Cork arrival in Bowen's novel *The House in Paris* (1935). In fact, "The Bride of the Innisfallen" seems to be in conversation with *The House in Paris* just as Welty was in conversation with Bowen as she worked on this story.

But the writers' affinity for each other and Bowen's impact upon "The Bride of the Innisfallen" extended beyond parallel passages in their fiction. The two women liked each other's work before they ever met. Early in 1949, Welty discussed Bowen's fiction in a letter to Diarmuid Russell: "Is Elizabeth Bowen your author in America by any chance? I think her so good, don't you?" A month later Welty again spoke of Bowen in a letter to Russell, observing that she "liked what G. Wescott said about her in some review, 'she never reveals anything too soon.'" Even though Welty felt that Bowen lacked "some feeling of joy," she found her "intelligent and sensitive," even at moments "tremendous." Bowen

---

9. Welty to Russell, n.d. [May 1951], restricted papers, Welty Collection, MDAH.

offered similar praise of Welty in a 1947 review of *Delta Wedding*, a review that Welty saw for the first time four years later. "'Delta Wedding,'" Bowen wrote, "is Eudora Welty's first novel—and what a beauty it is!" And Bowen went on to assert, "I don't imagine that anyone who is on the look-out for anything new and great in writing can by now have overlooked the work of this young American, or that anybody susceptible to the magic of writing can have forgotten hers, once met." Though neither Bowen nor Welty knew she was doing so, Bowen praised *Delta Wedding* for the joy Welty suspected was missing in Bowen's work: "There is a heart-breaking sweetness about this book, a sense of the momentum, joy, pain and mystery of life." In this same review, however, Bowen did express reservations about Welty's early work: "One or two of the stories in her second collection, *The Wide Net*," Bowen noted, "made me terrified that she might be heading for esoteric incomprehensibility." But even this reservation strengthened a bond between the two writers, for in 1951 Welty wrote to express her regrets at having missed this review and to tell Bowen how helpful the comments about *The Wide Net* might have proved.[10] In these expressions of affinity for each other's works, we see the method and tone of "The Bride of the Innisfallen" being struck. In this story, perhaps more than in any of her others, Welty guards against revealing anything too soon, she cultivates a sense of mystery, and she expresses a profound sense of joy.

The affinity between Welty and Bowen is also evident in the critical statements the two women have made about fiction. Welty's review of Bowen's *Pictures and Conversations* points to the important critical ties between the two writers. Commenting on Bowen's "Notes on Writing a Novel," Welty says that the notes are

> probing, unadorned, and succinct to the point where they could almost serve as passwords between writers. They have the currency today, as far as I can see, of pure gold. "Plot is the knowing of destination." Its object is "the non-poetic statement of a poetic truth." They are provocative to imagination. Characters,

10. Welty to Russell, 2 February [1949], 14 March [1949], restricted papers, Welty Collection, MDAH; Elizabeth Bowen, "Book Shelf," *The Tatler and Bystander*, 6 August 1947, 183; Welty to Bowen, 6 August [1951], Bowen Collection, Harry Ransom Humanities Research Center, University of Texas at Austin.

she thought, pre-exist for the novelist. "They are *found*. They reveal themselves slowly to the novelist's perception—as might fellow-travelers seated opposite one in a very dimly-lit railway carriage." Among the things I learned that startled me with their truth: "Nothing physical can be invented." (*ES*, 275)

A rare and full meeting of the minds is implicit in Welty's discussion of Bowen's notes, and the railway metaphor Welty quotes from those notes seems almost to describe the way travelers in "The Bride of the Innisfallen" come to understand each other as they journey from London to Cork.

Small wonder then that the two writers became close friends immediately upon meeting at Bowen's Court in 1950 and that in the friendship Welty was encouraged to follow new fictional paths. Eudora Welty, the sometimes solitary traveler, found great pleasure in her meetings with Elizabeth Bowen, and her 1951 journey to visit Bowen provided the raw material from which "The Bride of the Innisfallen" emerged. Though Welty herself is not a character in the story, in it she shares her inner landscape, emotions that were not new to her but that were particularly intense during this period of her life. The breaking away from confinement, the traveler's discovery of independence, and the joy implicit in an independent life all find expression in "The Bride of the Innisfallen," for Welty shapes, orders, and describes the actual journey so that it serves just these thematic purposes.

Travel for many characters in the story seems to provide an escape from oppressive relationships and a license for enjoyment. These characters are in transit, not in a stable environment that defines them, and they relish their freedom from rigidly defined worlds and roles. The lady whose raincoat creates a pavilion-like effect finds her fellow travelers of great interest: Every time she leaves the train compartment, she looks back as if to say, "Don't say a word, start anything, fall into each other's arms, read, or fight, until I get back to you." Later in the story, the same woman returns "beaming from her dinner" (*BI*, 52, 64). And this is the woman who bets on the dog races, who loves games of chance. On arrival in Cork, however, the woman is "confronted with a flock of beautiful children—red flags in their cheeks, caps on their heads, little black boots like pipes—and by a man bigger than she was" (*BI*, 79). The freedom she has relished during the voyage seems to have ended.

The Connemara man, who looks down on this Cork reunion and believes the woman now has her head "in the basket" (*BI*, 80), has similarly been entranced by the freedom of the voyage. During the train journey from London to the Welsh coast, he looks forward to the drink he can buy once the *Innisfallen* has left port. He glories in being free of his English wife, who, he suspects, has killed his talking bird. And he plans to have a night in Cork before he must visit another female oppressor, his mother. Travel is a source of joy and freedom for him.

Most important, the American girl on the boat-train is in quest of freedom, and she will find it by herself in her first visit to Cork. She has left London without her husband's knowledge, and arrival in Ireland seems to confirm the wisdom of doing so. For her it seems that Cork's streets "take off from the waterside and rise lifting their houses and towers like note above note on a page of music" (*BI*, 82). Though the young woman thinks she should explain herself to her husband, she eventually chooses not to do so. She denies the demands he has made upon her freedom, drops the letter she had planned to send, and walks into a pub, into a "lovely room full of strangers" (*BI*, 83). The greyhounds that the American, and the Connemara man, and the raincoat lady have heard on the boat, just as Eudora Welty did, come to seem the emblem of their quest for freedom in a world of chance. The dogs may or may not find any glory, but they move through the train corridors like "dangerously ecstatic old ladies" (*BI*, 56). The wanderers of "The Bride of the Innisfallen" may be in danger and may find their quests for freedom to be frustrated, but they may instead find ecstasy.

The story, in its emphasis upon freedom and self-definition, does not deny the importance or power of human relationships, and travel often leads to reunions. The American girl does not find a reunion but participates in the joy of those she imagines or witnesses in Cork. She looks at a bride who arrives in Cork on the *Innisfallen* and later thinks, "Yes, somewhere in the crowd at the dock there must have been a young man holding flowers: he had been taken for granted" (*BI*, 81). And when the American wife walks through Cork's Sunday streets, she sees "people busy at encounters, meetings, it seemed to her reunions. After church in the streets of Cork dozens of little girls in confirmation dresses, squared off by their veils into animated paper snowflakes, raced and danced out of control and into charmed traffic—like miniature and more conscious brides"

(*BI*, 80–1). These small girls who are part of the religious communion feel joy no less than the actual bride of the *Innisfallen*. The American wishes she could assume her husband's understanding of and communion in her emotional life, but knows she cannot; her husband, she recalls, claims that she always expects "too much" (*BI*, 82). As a result, she must find her joy as a solitary traveler. Her arrival in Ireland briefly threatens that joy; it makes her feel defined and "exposed," feel as if her marital difficulties have been revealed as they almost were on the train journey, but ultimately both the newly encountered land and the journey hold forth the possibility of rapturous fulfillment. The young wife knows a joyous solitude even though the telegram she tries to write to her husband can no more describe her emotional state than a news story can provide a comprehensive, historical analysis of today's events. When the *Innisfallen* comes into Cork harbor, a newspaper sinks into the water "with its drowned news." And when the wife abandons her effort to explain herself, she lets her message "go into the stream of the street" (*BI*, 79, 83). The mystery of emotion, whether shared in reunion or experienced alone, cannot be explained; it can only be felt. Openness, mystery, freedom, communion—this is the "too much" for which the American wife hopes and will continue to hope.

Welty links the sort of independence this young American feels with the creative independence of a writer following her fancy. In "Place in Fiction," an essay she wrote only three years after completing this story and an essay associated with her southern settings, Welty surprisingly seems to have "The Bride of the Innisfallen" in mind: "For the artist to be unwilling to move, mentally or spiritually or physically, out of the familiar is a sign that spiritual timidity or poverty or decay has come upon him; for what is familiar will then have turned into all that is tyrannical" (*ES*, 129). In "The Bride of the Innisfallen" Welty moves far from the familiar world of the South. For most of the story, she offers scant description of place at all. Train and boat are scarcely described; characters on the journey exist apart from place. Only Ireland, the journey's end, is described in some detail. It plays a special role in the development of the American wife; in fact, it seems to play the role that Welty believed foreign settings played for Hemingway: "Place heals the hurt, soothes the outrage, fills the terrible vacuum that . . . human beings make. It heals actively, and the response is given consciously, with the ardent care and explicitness, respect and delight of a lover. . . . The response to place has the added intensity that comes with the place's not being native or taken for granted, but found, chosen" (*ES*, 131). The young American responds to Cork with the "respect and delight of a lover," and she accepts the risks with which any lover is involved. This newly chosen place cannot shield or shelter her from life's dangers, but it may heal the hurt a "callous and insensitive, empty and cruel" husband has brought to her (*ES*, 131). Just as the young wife embraces risk-taking, so too did Eudora Welty in her choice and use of a non-southern setting. In her portrait of Ireland, as in her creation of the placeless boat-train, she had taken a new risk in a lifetime of risk-taking as a writer. As Welty wrote in "Place in Fiction," "No art ever came out of not risking your neck. And risk—experiment—is a considerable part of the joy of doing, which is the lone, simple reason all writers of serious fiction are willing to work as hard as they do" (*ES*, 130).

Welty began to revise "The Bride of the Innisfallen" almost immediately after completing it and sending it to her agent Diarmuid Russell. On May 4, 1951, she sent the story to Russell with a note saying, "The long paragraphs about Ireland toward the end I perhaps should take out, for the story's sake, & I don't suppose they make much sense to anybody either, but I left them in at present & you can see." Russell agreed with Welty's judgment, and she did revise the story before it appeared in the *New Yorker*. Not satisfied with these revisions, Welty returned to the story again before it appeared in *The Bride of the Innisfallen*. What those deleted paragraphs said of Ireland we don't know. We do know that Welty cut brief additional descriptions of Ireland before publishing the book version of her story. Clearly she sought to hold descriptions of place to a minimum. Place in "The Bride of the Innisfallen" served not to define character as it did say in *Delta Wedding*, but to represent a mystery, to promise fulfillment even as it threatened exposure. And when Welty did add information about setting to the story's final version, she did so with this concept in mind and with the desire to emphasize fulfillment more than danger. As the 1955 story concludes, the American wife thinks of Cork's beauty: "Out of the joy I hide for fear it is promiscuous, I may walk for ever at the fall of evening by the river, and find this river street by the red rock, this first, last house, that's perhaps a boarding house now, standing full-face to the tide, and look up to that window—that upper window, from which the mystery will never go. The curtains dyed so many times over are still pulled back and the window looks out open to the evening, the river, the hills, and the sea" (*BI*, 82). The upper window here possesses a "mystery" that "will never go," but this description is missing from the periodical version. And the window in the book looks out "open to the evening, the river, the hills, and the sea," but in the *New Yorker* it suggests instead that "some long, longer, more tragic, more rapturous story than she had yet guessed [was] still being repeated, printed, being made into history." The story's final emphasis thus lies more upon the promise of mystery than upon the threat of exposure. Additional cuts appropriately limit the exposure to which the American wife is subjected. In the *New Yorker*, the wife writes to her husband with a London pencil that reminds "her in its whole length and body of the flat, the cretonne, the linoleum, the fog (as if the disgusting powdery patches of where all her handkerchiefs had dried on the mirror were everything), the very beds—of where the letter must go." But this passage is gone from the book, and the American wife escapes exposure even to the reader. Place itself, whether Cork or London, serves as a kind of mystery in the story, and Welty wisely therefore limits description of it. Welty's world in this story is not a "world completed, full, closed upon itself" like the one which characters in *Delta Wedding* and *The Golden Apples* have unsuccessfully attempted to secure for themselves, but is a mysterious, unknowable one.[11] Welty's protagonist embraces this world, and at the story's close she walks into a "lovely room full of strangers" (*BI*, 83).

Within a year of completing "The Bride of the Innisfallen," Welty had written another travel story, but "No Place for You, My Love" did not begin in this fashion. "As first written," Welty recalled, "the story told, in subjective terms, of a girl in a claustrophobic predicament: she was caught fast in the over-familiar, monotonous life of her small town, and immobilized further by a prolonged and hopeless love affair; she could see no way out" (*ES*, 111). This plot seems vaguely reminiscent of *The Golden Apples* and seems the antithesis of "The Bride of the Innisfallen." But Welty found herself unable to continue in the earlier pattern, and she despaired of finishing the story. Perhaps the story was too close

11. Welty to Russell, 4 May 1951, restricted papers, Welty Collection, MDAH; Eudora Welty, "The Bride of the Innisfallen," *New Yorker* 27 (1 December 1951): 78, 77; Robbe-Grillet, 156.

to her. Welty's romance with John Robinson, which had been troubling in San Francisco, had seemed very promising when Welty joined Robinson in Florence in 1950. But late in 1950 or early in 1951, Robinson brought his Italian companion Enzo Rocchigiani with him when he sailed to Mexico. Rocchigiani would be with Robinson in New York City when Welty returned there from her second overseas trip in 1951, and he would remain Robinson's companion for life. Whatever lingering hope Welty had for a life with the man she loved was by the summer of 1951 doomed, and so it seemed was her story. Travel, however, saved the story. While spending some time in New Orleans, Welty made a trip to Venice, Louisiana. Two days after driving to land's end, she wrote Elizabeth Bowen about the adventure she had shared with a young Harvard professor named Carvel Collins:

> We . . . crossed the river on a good ferry at Pointe a la Hatche, full of Cajuns combing their hair and giving each other baskets of shrimp (what coals to Newcastle!)—we went into a remarkable cemetery that (but you must see it *just like this*) was two rows of elevated graves, like bureau drawers, with the fronts newly whitewashed, the cartracks [sic] paved between—car almost touched as we drove—straight down this alley to the church, green and white frame with poinsettias planted around it—and beyond the church was the priest's house with his cassock hung out on the clothesline to air—all in an enormous red sunset light—the white and the black and the vivid green, and the raging sound of all those crickets and locusts and what-all in the jungle around it. Crawfish scuttled across the road in front of us—Big okra patches high as your head and white as snow from dust—lots of little fishing boats right at any break in the forest—the water. The towns began with Arabi—and there was Port Sulphur, Jesuit Bend, Naomi, Alliance, Junior, Diamond, Socola, Happy Jack, Empire (a bad smell there, burning old fish?), Buros, Triumph, Concession, Phoenix, Nero, Ostrica and Venice. I don't mean we found all those—where were they? But they were on the map—maybe taking in both sides of the river. I wished for you. Except the mosquitoes were so thick, everybody on the road carried a branch of a palm to keep flailing around. . . . Huge sky, and the biggest moon came up—and after dark, the dust was like lakes all around us, with fires burning in their centers, and around the fires, cows—all untended—standing in a ring—in the heat and the night, to keep off mosquitoes—away off in the marshes,

you could see their horns standing up black against that lonely glow. Life is very gay in the villages—movies ("Rocket-Ship X-M"), Booga Red's Place, Te-Ta's Place, Paradise—cards and you could tell it was a dance floor too—slot machines. Juke boxes lit up. Full of children. They were going to have a Shrimp Dance the next night—I longed to return. Huge catfishes were lying on people's front porches. The whole place was amphibious—The people were dark, merry, with white teeth, teasing—one old man in the Paradise where we were having a bottle of beer at the bar came over and apologised to Carvel in a low voice for having just come in with a ribald remark—we didn't hear it, but his pals told him a lady was present. Everybody had on wonderful bright shirts— lavender, and such colors—I didn't see any women, I was possibly in the wrong place in the Paradise, it was for men and little children—holding each other up to play the slot machine—which *never once* paid off.[12]

The setting of the resultant story, one completed almost a year later and one almost wholly new, came directly from this experience. The ferry, the road of shells, the cemetery, the flora and fauna, the heat, the village life—detail after detail from Welty's letter is transcribed in her story. And in re-creating this setting, Welty has transformed the story she had originally set in a conventional small town. Though her new setting is very realistically described, no longer is it monotonous and conventional, and no longer does it define or confine her characters—it is wholly alien to them. Though her characters are still trapped, the story's focus is not on entrapment. Instead, the new story describes two individuals who fear that their entrapment may be revealed and who are engaged in "the vain courting of imperviousness in the face of exposure" (*ES*, 113). The bar in the story is not called Paradise, for the story is not about refuge or sanctuary but about exposure. As Welty has written in her essay about this story, "Secret and shadow are taken away in this country by the merciless light that prevails there, by the river that is like an exposed vein of ore, the road that descends as one with the heat—its nerve (these are all terms in the story), and . . . the heat is also a visual illusion, shimmering and dancing over the waste that stretches ahead. I was writing of a real place, but doing so in order to write about my

12. Welty to Bowen, 17 August [1951], Bowen Collection, Harry Ransom Humanities Research Center, University of Texas at Austin.

subject. I was writing of exposure, and the shock of the world; in the end I tried to make the story's inside outside and then leave the shell behind" (*ES*, 112–13). A contemporary travel experience thus moved Welty away from the portrait of a predictable world to a description of an environment that can neither define or shield its inhabitants.

Into this world that threatens exposure come two strangers. They meet over lunch in a New Orleans restaurant and then spend the afternoon and evening together, driving south of the city to land's end. Both the man from Syracuse and the woman from Toledo are unhappy in love. He has delayed his trip home so that his wife may entertain some old college friends; his marriage seems a passionless one. The woman from Toledo seems to be involved with a married man, and the bruise above her temple suggests that her love affair has taken a violent turn. The suffering that love has brought to both these individuals leaves them in quest of imperviousness; they want to avoid thinking about their situations, and they want to avoid exposing their situations to others. The man will not discuss his wife with the woman from Toledo, and the woman resents his intuitive recognition of her plight: "How did it leave us—the old, safe, slow way people used to know of learning how one another feels," she wonders (*BI*, 3–4). But as much as they may desire to shield themselves, a relationship springs up between them, and they know that "even those immune from the world, for the time being, need the touch of one another, or all is lost" (*BI*, 22).

Welty's metaphoric apprehension of the very real landscape through which these two characters travel focuses upon the question of immunity and exposure. The story's crayfish seem "grim and bonneted," and the alligators seem to be "crawling hides you could not penetrate with bullets or quite believe" (*BI*, 7–8). These creatures seem to have the very imperviousness that Welty's travelers seek. But neither the crayfish nor the alligators are impervious: Cars routinely run over and crush crayfish in the road, and on the river ferry an alligator is held captive on a leash. For Welty, therefore, this region "south of South" (*BI*, 25) promises exposure, not imperviousness. The "amphibious" land seems to deny the couple "all other bearings" (*BI*, 24). The mounds of shells and the shell roads are further testimony of failed protection, of the impossibility of imperviousness. The couple is exposed to light, to insects, to everything about the environment, and to each other. Though they seek not to feel, not to reveal their histories to each other, not to become involved with each other, they begin to respond as one to the events of the afternoon and evening. In the early evening, having arrived at land's end and entered a bar, they dance formally, "imperviousness in motion," but they dance "too well" together (*BI*, 22, 21). And even when that new relationship is over and the couple has returned to New Orleans and regained their bearings, their attitudes toward their lives have been altered. The woman seems to walk confidently toward the lover who has mistreated her, and the man is able to recall "the lilt and expectation of love" he had felt as a young man (*BI*, 27). The journey into an unknown and unexpected world convinces the two people of the significance of intimacy and enables them to cope more effectively with the involvement they have fled during their day together. The relationships in which these two are separately engaged may have caused much pain, but the brief, tentative relationship they share going to and returning from Venice reestablishes for them the value of love, whatever its outcome.

The mysterious and little known world of "No Place for You, My Love" seems very contemporary, and so too does the story's conclusion. Driving out of the primitive landscape, the woman from Toledo and the man from Syracuse return to the confines of New Orleans, a city where people shelter themselves from light and heat, where they keep the roofs up on their convertible cars, sit in restaurants under fans, and go home to sleep in "flaked-off, colored houses" that are "spotted like the hides of beasts" (*BI*, 5–6). This return dooms their relationship, but the relationship itself is reluctant to die: "Something that must have been with them all along suddenly, then, was not. In a moment, tall as panic, it rose, cried like a human, and dropped back" (*BI*, 26). When Welty recalled the story in her essay "Writing and Analyzing a Story," she paid particular attention to this human-like cry:

> I admit that I did expect to sound mysterious now and then, if I could: this was a circumstantial, realistic story in which the reality *was* mystery. The cry that rose up at the story's end was, I hope unmistakably, the cry of that doomed relationship—personal, mortal, psychic—admitted in order to be denied, a cry that the characters were first able (and prone) to listen to, and then able in part to ignore. The cry was authentic to my story: the end of a journey *can* set up a cry, the shallowest provocation to sympathy and love does hate to give up the ghost. (*ES*, 114)

The courting of mysteriousness and the depiction of an apparition link "No Place for You, My Love" with those stories we today place in the camp called magical realism. This story, of course, is not a full-fledged ghost story like Toni Morrison's *Beloved*, but Welty herself called it a ghost story when she sent it to her agent. And Diarmuid Russell's response to the story took note of its other-worldly qualities: "I thought this new story quite lovely, and sort of mysterious, both in the heat and the ride, a curious dreamlike affair with the effect on me that something was hovering in my mind ready to be said. But it is good and holds together wonderfully, just right." What Russell found to be just right for this story is the indeterminacy that today we associate with postmodernism, and it is no surprise that "No Place for You, My Love" is the favorite Welty story of those southern postmodernists Barry Hannah and Richard Ford.[13]

Just as Welty transcribes her travel experiences quite faithfully in "The Bride of the Innisfallen" and "No Place for You, My Love," so too does she rely upon autobiography in "Going to Naples." When Welty sailed for Europe on her Guggenheim grant, she sailed on the *Italia*, an old ship that had been in use during World War II. Almost everyone on the boat was Italian or Italian-American, and a large percentage of the people were Sicilian. Welty, in fact, was almost the only third-class passenger who spoke no Italian. A shipboard friendship with a New York actor, Gemi Festa, stood out in her memory, and she recalled her fun dancing with Festa and singing songs from *Annie Get Your Gun* with him. There were women very much like Gabriella and her mother on board, and the mothers were very much interested in arranging marriages for their daughters. Old people returning to Italy, returning to die in their homeland, and Holy Year pilgrims also dominated the boat's population. And the arrivals in Palermo and Naples were just as Welty delineates them in her story. In 1949, while still on the *Italia*, Welty wrote to describe the events to Diarmuid Russell:

> If only I could write the exact account of that voyage, with names—(how could it be written without using Mrs. Crocefissa Virga? just for instance.) It was a

13. Russell to Welty, 23 July 1952, restricted papers, Welty Collection, MDAH, and as cited by Kreyling, *Author and Agent*, 160; Barry Hannah and Richard Ford, interviews with author on Public Radio in Mississippi, 4 March 1986.

grand experience, and for me I know it's the only way to travel that would be so interesting, Turistica with passengers of another country. You would have been delighted at the welcome to Palermo—boatloads of family connections rowed out into the harbor to meet us, and such cries and such wavings— "Umberto!"—"Pepiiiiita!" one rowboat had 13 big fat Sicilians in it rowed by one poor man, the rest wildly waving and almost upsetting. It was dramatic. We had a good time in Palermo and a nice stop too in Naples—and I got to see Vesuvius at sun-up. My best friend on board was a 23-year old dancer of Neapolitan descent, who was going over to Rome to be in a movie—he'd just graduated from Columbia on the GI bill, and was the most exhuberant [sic] soul I've had the pleasure to see in a long time. His family are out in the country from Naples, some big place I gather, where all is made at home, cheese, wine, bread, candles, and much to-do at holidays—he's invited me to visit at Christmas or Easter or such—would be wonderful to see the real life in the country.

There was also a nice member of the crew I got to know a little, who was a real poet at heart. The mean old woman on board, I guess there's always one, to speak the evil about everybody, he called La Secconda, which means "the dried-up one," and the actress, who had an ocelot skirt and purple lipstick, he called La Funeria. He knows all the ports, and was the one who took us to dinner in Palermo, that is, we took him. He has read all kinds of American books in translation, an interesting man. A machinist.[14]

Vivid as this experience was and as much as she wished to write about it, for several years Welty found herself unable to transform it into a story. Perhaps, in fact, she needed to partake of the traveler's freedom for an extended period before she could fully appreciate the meaning of her first European voyage. Whatever the case, four years after first sailing to Europe, Welty completed and subsequently published "Going to Naples."

"Going to Naples" is a very personal story. Indeed, Welty wrote herself, in a sense, into the story, and she looks at herself in a rather bemused fashion. The traveler Eudora Welty was, like the story's Miss Crosby, an "unattached lady who could not speak a word of Italian" (*BI*, 164). And when Miss Crosby leaves

14. Eudora Welty, interview with author and with Mary Hughes Brookhart, Jackson, Mississippi, 23 July 1983; Welty to Russell, [31 October 1949], restricted papers, Welty Collection, MDAH.

her reading, rises from the forward deck where she has been seated, and comes over to Gabriella "on her long legs" (*BI*, 173), she resembles Welty who spent a good bit of her voyage reading *Moby-Dick* (not *First Lessons in Italian Conversation* as Miss Crosby does) and who was also a rather tall woman. Although Miss Crosby is peripheral to the story's main action and although she is not the story's narrator, she seems to embody traits Welty associates with narrators. In *One Writer's Beginnings*, Welty says of herself: "My temperament and my instinct had told me alike that the author, who writes at his own emergency, remains and needs to remain at his private remove. I wished to be, not effaced, but invisible—actually a powerful position. Perspective, the line of vision, the frame of vision—these set a distance" (*OWB*, 87). Yet, if Miss Crosby is at a remove from her fellow passengers, she is also at a remove from her creator. Unlike Welty, Miss Crosby does not dance, participate in the social life of the boat, go out to eat with the ship's machinist, or receive invitations to visit Italian homes. Welty also removes Miss Crosby from any southern background. We know nothing of Miss Crosby's heritage. She exists for us only on the ship, which Welty renames the *Pomona*. In distancing herself from Miss Crosby, Welty thus maintains the "powerful position" that she could not have had as a character in her own story. Welty's stance in the story allows her to deal with personal experience without being self-absorbed. For Faulkner, David Minter argues, travel was associated with self-absorption.[15] Not so for Welty. She describes early train journeys and says that a key moment in her development as a writer came when she realized the world was not passing by her train window, but that "it was *I* who was passing." At that moment, Welty tells us, "my self-centered childhood was over" (*OWB*, 76). Through Miss Crosby, Welty dramatizes this realization; through Miss Crosby, Welty is both in and out of the story. In her ironic portrait of this unattached American lady, Welty may be undercutting her own narrative authority and engaging in a sort of frame breaking. More importantly, perhaps, Welty uses Miss Crosby to develop key thematic issues that emerged from personal experiences. In contrasting the isolation and reserve of middle-aged Miss

15. David Minter, *William Faulkner, His Life and Work* (Baltimore: Johns Hopkins University Press, 1980), 75.

Crosby with the youth and exuberance of Gabriella, Welty certainly raises the issues of love and separateness, time and mortality.

Love and separateness, time and change are hardly new issues in Welty's fiction, but in "Going to Naples," Welty wholly divorces these issues from a southern setting. The *Pomona* in fact is a sort of no place. As the story opens, Gabriella Serto bewails her departure from the known world of Buffalo, New York, as she and her mother walk "along the passages—where of course everybody else, as well as the Sertos, was lost" (*BI*, 156–57). Although Gabriella believes this journey on the *Pomona* involves a farewell to liberty—she screams and waves good-bye to the Statue of Liberty as the *Pomona* leaves New York harbor—her time on shipboard may provide the greatest freedom she has known or will know. Her destination, whether it be Italy or marriage, seems a real threat to freedom, but the journey itself does not. On shipboard, there is no authoritarian father who will hit the ceiling if she flunks typewriting. Her mother is present, but Mama knows when to fall back and at a key moment is indisposed. Gabriella and her mother have trouble walking through the ship together, but "the long passage through the depths of the ship, that was too narrow for Mrs. Serto and Gabriella to walk without colliding, seemed made for Gabriella and Aldo" (*BI*, 170). On the ship, Gabriella is free to pursue a romance without her mother at her heels. Ultimately, she is also free to be happy without pursuing a man. Only on the ship and with the license of Gala Night could Gabriella dance alone as she does: "For an unmarried girl, it was danger. Some radiant pin through the body had set her spinning like that tonight, and given her the power—not the same thing as permission, but what was like a memory of how to do it—to be happy all by herself" (*BI*, 186). Instead of the power "to be happy all by herself," Italy offers Gabriella hierarchy and obedience. But for the length of her journey Gabriella is remarkably free. Significantly, when Welty wrote Diarmuid Russell to describe her own voyage to Naples, she never mentioned an event like Gabriella's Gala Night dance. It was only in retrospect, only after she had journeyed to Europe again and only after her romance with Robinson was clearly over, that Welty either recalled the importance of the event or created an event to convey her concern with the single woman who can "be happy all by herself."

Welty, however, does not merely exult in freedom from place. She describes the *Pomona*'s arrival both in Palermo and in Naples in considerable detail. If a very real destination promises to deny Gabriella the kind of freedom she has known on shipboard, it will bring her a knowledge of time and of love. After the Gala Night has ended, Gabriella thinks seriously about the meaning of time: "Was now the time to look forward to the doom of parting, and stop looking back at the doom of meeting? The thought of either made sorrow go leaping and diving, like those dolphins in the water. Gabriella would only have to say 'Good-by, Aldo,' and while she was saying the words, the time would be flying by; parting would be over with almost before it began, no matter what Aldo had in store for an answer" (*BI*, 192). But Gabriella also learns that despite time, despite the separation which time makes inevitable, the moment of communication, even if only of saying good-bye, is worth the pain occasioned: The "golden moment of touch" when she and Aldo say good-bye in Naples seems to transfigure her experience. And the continuity of family ties seems more blessed than oppressive. Introduced to her Italian grandmother, Gabriella thinks, "Nonna was still the mother. Her brown face might be creased like a fig-skin, but her eyes were brighter now than tears had left Mama's, or than the lightning of bewilderment that struck so often into the eyes of Gabriella. Surely they knew everything. They had taken Gabriella for granted" (*BI*, 206). As she and her mother and grandmother turn away from the *Pomona*, a "golden moment," Gabriella feels, "seemed to go ahead of them as they walked, to tap without sound across the dust of the emptying courtyard, and alight in the grandmother's homely buggy, filling it" (*BI*, 207). The dusty courtyard, the yellow leaves of its plane trees, the black country horse hitched to the buggy, the church bells of Naples that strike each hour—this place of the "golden moment" is hardly a contemporary no man's land. And this place represents values that are quite traditional; this place not only defines and shelters, but also leads to a kind of transcendence.

As we have seen, Welty concludes *The Bride of the Innisfallen* with a safe arrival in Naples, but the book's route to Naples has involved journeys to magical islands and through exotic amphibious landscapes; it has involved travels via the no man's land of train and ship, travels in which time seems suspended and place alien or almost irrelevant. In this 1955 work, her characters are not, as they typically were in her earlier books, trapped by a confining and defining place or engaged in revolt against it. Her own experience as a traveler freed from the known world of home and as a writer freed from conventional expectations led her to depict protagonists who either felt secure in identities not defined by place or who relished their freedom from place and their freedom to create, if only temporarily, their own worlds. In *The Bride of the Innisfallen*, Eudora Welty thus surely anticipates the issues upon which critics of the 1980s and 1990s have focused, but she does so in a way far richer and far more hopeful than we have come to expect in contemporary literature.

 VII

# The Insistent Present and the
# "Huge Fateful Stage of the Outside World"

Throughout her life Welty was interested in politics and in the course of political events. As we have seen, her fiction from the start confronted issues of racism and poverty, issues of self-aggrandizement and the abuses of power. And as we have also seen, Welty upon at least one occasion publicly denounced two Mississippi demagogues. But, of course, Welty was not a political activist, and her fiction of the fifties seems largely removed from the political arena. Her interest in politics during the fifties, however, remained keen, and in the 1960s Welty's political involvement intensified greatly as the civil rights movement focused upon Mississippi. Ultimately, Welty's political concerns would become the subject of the only two stories she published during the sixties.

Adlai Stevenson provided the spark for Welty's political activity in the 1950s. In New York City during the fall of 1952, Welty canvassed for Stevenson and sold tickets for Stevenson fund raisers, attending watch parties on election night, hoping against hope for his victory. For Welty this was a moment of convergence; Stevenson brought to the public stage the very values that animated her fiction. She admired his forthright nature, his acceptance of diversity, his keen intellect and complexity of thought, and his use of the English language. As a result, Welty for the first and only time in her life actively joined a political campaign.

The defeat of Stevenson was a bitter pill, but her loyalty to the candidate and her hope that he might one day lead the country were unquenched. She expressed that loyalty openly one more time, this time in print when the *New Republic* requested that she and other writers send New Year's greetings to Governor Stevenson. In her message, Welty told the governor that in his campaign his supporters saw "their chiefest inner convictions translated for the time being to the huge fateful stage of the outside world" and that Stevenson "had got up and represented those convictions and brought them to bear on the scene, life-size and first-hand." In writing about inner conviction translated to the "huge fateful stage of the outside world," Welty might have been describing her own attempts in fiction. In *One Writer's Beginnings*, she notes that "the outside world is the vital component of my inner life. My work, in the terms in which I see it, is as dearly matched to the world as its secret sharer. My imagination takes its strength and guides its direction from what I see and hear and learn and feel and remember of my living world" (*OWB*, 76). This "charged dramatic field of fiction" (*OWB*, 102) converged with "the huge fateful stage of the outside world" in the election of 1952, so that Eudora Welty supported a candidate she characterized in her New Year's greeting as having "intelligence . . . charged to communicate, . . . shaped in responsibility and impelled with learning and curiosity, [and] . . . alight with imagination."[1] Stevenson, Welty saw, was concerned with communication and "alight with imagination," and such concern and such imagination, she felt, made not merely for great literature, but also for credible political leaders, for effective political communication, and for innovative political policies.

Stevenson, as Welty recognized and admired, possessed the courage of his convictions, but expressing those convictions damaged his chances for victory. Though the selection of John Sparkman as his running mate on the Democratic

---

1. Eudora Welty, "What Stevenson Started," 8.

ticket was designed to appease southern Democrats, Stevenson's majority in Welty's Mississippi, was restricted by "a significant Republican showing for the first time in the century." Many Mississippians were like voters nationwide— not only attracted by Dwight David Eisenhower's war record, but also alienated by the Democratic candidate's public pronouncements. As David Halberstam reports, Stevenson "went before the American Legion, a citadel of jingoism and political reaction, and told the audience that McCarthy's kind of patriotism was a disgrace." The American Legion was not alone in hearing such frank comments. Stevenson biographer Jean Baker observes that

> In his childhood Adlai Stevenson had learned the virtues of self-criticism, and so throughout the campaign he offered the language of business to labor, remarking that "goons and violence and property damage are as wrong and as intolerable in labor disputes as anywhere else." In New Haven he promised an audience of loyal party men that he would support only worthy Democratic candidates. In New Orleans he spoke on civil rights and tidelands oil. At a town hall luncheon in Los Angeles, he informed party activists that the people got the kind of leaders they deserved. "Your public servants serve you right; indeed they often serve you better than your apathy and indifference deserve."

Stevenson was a rare candidate, one who sought to challenge his listeners, not pander to them. That such a candidate went on to national defeat raised for Welty a crucial question: "How soon and how fully can we accommodate greatness—honor it, not punish it, because it *is* greatness," she asked.[2]

For Welty, Stevenson's greatness lay in his recognition that political situations were too complex for simplistic answers. For example, the war in Korea was central in the mind of the electorate in 1952, but Stevenson offered no easy answers for this problem. A speech he gave in Louisville, Kentucky, is typical. There, as Baker reports, "he offered his special brand of the politics of unresolved modern dilemmas: 'I promise no easy solutions, no relief from burdens and anxieties, for

2. William F. Winter, "New Directions in Politics, 1948–1956," in *A History of Mississippi*, ed. Richard Aubrey McLemore, vol. 2, p. 149; David Halberstam, *The Fifties* (New York: Villard Books, 1993), 236; Jean H. Baker, *The Stevensons* (New York: Norton, 1996), 323; Welty, "What Stevenson Started."

to do this would be not only dishonest; it would be to attack the foundations of our greatness.' It was typical of Stevenson that he carefully and thoughtfully dissected the Korean War—its history, its manipulation by the Soviets (this was an era in which Americans misunderstood the tensions among Communist countries and exaggerated the power of the Soviets), and its necessary resolution by military containment under the United Nations."[3] Stevenson's discussion of the multi-faceted and perhaps impenetrable nature of reality held vital appeal for Welty, whose character Virgie Rainey knew that "all the opposites on earth were close together" (*GA*, 234) and who herself would later write: "Relationship *is* a pervading and changing mystery. . . . Brutal or lovely, the mystery waits for people wherever they go, whatever extreme they run to" (*ES*, 114).

Finally, Stevenson's love of language, of its imaginative and precise use, set the note of the campaign in which Welty had so ardently participated. According to Baker, Stevenson paid more attention to the written text of his speeches than to their effective delivery. When his advisors argued that his defects as an orator limited his appeal to voters, "Stevenson's reaction was expectable: 'If they don't like me as I am, *tant pis*! I won't pretend to be anything else.'" Concern for language defined Stevenson. As Baker notes, "Intent on creating carefully crafted political essays graced with complex vocabulary—the language of the university, the Washington-based institutes, and the nation's best writers . . . , Stevenson paid no attention to the important consideration of advancing himself as a future president. Always the presentation of his words was secondary to the words themselves."[4] Such a stance clearly made Stevenson a writer's candidate.

If public and private thus converged for Welty in the campaign of 1952, if the fiction writer found some of her most interior values being championed on the "huge fateful stage of the outside world," she herself championed an inner conviction on a somewhat smaller Mississippi stage in the 1960s. That stage was literally located in the Christian Center of Millsaps College, and there Eudora Welty on April 18, 1963, and December 2, 1964, made powerful, yet complex

3. Baker, 333.
4. Baker, 325, 320.

statements in favor of civil rights, an issue upon which Stevenson had not so clearly spoken.[5]

When Welty took the podium in 1963, it was with a background of interracial relationships more diverse, extensive, and empathetic than most white Mississippians possessed. During her student days at Columbia University and later during visits to New York City, Welty had often gone to Harlem: She loved to hear jazz played at the Cotton Club and Small's Paradise, and she had been thrilled to see an African-American production of *Macbeth*. In Jackson, Welty had frequented music stores in the black business district so that she could buy what were called "race records," and she had moved easily in and out of black neighborhoods, homes, and churches, photographing many a black Mississippian. Sometime in the 1940s, her editor John Woodburn introduced Welty to Ralph Ellison and took her to dinner at the Ellisons' New York apartment. It was her first social contact with African Americans, and she and Ellison became friends.[6]

Moreover, late in the 1950s, Welty, often in the company of Millsaps history professor Ross Moore and his wife, began to attend events at Tougaloo Southern Christian College, an African American institution just north of Jackson. She also gave at least two lecture/readings there, one of which was sponsored by the Social Sciences Forum. According to Millsaps political science professor John Quincy Adams, Tougaloo's Professor Ernst Borinski had designed the Forum as part of an effort to provide a "model of an integrated society," and Millsaps professors of history, sociology, and political science had been frequent speakers. The invitation for Welty to speak about her work was a very unusual one for the Social Sciences Forum—her fiction and her creative process had little to do with the social sciences—but simply by addressing the group, Welty was issuing a call for integration. In fact, this lecture came only five months after a 1958 furor about the Millsaps College Religious Forum that had dared to invite integrationists to speak, and her lecture seems almost to have been a response to the clamor raised by local newspapers, a clamor that had prompted Millsaps to close its

5. See Baker, 341–3.

6. Eudora Welty discussed this and other biographical information with me in many conversations held between 1983 and 2001.

public events to African Americans and to discourage its professors from teaching or speaking at Tougaloo. Welty clearly regretted that Millsaps would no longer provide a "model of an integrated society," but she participated in such a model at Tougaloo, even though speaking at Tougaloo involved some personal danger. By 1958, white visitors to Tougaloo might have expected to have their visits monitored by the State Sovereignty Commission or its informers. Welty's friend Jane Reid Petty recalled that she and others often carpooled when going to Tougaloo, varying the car they took as often as possible so that the sheriff, whom they suspected of recording the tag numbers of white visitors to Tougaloo, would not see a pattern in their visits. Though the possibility of harassment loomed in the offing, neither Welty nor her friends were deterred from this activity.[7]

Despite a history of refusing to capitulate to racist pressure, Welty must have been keenly aware that her April 18, 1963, appearance at Millsaps occurred at a particularly tense moment in the history of both the state and the college. In the fall of 1962, there had been riots and two deaths at the University of Mississippi when James Meredith had arrived to enroll. In December 1962, a black boycott of downtown Jackson stores had begun and would be the source of much hostility for more than six months. In January 1963, twenty-eight young white Methodist ministers caused outrage in the white community when they published a "*Born of Conviction* statement . . . , in which they asked for a free and open pulpit in the racial crisis and full support of the public schools instead of the private schools that were being established to maintain segregation."[8]

At Millsaps, there was tension as well. Both faculty and administration overwhelmingly supported efforts for integration, but the administration, in particular, feared both violence and the loss of its financial base if integration came to

7. Social Sciences Forum Announcements, Tougaloo College Archives, Tougaloo, Mississippi; John Quincy Adams, Papers and Audio Tapes, Faculty Papers, Series F, Millsaps College Archives, Jackson, Mississippi; Laura G. McKinley, "Millsaps College and the Mississippi Civil Rights Movement" (honors thesis, Millsaps College, 1989), 5–6; "Millsaps President and Wright Protest," *Jackson Clarion-Ledger* 9 March 1958, sec. A; Jane Reid Petty and Patti Carr Black, personal conversations with the author, March 1997.

8. W. J. Cunningham, *Agony at Galloway* (Jackson: University Press of Mississippi, 1980), 8.

the school. Nevertheless, on January 24, 1963, the Millsaps faculty voted 36–22–1 to support the twenty-eight Methodist ministers who had signed the *Born of Conviction* statement. The Millsaps resolution read, in part: "We are concerned . . . that encroachments upon the liberties of ministers to speak freely their sincere interpretations of the Christian gospel constitute but one manifestation of those evil tendencies which would deny men freedom in every sphere. Such tendencies are a constant threat, not only to a free and valid church, but also to a democratic society." Nor was this the end of consternation felt by Millsaps faculty over the racial situation in Mississippi. On April 2, 1963, a professor and several African American students from Tougaloo College were turned away from a play at Millsaps, and on April 11, the Millsaps AAUP chapter passed another controversial resolution, this time asking the college president to appoint a committee to study the possibility of integrating the Millsaps student body.[9] A week later, it was time for the college to host the Southern Literary Festival, which was directed by Millsaps English professor and Welty friend George Boyd, one of the signers of the AAUP resolution. The college thus faced a dilemma—whether to abide by its policy of segregation, so recently enforced, or to allow open admission to Eudora Welty's April 18 address because it was sponsored by the Southern Literary Festival rather than Millsaps.

Early on that day, officials from Millsaps called upon Welty to discuss the prospect of an integrated audience—they feared conflict. Welty, nevertheless, asked that her lecture be open to all, and it was. That lecture, published almost a year earlier under the title "Words into Fiction," seems detached from any sort of political situation. In it, Welty acknowledges that a reader may have a conception of a novel that differs from that of the writer, but she contends that this difference "is neither so strange nor so important as the vital fact that a connection has been made between them" (*ES*, 144). The novel, she argues, is "made by the imagination for the imagination" (*ES*, 145). After delivering this address, however, Welty went on to show her audience the political import a work made by the imagination for the imagination could have—she read the story "Power-

9. Minutes of Faculty Meeting, 24 January 1963, Series B, Millsaps College Archives, Jackson, Mississippi; H. E. Finger, Jr., Papers, Administrative Papers, Series A1, Millsaps College Archives, Jackson, Mississippi; Adams, Papers and Audio Tapes.

house" to the interracial audience, which included a contingent from Tougaloo Southern Christian College.[10]

Written in 1940 and inspired by a Fats Waller concert Welty had attended, "Powerhouse" is the story of an African American pianist and his band playing at a segregated dance; it focuses on the white audience's simultaneous fascination with and repulsion by the band leader, Powerhouse, and on the band's ability to find intermission conviviality and refreshments only at a black café. In reading this story at the festival, Welty took a considerable risk. "The point of view of this story," she has noted, "is floating around somewhere in the concert hall—it belongs to the 'we' of the audience," and that audience is a racist audience.[11] Powerhouse, on the other hand, is drawn from Welty's own experience as a writer. Welty has said that she is driven by "the love of her art and the love of giving it, the desire to give it until there is no more left" (*OWB*, 101), and Powerhouse is a performer who "gives everything" (*CG*, 257). Thus, the narrative voice located in the story's white racist audience might have offended black listeners at Millsaps even as the author's clear identification of Powerhouse as representative of artists like herself might have offended whites. But Welty trusted in the ability of her listeners, and she might well have expected the story to bring together the two factions attending the lecture and reading.

In "Powerhouse," Welty suggests that a shared act of imagination can break through, if not bring down, the walls between individuals. Though both Powerhouse's white audience at the dance and his black admirers at the World Café at first feel separated from him, either by race or by fame, his performances involve them fully and variously bring them "the only time for hallucination," leave them in a "breathless ring," send them "into oblivion," and cause them to moan "with pleasure" (*CG*, 254, 265). The song that closes Welty's story seems indirectly to anticipate the communication that imagination can initiate and sustain. "Somebody loves me," Powerhouse sings and then concludes, "Maybe it's you!" (*CG*, 269) Despite the odds, maybe Powerhouse will have a profound and en-

10. Eudora Welty, personal conversation with author, and R. Edwin King, personal conversations with author, 20 March 1997, 7 April 1997, 19 June 1997; Jerry DeLaughter, "Miss Welty Opens Literary Festival," *Jackson Clarion-Ledger* 19 April 1963, sec. A.

11. Eudora Welty, William E. Massey Lecture III, p. 6, Welty Collection, MDAH.

during effect on his audience, at least upon some members of it. Surely the origin of this story demonstrates that imagination had transcended the boundaries of race in one instance: The Fats Waller concert in Jackson brought forth a lasting and powerfully creative response from Eudora Welty.

More than twenty years after writing this story based on the Waller concert, Welty read it to her 1963 Millsaps audience, black and white, as if to proclaim the destructiveness of segregation and the enriching effect of imagining oneself into other and different lives. Combining her story with a lecture about the power of the imagination to unite reader and writer was a political act for Welty, an act of courage and vision, an act that built upon the integrated readings she had earlier given at Tougaloo College. And Welty's presentation at Millsaps did unite, however briefly, black and white Mississippians. John Salter, the professor who led the Tougaloo contingent on April 18, reported that "Eudora Welty gave an excellent lecture, including a reading of one of her short stories—which we could follow as she read since we had brought along several copies of her work. When the evening was over we walked slowly outside. A group of Millsaps students came up and indicated that they were quite glad that we had attended. Other than that, no one appeared to notice us, and that, in its own small way, marked a significant breakthrough in Mississippi." Welty's part in this breakthrough won her the enduring respect of Tougaloo Chaplain Edwin King, who attended the event along with Salter and black students from Tougaloo, and of Anne Moody, one of those black students, who in a February 1985 appearance at Millsaps recalled how important it was for her to hear Welty read.[12] Nevertheless, despite Welty's actions in support of integration and despite the standing ovation she received from blacks and whites at the festival, Millsaps College would less than one month later turn away African Americans who sought admission to a theatrical production by the Millsaps Players.

Off the Millsaps campus, infinitely more virulent acts of racism soon occurred. On May 28, 1963, a faculty member and some students from Tougaloo

12. John R. Salter, *Jackson, Mississippi* (Hicksville, N.Y.: Exposition Press, 1979), 102; Edwin King arranged for Moody to speak at Millsaps, attended the lecture with her, and told me of her comments about Welty's importance to the Tougaloo contingent (19 June 1997).

were beaten and one student arrested when they attempted to integrate the lunch counter at Woolworth's variety store. On June 12, Medgar Evers, field secretary of the Mississippi NAACP, was assassinated. And on June 18, John Salter and Edwin King, leaders of the Tougaloo contingent that sought to integrate Millsaps and Jackson's commercial establishments, were injured, King very seriously, in a suspicious car accident. In the wake of these events, Eudora Welty courageously published "Where is the Voice Coming From?" a devastating portrait of the racist mind-set.

Even before Welty's story was in print, her friend and agent Diarmuid Russell expressed concern about violence in Jackson and about Welty's safety. Welty, on the other hand, was afraid not for herself, but for her mother. For months she had been consumed with anxiety about her mother's health and spirits, and that anxiety coupled with alarm for her mother in the local climate of hatred prevented Welty on one occasion from undertaking what would have inherently been a symbolic act in support of integration. In late July 1963 (the time frame that seems most likely), she decided at the last minute, after much agonizing and with deep regret, not to be interviewed by Ralph Ellison on national television. She worried that a nationally televised appearance with this fellow writer, an African American man, would create a good deal of white hostility in Mississippi, hostility that she feared would be deflected from daughter to mother. She worried that such hostility would affect her ability to hire desperately needed caregivers for her mother, who in August was coming home from a five-month stint in a convalescent facility, and that it might affect the quality of care her mother received in the future. Although she and her mother had long been of one mind on the issue of civil rights, Welty sought to ensure that she alone would pay the price for their shared convictions. A desire to shelter her ailing mother from a volatile environment of racial tension and especially from white recrimination governed her decision, as she confided to Reynolds Price, not to be interviewed by Ellison. Ellison for a brief time was understandably mystified by Welty's decision. Shortly after the cancellation, Ellison told Price how open and outgoing Welty had always been with him, and he worried that he might have in some way unwittingly offended her. Price explained Welty's situation to him and also told Welty of Ellison's worries. According to Price, Welty then wrote to Ellison to explain her deep-seated apprehensions for her mother, and the Welty/Ellison friendship endured.[13]

Welty's relationship with the state of Mississippi, however, seemed in danger. On August 14, 1963, and again on August 28, she wrote her friend and former *Harper's Bazaar* fiction editor Mary Lou Aswell about the impossible, but desired prospect of moving her mother and herself away from Mississippi and its racist political leaders. And in the following spring, Welty continued to worry about the effect of social unrest upon her mother. In March 1964, she wrote to Aswell about her anxieties. She wanted, she wrote her old friend who had settled in Santa Fe, to move her mother to "some convalescent home in that part of the world." The fact that her mother was fifty miles away in a Yazoo City nursing home, that Yazoo City was "reputed to be now the headquarters of the Ku Klux Klan," that "our state is now authorized to . . . arm the highway patrol," and that violence might prevent her from reaching Yazoo City and her mother played heavily upon Welty's mind. Recalling riots both black (Jacksonville, Florida) and white (Oxford, Mississippi), Welty wrote that she wanted to "bring my little mother to some safe spot where she won't hear of this even."[14]

But Welty did not leave Mississippi or the South; neither did she abandon a public stance in favor of an open society. Late in 1964, she returned to the Millsaps College Christian Center, this time as the college's Writer-in-Residence. Though she did not on this occasion have to request unrestricted attendance—Millsaps now welcomed all to its public events—she once again spoke during particularly tense times.[15] The previous summer had seen the murders of three civil rights workers in Philadelphia, Mississippi, the fire-bombing of forty black

13. Russell to Welty, 17 June 1963, restricted papers, Welty Collection, MDAH; Welty's 1963 correspondence with Russell and with Mary Lou Aswell (restricted papers, Welty Collection, MDAH) suggests a July decision by Welty; Reynolds Price, personal conversation with author, 25 October 1998. According to Price, the *Paris Review* intended to publish the interview with Ellison. Instead, Hildegarde Dolson conducted the Camera Three interview, and the *Paris Review* decided against publication. The interview aired on Sunday, August 18, 1963.

14. Welty to Aswell, 14 August 1963, 28 August 1963, [24/25 March 1964], restricted papers, Welty Collection, MDAH.

15. Finger Papers, 9 August 1963; Sara Ann Weir covered this lecture for the Millsaps College paper. See "Miss Welty Tells Position of Southern Writers Today," *Purple and White*, 8 December 1964.

churches, and the white Citizens' Councils' intimidation of whites known to have "moderate" sensibilities, intimidation that had not ceased.

In her December 2, 1964, lecture, titled "The Southern Writer Today: An Interior Affair," Welty delivered comments that she would later publish as "Must the Novelist Crusade?" Here, she ostensibly rejected a political purpose for fiction, arguing that "there is absolutely everything in great fiction but a clear answer," that fiction is concerned more with the complexities of human experience than with proposing solutions to human difficulties (*ES*, 149). Welty followed this address with a reading of "Keela, the Outcast Indian Maiden," which, appropriately, examines the complexities of human relationships. The story describes a crippled black man who was once kidnapped into carnival work as a geek called Keela, the Outcast Indian Maiden, and who, notwithstanding the horror of his past, feels nostalgic about the carnival experience in which he was noticed as now within his own family he is not. The story further deals with the guilt felt by Steve, the carnival barker, and with his inability, nevertheless, to overcome the separation of race, and finally, the story depicts a bystander's courting of detachment from the horror and guilt Keela represents.

Complex though it is, however, "Keela" makes an important political statement—the dehumanizing nature of racism is infinitely more grotesque than a carnival side show. Certainly, Steve recognizes that by acquiescing to this evil, he has become part of it: " 'It's all me, see,' said Steve. 'I know that. I was the one was the cause for it goin' on an' on an' not bein' found out—such an awful thing. It was me, what I said out front through the megaphone.' " On the other hand, his acquaintance, Max, the owner of Max's Place, represses any guilt that might be his: " 'Bud,' said Max, disengaging himself, 'I don't hear anything. I got a juke box, see, so I don't have to listen' " (*CG*, 77). Max, in his disengaged state, might be speaking for many white Mississippians in 1964—they did not want to recognize their own complicity with evil, they did not want to accept the guilt they shared with Steve. But in reading this 1940 story to her 1964 audience, Eudora Welty called attention to that guilt. She did not ask that her audience become political activists, but she did ask, implicitly, that they refuse to be part of racist activities, that they recognize the humanity and complexity of all individuals. Millsaps College had already recognized the wisdom of positions like Welty's—within three months it would announce that African American students were welcome to enroll at the college.

It is important to recognize that Welty's call for nonracist behavior was not a call to crusade, for she herself had chosen not to take to the streets. In a June 1965 letter to Mary Lou Aswell, Welty pondered her lack of stridency in the civil rights movement and concluded: "I'm to blame, I suppose, for not dashing into it and doing some of the shrieking, but I don't really think so, because it would not mean with me any change of heart. I've always felt as I do now, and I hope my feeling has been all the time in my work."[16] Welty's belief in the power of fiction was more important to her than public pronouncements. Even the aborted Ellison interview was to have focused on fiction, and in her public appearances at Millsaps, Welty had demonstrated how effectively her short stories expressed support for the civil rights movement.

As one who did not march on Washington, organize voter registration drives, or challenge Mississippi mores on national television, Welty continued to find meaningful ways to act against racism, speaking at the 1965 Southern Literary Festival, supporting interracial audiences and casts at New Stage Theatre from its planning stages in 1965 to her death, describing segregationists' benighted resistance to change as part of her 1966 story "The Demonstrators," and inaugurating in 1967 a series of Wednesday programs open to black and white at Jackson's St. Andrew's Episcopal Cathedral.[17]

16. Welty to Aswell, 8 June 1965, restricted papers, Welty Collection, MDAH.

17. Tragic circumstances prevented Eudora Welty from being present on January 25, 1966, opening night at New Stage Theatre. Her mother died January 20, 1966, and her brother Edward died January 24, 1966. Although she could not attend the opening, which she had helped to make possible, Welty's public and private support for the theater never faltered and continued throughout her life. In its early days, New Stage encountered white opposition to its racial policies. A bomb threat on opening night occurred even though no African Americans were in the cast; the fact that tickets were available for both blacks and whites, as Jane Reid Petty and Patti Carr Black told me in March 1997, was enough to generate the threat. (Both Petty and Black were among the founding members of New Stage Theatre.) The theater, nevertheless, continued its open-door policy, and African Americans, though relatively few in number, were in its audiences from the inaugural year onward. The regular appearance of African Americans in New Stage casts began in 1969, making New Stage the first theater group in Mississippi "other than academic departments" to have both integrated audiences and casts (Martha H. Hammond, "Dialogue: New Stage Theatre and Jackson, Mississippi" [Ph.D. diss., University

Welty's speech at the April 1965 Southern Literary Festival, held in Oxford, Mississippi, in honor of William Faulkner, is particularly instructive. Robert W. Hamblin has discussed the powerful statement for civil rights embedded in Robert Penn Warren's Festival address, an address made twenty-four hours after a mob harassed the Tougaloo College delegation that had hoped to participate in the festival. Hamblin might also have cited Welty's remarks, for they reiterated her faith in fiction's power to expose and combat racist hatred. In the midst of a wide-ranging discussion alluding to many Faulkner texts, Welty called the audience's attention to the brutal murder of Joe Christmas, "waiting with his hands in chains, 'bright and glittering,' . . . as Percy Grimm arrives with his automatic." Later she noted that Faulkner's characters "are white, Negro, Indian, Chinese, Huguenot, Scotch, English, Spanish, French, or any combination of these, and known always or at any point of their time on earth from birth till death and in between." And she added that these characters constitute "a population that has *reality* as distinguished from *actuality*: they are our hearts made visible and audible and above all dramatic; they are ourselves translated, and, at

---

of Southern Mississippi, 1994], 196). In 1970, when highway patrol and city police gunfire at Jackson State College took two lives, a black Jackson State student who was then a cast member of *The Ponder Heart* resolved to continue in her role, living with a white cast member for the run of the show (Hammond, 181). Frank Hains, the director of the play, devoted a regular *Jackson Daily News* column to his deep sorrow at the violence that had just taken place, to the decision of Florence Roach to continue in her role, and to the play's relevance to this Jackson crisis. *The Ponder Heart*, he wrote, though it seemed far removed from questions of "race relations or problems of the day," actually had "everything to do with them." This play, he continued, was "all about love and Uncle Daniel's unbounded love for all the world—and it's a reflection of the great love of humanity which lifts its author, Eudora Welty, into a state of grace few achieve on this earth." In print, Hains proclaimed the role that New Stage Theatre hoped to play in defining race relations, and human relations more generally, in terms of love, not hate and violence, and he identified Eudora Welty as a person living and writing by such a code. See "On Stage—Eudora Welty's 'Ponder Heart': A Message of Love Needed Now," *Jackson Daily News* 17 May 1970, sec. C.

In 1967, at St. Andrew's Cathedral, organizers wholeheartedly supported open admission to the series of readings, lectures, concerts, and plays, and they hoped that African Americans would attend. As it turned out, however, Welty read to an all-white audience (September 1999 personal conversation with Ann Morrison, chair of the 1967 Wednesdays at St. Andrew's programs).

times, transmogrified."[18] Welty thus suggested that race is as artificial a concept as nationality and that to whatever race or nationality Faulkner's characters belong, they represent our common humanity.

Such local actions were tremendously significant. As David Chappell notes in his book *Inside Agitators: White Southerners in the Civil Rights Movement*, white southerners who "were sickened by segregation" together with white southerners who "found it terribly inconvenient in practice" provided the civil rights movement with a strategic "moral and political resource." Knowing of the existence of such whites, he writes, "gave millions of black southerners, despite a dispiriting history of crushed hopes and broken promises, confidence in their ability to win—not simply confidence in the righteousness of their cause but in the usually unrelated prospects of that cause for victory in the real world."[19] Eudora Welty, one of those white southerners who was sickened by segregation, thus played her own small but crucial and courageous role in the move toward integration. By repeatedly refusing to comply with racism in her private life and by encouraging others to refuse as well, she became one of many who helped to create a climate for change and for progress.

Most particularly, Eudora Welty in her 1963 and 1964 Millsaps lecture/readings experienced the same sense of convergence that she had known in 1952. In 1952 she found the fiction writer's values and the public domain pulled together by Adlai Stevenson, and she actively supported the convergence he represented. In the sixties, however, Welty herself pulled the private and public together. She pulled together aesthetic and political concerns, stories from the past and contemporary conflicts, fiction and politics, and she sought to part the curtain that divided Mississippi's blacks and whites. Beyond that time, Welty's public political statements were relatively few. For many years after William Winter's election as a progressive Democratic governor of Mississippi, Welty continued to sport a Winter bumper sticker on her car; in 1988 a full page ad in the *New York*

18. Robert W. Hamblin, "Robert Penn Warren at the 1965 Southern Literary Festival: A Personal Recollection," *Southern Literary Journal* 22 (Spring 1990): 53–62; Eudora Welty, untitled speech, p. 7, Southern Literary Festival, 23 April 1965, Welty Collection, MDAH.

19. David L. Chappell, *Inside Agitators: White Southerners in the Civil Rights Movement* (Baltimore: Johns Hopkins University Press, 1994), xxv.

*Times* contained Eudora Welty's signature in support of the word *liberal*; and a 1992 Clinton-Gore bumper sticker greeted those who knocked on her front door both before and long after election day. The convergence of public and private continued to be a factor in Eudora Welty's life, but it was most ardently felt and acted upon in 1952 and 1963–64. For Welty, Stevenson's campaign for the presidency and the civil rights struggle of the sixties were causes that transcended the writer's need to be a "privileged observer" (*OWB*, 21).

Occupied by family responsibilities, worried about the very serious health problems faced by her mother and brothers, and ultimately having to cope with their deaths, Welty published only two stories between 1955 and 1969, but in writing both she must have felt the same sense of convergence that she had felt during the Stevenson campaign and in her 1963 and 1964 Millsaps lecture/readings. The two stories she published in the sixties deal simultaneously with long held, deep-seated personal values and with a contemporary public political situation. "Where is the Voice Coming From," published in the wake of Medgar Ever's assassination and dealing quite explicitly with it, expresses the same horror Welty had felt during World War II at the ways self-glorification and ethnocentrism destroy lives. And "The Demonstrators," published in 1966 and focusing on racial tensions in a small southern town, suggests the ways in which clannishness and fear of the other can warp the private and personal lives of individuals. These stories, like Welty's earliest fiction, sprang from the present moment. But unlike the early stories, the sixties stories are explicitly rather than implicitly political. Both stories offer portraits of Mississippians caught up in a national crisis. One of those Mississippians is an ardent racist and murderer, the other a white moderate who has great difficulty coping with social change.

Welty wrote "Where is the Voice Coming From?" as an immediate response to the murder of Medgar Evers. Horrified by this violent event, she felt compelled to depict both the social setting that fostered the assassination and the individual who was capable of committing it. In her story, Welty clearly indicates that the local press has encouraged a climate of hatred and violence directed against African Americans. In fact, the murderer's wife reminds him that the newspaper has endorsed the murder he has committed:

"Well, they been asking that—why somebody didn't trouble to load a rifle and get some of these agitators out of Thermopylae. Didn't the fella keep drumming it in, what a good idea? The one that writes a column ever' day?"

I says to my wife, "Find *some* way I don't get the credit."

"He says do it for Thermopylae," she says. "Don't you ever skim the paper?"

I says, "Thermopylae never done nothing for me. And I don't owe nothing to Thermopylae. Didn't do it for you. Hell, any more'n I'd do something or other for them Kennedys! I done it for my own pure-D satisfaction." (*CS*, 605)

Though the murderer prefers to think that he has acted independently, self-reliantly, for his own "pure-D satisfaction," he is clearly a product of his society. He has acted for white Thermopylae; he has committed an act that many middle-class whites would not commit themselves, but that they are happy to have done for them. He has answered the newspaper's request.

The *Jackson Clarion-Ledger*, like the paper in Welty's story, fostered a similar climate for violence. On May 29, a day after a group of student protesters attempted to integrate the lunch counter at Woolworth's in Jackson, Tom Ethridge wrote in his "Mississippi Notebook" column, "Lines are drawn and it is time for Jacksonians to stand up and be counted—either for or against keeping the peace, safeguarding personal freedom and protecting property rights." The call to keep the peace sounds innocuous enough, but it was directed against the non-violent protests of civil rights workers, and it indirectly condoned violence against the protesters. Other *Clarion-Ledger* columns did the same. On June 6, 1963, just six days before the murder of Medgar Evers, Charles Hills wrote

We see in the papers that Lena Horne is going to come down here and try to dazzle our colored folks into committing acts on the spur of the moment which they may repent at leisure in the city or county bastille.

Be that as it may, we are reminded of an incident described by Lt. Gov. Paul Johnson at a Citizen's Council Meeting recently.

It seems that a Negro woman singer of the Horne variety, ambled into a New York department store.

Espying a large mirror she sashayed up to the looking glass with:

"Mirror, mirror on the wall, who's the fairest of them all?"

> Answered the mirror:
> "Snow White, Negro . . . and don't you forget it!"

And after relating this racist joke, Hills went on to offer more overtly intimidating words:

> We attended the Shrine convention here last week, but didn't see an incident . . . although we hear much of it—
>
> Seems that a diminutive Shriner made some remarks about Negro demonstrators who were being hauled into the paddy wagon.
>
> A big bruiser standing nearby reportedly started buffeting the little fellow around.
>
> Whereupon, a bigger hulk of a man, also wearing a Shrine fez, is said to have grabbed the aggressor with an arm-lock and hiked the fellow on tip-toes to the paddy wagon, meantime administering swift kicks almost every step of the way.
>
> Lo, we are told, on release, the "bad boy" lost no time at all producing for police his identification as a federal marshal.
>
> There are a lot of mistakes being made around here of late, but, you never can tell.[20]

The Jackson newspapers which might have called for reasoned discussion, which might have helped to prevent conflict, instead abetted it, threatening that those who supported the civil rights struggle might become victims of "mistakes." Welty's story illuminates the intimidating role of the Jackson press.

Ironically, of course, the newspaper that encouraged aggression on the part of whites attacked African Americans as inherently destructive and irrational. White use of force it labeled peace-keeping; a black demonstration was to the *Clarion-Ledger* a "moving mass of hysteria."[21] Similarly, the story's narrator, himself a killer, longs to see what he regards as the murderous nature of blacks exposed: "I won't be sorry to see them brickbats hail down on us for a change. Pop bottles too, they can come flying whenever they want to. Hundreds, all to

20. Tom Ethridge, "Mississippi Notebook," *Jackson Clarion-Ledger* 29 May 1963; Charles Hills, "Affairs of State," *Jackson Clarion-Ledger* 6 June 1963, sec. A.

21. "Jackson Is Unique in its Unity," editorial, *Jackson Clarion-Ledger*, 29 May 1963.

smash, like Birmingham. I'm waiting on 'em to bring out them switchblade knives, like Harlem and Chicago. Watch TV long enough and you'll see it all to happen on Deacon Street in Thermopylae. What's holding it back, that's all?—Because it's *in* 'em" (*CS*, 607). He is threatened by the peaceful protest; he wants to see blacks as violent, but does not recognize his own violence.

Of course, the story also illuminates class issues in white resistance to social change. The poverty that long might have linked poor whites and blacks in a populist coalition instead continued to divide them. The story's narrator is a poor, uneducated, ungrammatical white man who feels threatened by the possibility of political and economic equality for African Americans. He resents the prominence and prosperity of civil rights leader Roland Summers. He is threatened by a black man who no longer accepts his position of inferiority and who in fact seems clearly superior. He resents Summers' fame, his face on T.V. He resents Summers' paved street and drive, his lush green lawn, his new white car. Killing Summers lets him feel "on top of the world myself. For once." And he tells the dead Summers, "There was one way left, for me to be ahead of you and stay ahead of you, by Dad, and I just taken it. Now I'm alive and you ain't" (*CS*, 604).

Welty wrote this story immediately upon learning of the Evers assassination, and her agent quickly sent it to the *New Yorker*. Revisions to the story were made over the phone. The names of actual people, streets, and businesses were changed to fictional ones. Evers became Summers, Red Hydrick became Goat Dykeman, Jackson became Thermopylae, Delta Drive became Nathan B. Forrest Boulevard. Legal considerations governed the changes, but revisions did not affect plot or characterization. Having satisfied the *New Yorker* legal department, the story was published on July 6, 1963, less than a month after the Evers assassination. Publishing such a story was a courageous act by Welty, but she characteristically downplayed her own bravery, telling a reporter not to worry about her: "The people who burn crosses on lawns don't read me in *The New Yorker*."[22] True, the people who burn crosses on lawns may not read the *New Yorker*, but

22. See untitled, original typescript of "Where is the Voice Coming From?" in the Welty Collection, MDAH, which contains holograph revisions to names of actual people and places; Walter Clemons, "Meeting Miss Welty," in *Conversations with Eudora Welty*, ed. Prenshaw, 31.

they may certainly hear about white southern ladies who unsympathetically depict them there. Eudora Welty published her story nevertheless.

"The Demonstrators," published in 1966, is the story of Dr. Richard Strickland of Holden, Mississippi, a Delta town. The story begins when Dr. Strickland, who has been attending the aged Miss Marcia Pope, encounters a Negro child who tells him, "We got to hurry" (CS, 608). And hurry they do—to the unlighted, poor, black section of town. There Strickland attempts to save the life of Ruby Gaddy, but the wound her lover Dove Collins has inflicted with an ice pick is clearly a mortal one. Strickland treats Ruby and then leaves, but his involvement in this incident is not over. He soon meets Dove, only to see him hemorrhage through the mouth, a victim of Ruby's retaliatory wound.

The time and place Welty specifically recreates in this story are indelible. In this story, Welty depicts not an assassin, but a typical Mississippi town. A spirit of fear and hatred pervaded the state during the 1960s, and "The Demonstrators" captures that spirit. The whites of Holden, Mississippi, are particularly insensitive and self-serving in their response to a black tragedy. When Ruby and Dove kill each other, the whites are both relieved and reassured. The town newspaper rejoices that these deaths cannot be blamed on white racists and sees the violent event as proof of white superiority:

An ice pick, reportedly the property of the Holy Gospel Tabernacle, was later found by Deacon Gaddy, 8, brother of Ruby Gaddy, covered with blood and carried it to Marshal Stubblefield. Stubblefield said it had been found in the grounds of the new $100,000.00 Negro school. It is believed to have served as the instrument in the twin slayings, the victims thus virtually succeeding in killing each other.

"Well, I'm surprised didn't more of them get hurt," said Rev. Alonzo Duckett, pastor of the Holden First Baptist Church. "And yet they expect to be seated in our churches." County Sheriff Vince Lasseter, reached fishing at Lake Bourne, said: "That's one they can't pin the blame on us for. That's how they treat their own kind. Please take note our conscience is clear." (CS, 621)

Here as in "Where is the Voice Coming From?" Welty focuses upon the slanted and ungrammatical newspaper reporting that typified the sixties. And her characters Duckett and Lasseter might well have belonged to one of the white Citizens' Councils, which controlled Mississippi politics at the time and which used their political power to fight integration. Though Welty does not here describe horrendous, racially motivated acts of violence—during the summer of 1964 forty black churches were firebombed and three civil rights workers were murdered in Mississippi—she clearly establishes the psychological violence, "the bitterness, intractability that divided everybody and everything" (*CS*, 617).

Dr. Strickland himself has been the victim of this intractability. Prior to the major events of the story, he has been harassed by white townspeople who consider him too moderate on the issue of civil rights. After attending to Ruby Gaddy, Strickland recalls entertaining a young, Freedom Summer civil rights worker and subsequently finding broken glass spread over the length and breadth of his driveway. And such pointed harassment was once common in Mississippi. Indeed, many autobiographical accounts of the sixties tally with Welty's fictional portrait. John Emmerich, for instance, recalled this era as it existed in McComb, Mississippi. In a 1984 *Jackson Clarion-Ledger* editorial, he reported that "The Mississippi summer of 1964 was a time of racial fear, mistrust among friends and near public hysteria." And Emmerich went on to describe this hysteria: "My friends, Albert and Malva Heffner, unwittingly became scapegoats of the community fear. At the Episcopal church, they met two young visitors and invited them home to a church spaghetti supper. The visitors were summer civil rights volunteers. Even though the Heffners were respected and well-liked in the community and were parents of the reigning Miss Mississippi, they were harassed to the point of leaving town, never to return." Hodding Carter, in his 1965 book *So the Heffners Left McComb*, describes the Heffners' attempts to foster understanding between the community and the Freedom Summer workers, and he provides a more detailed picture of the consequences. He cites the mysterious death of the Heffners' dog, the anonymous telephone calls, the family's social isolation, and the devastating boycott of Heffner's business.[23] Welty's Dr. Strickland does not encounter such enduring hostility, and he never leaves Holden, Mississippi. But his experiences effectively represent the hysteria that had overcome white Mississippi.

23. John Emmerich, "McComb Editor Sought Moderation in Explosive Summer," *Jackson Clarion-Ledger* 1 July 1984, sec. H; Hodding Carter, *So the Heffners Left McComb* (New York: Doubleday, 1965).

Of course, civil rights workers could be guilty of their own distortions of the truth. Strickland takes the young civil rights worker to task for just this reason.

"Speaking of who can you trust, what's this I read in your own paper, Philip? It said some of your outfit over in the next county were forced at gunpoint to go into the fields at hundred-degree temperature and pick cotton. Well, that didn't happen—there isn't any cotton in June."

"I asked myself the same question you do. But I told myself, 'Well, they won't know the difference where the paper is read,'" said the young man.

"It's lying, though."

"We are dramatizing your hostility," the young bearded man had corrected him. "It's a way of reaching people. Don't forget—what they *might* have done to us is even worse."

"Still—you're not justified in putting a false front on things, in my opinion," Dr. Strickland had said. "Even for a good cause." (*CS*, 617)

Welty has not manufactured this exchange out of thin air. In the *Jackson Daily News* of June 1,1961, Hinds County Sheriff J. R. Gilfoy derided a black Freedom Rider who "said he had been forced to pick cotton for three days in 95-degree weather while guards held shotguns on him."[24] Though the *Daily News* and the Jackson authorities were then prone to distort evidence, Welty herself had heard of civil rights workers making such blatantly false charges—there is no cotton to be picked in June, however bad the heat and however hostile the authorities.

Eudora Welty recreates not merely this troubled time in Mississippi's history, but she also recreates the Mississippi setting itself. Her story takes place in the Delta, in the rich cotton country between the Yazoo and Mississippi Rivers. It is in this area that Mississippi's black population is most concentrated, and Welty's story of racial strife appropriately is set here. Holden, like most Delta towns, is dominated by cotton. Cotton fields come right up to the edge of the town, the smell of the cottonseed mill spreads "over the town at large—a cooking smell, like a dish ordered by a man with an endless appetite" (*CS*, 615), the sound of

24. W. C. Shoemaker, "Mix Riders Lose Appetites in Jail," *Jackson Daily News* 1 June 1961, sec. A.

the cotton gin is difficult for townspeople to escape, and shreds of cotton hang from telephone wires and are strewn along the roadside. Cotton is especially important in the life of Dove Collins. In life and death, Dove is tied to cotton. He is an employee of the Fairbrothers Cottonseed Oil Mill, he hides from the law and from avenging blacks at the mill, and he dies covered with yellow cottonseed meal. Dove is killed by Ruby Gaddy, but a life in service to the cotton economy, the story indirectly suggests, is itself a deadly existence. In death neither Dove nor Ruby stimulates the sort of paternalistic concern or regret that might have typified Delta whites of an earlier era. Stories of kindly aristocrats and their devoted servants, according to Neil McMillen, "bespoke much nostalgic foolishness, but some truth. Strained by emancipation and Reconstruction, the old paternalism persisted feebly into the twentieth century. No doubt it occasionally still softened the harder edges of white supremacy, particularly in the plantation counties. As a social ideal, however, it was no match for the more savage impulses of racism; after 1890 it was honored more often in the breach than in practice." And certainly by 1965 and the writing of "The Demonstrators," the need for a tenant force and the paternalistic system were both largely gone. As African Americans moved to jobs in other regions and as land owners came to rely upon mechanical cotton pickers and to some extent upon less labor-intensive crops than cotton, the tenant farmers who frequented small Mississippi towns declined in number—from 225,617 in 1930 to 25,634 in 1964.[25] Similarly, fewer and fewer black field hands were needed. Whites thus felt less need to display a fatherly, if condescending, interest in their workers, and civil rights leaders, who became increasingly assertive after the *Brown v. Board of Education* decision, rejected the white mask of benevolence and encouraged blacks not to abase themselves and not to feign gratitude. Whatever remained of the old paternalism was breaking apart, and the physical decay of Holden, Mississippi, literally and figuratively reflects that breakup.

The story's courthouse town, with its square, its row of shops under a tin awning, its drygoods building with an ornamental top that looks "like open

25. Neil R. McMillen, *Dark Journey: Black Mississippians in the Age of Jim Crow* (Urbana and Chicago: University of Illinois Press, 1989), 7; Howard Glenn Adkins, "The Historical Geography of Extinct Towns in Mississippi," Ph.D. diss. University of Tennessee 1972, 74.

paper fans," has known better days. The highway now bypasses it and its movie house has shut down. Dr. Strickland at times longs for the past, for the old system, for its seeming harmony, but even the appearance of harmony can scarcely be found. Strickland provides medical assistance to Ruby, but even he has trouble recognizing this woman who is the maid in his own office. And Strickland makes no extraordinary efforts on Ruby's behalf—no effort even to see that she be taken to a hospital that accepts blacks.

Just as Welty incorporates the Delta of the sixties into "The Demonstrators," she also incorporates details remembered from the 1930s and 1940s. Throughout the thirties Eudora Welty moved freely in and out of African American homes, churches, theaters. She photographed blacks in Jackson, the Delta, along the Natchez Trace. And images from these experiences surface in "The Demonstrators." The preacher with heel taps seems very similar to the preacher whose photograph appears in *One Time, One Place* (83) and who used heel taps to signal the congregation that they should respond in unison to his preaching. The guinea pigs that run across the floor of Ruby Gaddy's house recall the guinea pigs Welty saw in a Jackson fortune teller's house (*OTOP*, 64). The black woman who was once "sole factotum at the Holden depot" (*CS*, 614) is the woman Welty herself saw numerous times in the Meridian, Mississippi, depot (*OWB*, 95). And the tambourine hanging from Ruby's bedpost recalls Welty's photograph of a young African American playing a tambourine in the streets of Jackson. In addition, Ruby's two-room house, decorated with a valentine and supplied with what may be the Strickland's old china, recalls Partheny's house in *Delta Wedding* (1946), though a gas heater has replaced Partheny's fireplace. Perhaps Welty relies upon such details because she herself was freer to visit black Mississippians during the thirties and forties than she was in the sixties. But although Welty's knowledge of Mississippi blacks dates in part from that earlier time when she was active as a photographer, her picture of African American living conditions, employment opportunities, recreational and religious pursuits, is absolutely realistic. One has only to read Anne Moody's *Coming of Age in Mississippi* or L.C. Dorsey's *Freedom Came to Mississippi* to see how realistic. Welty's choice of thirty-year-old details indicates her awareness that black life had remained unchanged, often tragically unchanged, in many ways.

When "The Demonstrators" appeared in the *New Yorker*, Welty's friend and former editor Mary Louise Aswell wrote her to praise the story. Welty replied, "It was a difficult story because I wanted to show however imperfectly the complexity of what it's like today—the breakdown of the old relationships and the false starts and the despairs and the self-delusions of what it's like. . . . I called it 'The Demonstrators' because that's what I feel everybody is reduced to being." In this story, Welty seeks to dramatize the complexity of Mississippi life in the sixties and the frustrated desire to escape that complexity. Still, cruelty and suffering and hostility are realities that cannot be explained or eradicated. Dr. Strickland, the story's protagonist, numbly recognizes, regrets, and accepts the darkness of experience, yet even he longs to escape this knowledge and to go back to the mythic, orderly, paternalistic Delta he believes once existed. Given the present climate of "bitterness, intractability," he can only treat the wounded Ruby Gaddy in an "absent" fashion. He allows himself no emotion. He has anesthetized himself, and the grass fire he sees as he drives away from the Gaddy house is "like anesthetic made visible" (CS, 616). But when a passing train blocks his path and the fire from his view, Strickland comes out from under the anesthesia and begins to remember and nostalgically to feel. He thinks of the charity his family has shown its black servants. He recalls that a child at Ruby's house had brought him water in a cup that "might have been his own mother's china or his wife's mother's" (CS, 616), and he knows that he carries on his father's benevolent practice of medicine. Nostalgically remembering his family's paternalism, or the caring that was part of it, gives the doctor a "feeling of well-being" (CS, 616). He feels "as though someone had stopped him on the street and offered to carry his load for a while—had insisted on it—some old, trusted, half-forgotten family friend that he had lost sight of since youth." And he has the sense "that there was still allowed to everybody on earth a *self*—savage, death-defying, private" (CS, 618). Strickland never confronts the self-deception and self-interest that characterized the white society of his youth, but neither does he remain in the past. When the train has passed, he is again anesthetized to some extent ("feeling gradually ebbed away," [CS, 618]), but he attempts to minister to the dying Dove, and he refuses to join the white chorus of condescension or to deny the existence of trouble (as mill owner Herman Fairbrothers does). The morning after the double murder, he makes his daily retreat to that part of his house from which neither the gin nor highway traffic can be heard, but he is soon ready to venture out upon his rounds once again. Strickland needs an anesthetic if he is to cope with reality, but the anesthetic he adopts is a metaphoric rather than literal one.

Others require stronger medicine. Some blacks of Holden, Mississippi, quite literally depend upon a strong medicine, paregoric. They litter the banks of a creek near Ruby's house with "narrow bottles, the size of harmonicas, in which paregoric was persistently sold under the name of Mother's Helper" (CS, 615). Trapped in a society in which work is scarce and in which their chances for improvement are almost nonexistent, they retreat to a pain reliever. Other blacks find neither an opiate nor an anesthetic but an escape from the barren quality of their lives, an escape into the transports of religion at a church "where the sounds of music and dancing" can be heard "on many another night besides Sunday" (CS, 615).

Dr. Strickland's wife and the civil rights worker who visits them find still another retreat from life's incalculable and tragic nature. They gain a sense of order and security by devoting themselves to an idea. Young Philip will countenance lying if lying dramatizes white "hostility" toward blacks and thereby advances his cause. And Irene Strickland, after devoting her life to a daughter who "until her death . . . had never sat up or spoken," turns "not to a human being but to an idea" (CS, 616–17). She shares the activist's devotion to ideas and leaves her husband who does not. She shares the belief that one can demonstrate the reality of a "Truth," though her faith seems short lived. She ultimately retreats to a series of parties given for her in her hometown.

Far less rational but equally devoted to an idea which gives life order are the story's white racists who comfort themselves with the notion of white supremacy. For the racist, as for Mrs. Strickland, the cause provides purpose and order; it removes its devotees from the ambiguity, the confusion, the disorder of human life. These individuals are like the novelist who tries to crusade. As Welty wrote in 1965, "there is a good deal that we as the crusader-novelist must be at pains to leave out. Unavoidably, I think, we shall leave out one of the greatest things. This is the mystery in life. Our blueprint for sanity and of solution for trouble leaves out the dark" (ES, 151).

Whatever the anesthesia or mode of escape, Welty suggests, events remain beyond human understanding. The befuddlement Dr. Strickland feels when he enters Ruby Gaddy's shanty-like home is merely a more intense version of the befuddlement we all feel in facing the conditions of our lives. At Ruby's house, Strickland asks question after question, but receives few answers: "Too much excitement to send for the doctor a little earlier?" "Who did this to her?" "Where? Where did it happen? How did she get here?" "She married? Where's her husband?" "Is Dove who did it?" "Where'd he get to—Dove?" (*CS*, 609–12) But Ruby's house is not the only place where questions are unanswered. The story itself raises many issues for which there are no satisfactory responses. Why has the Strickland's daughter been injured at birth and left to exist for thirteen years without movement or communication? What has prompted the fight that leaves both Ruby and Dove dead? What will become of Ruby's child? Why must mill owner Herman Fairbrothers suffer so horribly from disease? Why are so many whites unable to accept the humanity of their black neighbors? Why cannot white Holden recognize the crippling effects of poverty in its African American community? These are the dark mysteries that Welty's story confronts but sadly cannot resolve.

In "Where is the Voice Coming From?" and "The Demonstrators," Welty found her inspiration in the insistent present of the 1960s. Although Welty had proclaimed that fiction should not crusade, she firmly believed that it must register a moral vision. And her two stories of the sixties do just that. They show a social order based upon hatred and fear and insecurity; they show the southern press playing upon and exacerbating those emotions; and they show the "despairs and the self-delusions" with which individuals faced the coming of social change. Though "Where is the Voice Coming From?" and "The Demonstrators" may be too complex to serve as direct calls to action or to provide a "blueprint for sanity and of solution," they nevertheless establish the need for racial equality and racial harmony. And publicly expressing that need in fiction, as well as in lecture halls, was "so true and powerful" a moral and political act that in 1966 a young Chicago civil rights leader named Jesse Jackson wrote the editors of the *New Yorker*, praising them for printing "The Demonstrators."[26] In this one story, Jackson saw the courage that Welty had repeatedly displayed. Eudora Welty, the private individual, was in her own way an "inside agitator."

26. Welty sent Mary Lou Aswell a Xerox copy of Jackson's handwritten letter to the *New Yorker*, and it is included in the restricted Aswell papers in the Welty Collection at the Mississippi Department of Archives and History.

 VIII

# A Season of Change
*Losing Battles*

Many contemporary scholars reject Allen Tate's notion that the Southern Renaissance arose as the South found itself poised on the edge of change, change from a traditional society to a modern one. Yet the essence of Tate's concept—the notion that writers are productive at "a crossing of the ways"—provides tremendous insight into Eudora Welty's career. Dealing with postwar change had been crucial to Eudora Welty's achievement in *The Golden Apples* (1949), the civil rights movement had inspired her only two short stories of the 1960s, and change, both personal and social, prompted the books that Welty published in 1970 and 1972. For fifteen years after *The Bride of the Innisfallen*, events that were personally devastating and socially disturbing threatened to leave Welty without words or with words that were predominantly dark and ironic. Nevertheless, *Losing Battles* emerged from this time of change and emerged with a vision not of despair but of affirmation. In the course of writing this novel, Welty came to a renewed faith that life's compensations outweighed its sorrows and that memory and storytelling could serve as stays against losses to time. She came to celebrate "the human being who can cope with any condition, even ignorance, and keep a courage, a joy of life, even, that's unquenchable." She moved from a vision that might have become what Richard Boyd Hauck calls a "cheerful nihilism" to a vision that celebrates "each life . . . [as] very valuable in itself, regardless, and in spite of everything."[1]

As Welty began writing *Losing Battles* in the mid-1950s, her brother Walter was suffering from rheumatoid arthritis, the complications of which would lead to his death from a heart attack in 1959. And by the early sixties Welty's mother had to cope with eye problems, a stroke, and resultant depression while her surviving brother Edward faced the same arthritis that had tormented Walter. In January 1966, Chestina Welty and Edward Welty died within days of each other, leaving Eudora as the sole surviving member of her immediate family. During the long siege of family difficulties, the kind of extended travel that had been the source for so many of the stories in *The Bride of the Innisfallen* was impossible. Instead, except for visits to New York or engagements at distinguished universities, Welty was largely confined to the home place. And ultimately the loss of her mother and two brothers threatened to thwart her ability to write. But Welty eventually found words and was able to complete *Losing Battles*. This novel marks her return from the no places of *The Bride of the Innisfallen* to the world of Mississippi, from the stories of solitary travelers to a story of family and home ties. And Welty's examination of home was prompted by more than her actual confinement to it. The suffering of her much loved family members and their eventual deaths surely pushed Welty to examine the meaning of family and to look rather specifically at her own family history.

As Tom McHaney has perceptively noted, the 1930s rural setting of *Losing Battles* is not merely North Mississippi; in many ways this setting seems based upon Clay County, West Virginia, where Welty's mother grew up. Even the map Welty drew for *Losing Battles*, McHaney argues, resembles a map of Clay County. And there are other, more personal, echoes of Welty's own family stories running throughout *Losing Battles*. Though Welty's Andrews forebears were

1. See, for instance, Michael O'Brien's "A Heterodox Note on the Southern Renaissance," *Perspectives on the American South* 4 (1987): 1–17, for a view opposed to Tate's; Allen Tate, "The New Provincialism," in *Essays of Four Decades* (Chicago: The Swallow Press, 1968), 546; Bunting, 48; Richard Boyd Hauck, *A Cheerful Nihilism* (Bloomington: Indiana University Press, 1971).

an educated and well-read family, unlike the Renfros and Beechams, the dog-trot house in which the Renfros live, Uncle Noah Webster playing the banjo, and Grandpa praying in the barn recall details from Chestina Andrews's life in Clay County (*OWB*, 52, 59). In fact, by selecting details of setting and character and plot from her family's past, Welty may have been doing exactly what the reunion participants are doing within the novel—seeking continuity in time by telling stories. Welty's novel is in part her own attempt to cope with losses to time. She suggests as much in a *Delta Review* article published shortly before *Losing Battles*. In that article, she asserts that in the South

> stories could be watched in the happening—lifelong and generation-long sto-ries watched and participated in, first by one member of the family and then without a break by another, allowing the continuous and never-ending recital to be passed along in full course and to grow. The event and the memory and the comprehension of it and taking a role in it were scarcely marked off from the other in the glow of hearing it again, telling it anew, anticipating, knowing the whole thing by heart—and all right here where it happened. A family story is a family possession, not for a moment to be forgotten, not a bit to be dropped or left out—just added to. No good story ever became *diminished*.[2]

Having faced the death of her mother and brothers, having endured the loss of every member of her immediate family, Welty in completing *Losing Battles* was in a way recapturing and giving life to her past. Her descriptions of both Julia Mortimer and Beulah Renfro, most importantly, rely upon stories Welty had heard or herself told about her mother. Like Julia Mortimer, Chestina Welty taught in a one-room rural school, rode on horseback to her job each day, and used brave methods to insure discipline. Welty's description of Chestina closely parallels the portrait of Julia: "My mother . . . piled up her hair and went out to teach in a one-room school, mountain children little and big alike. The first day, some fathers came along to see if she could whip their children, some who were older than she. She told the children that she did intend to whip them if they became unruly and refused to learn, and invited the fathers to stay if they liked

---

2. Thomas McHaney, "The Tishomingo of Welty's Imagination," unpublished ms.; Eu-dora Welty, "From Where I Live," *Delta Review* 6 (1969): 69.

and she'd be able to whip them too" (*OWB*, 51). Julia too encounters recalcitrant fathers, and after whipping their children, she tells the fathers, "If any of these fathers who were so brave as to come to school this morning feel prompted to step up too, I'm ready for them now. Otherwise, they can all stay right there on the back bench and learn something" (*LB*, 274). Just as the heroic proportions of Julia Mortimer's teaching come in good part from Chestina Welty, so do the heroic proportions of her suffering. Though Chestina Welty did not have to endure anyone like Lexie Renfro, her final years were unhappy ones, and she was dissatisfied in the care of anyone but her daughter. She especially dreaded being attended by a woman advertising herself as "a settled white Christian lady with no home ties." It is no coincidence that *Losing Battles* echoes Mrs. Welty's dread. In the novel, the Presbyterian sisterhood of Alliance puts out a call for just such a lady and hires the cruel Lexie to care for Julia Mortimer.

If Chestina Welty is a source for Welty's characterization of Julia Mortimer, she is also a source, as Ann Romines points out, for Welty's portrait of Beulah Renfro. This link is less direct than the connection between Chestina and Julia, but it is a powerful connection nonetheless. Beulah's lifelong guilt over the fate of her brother Sam Dale recalls Mrs. Welty's devastating guilt after her husband died during a blood transfusion. As Romines notes, "Like Beulah Beecham Renfro, who agonized throughout her life because she could not protect Sam Dale, Mrs. Welty emerges from her daughter's book as an ardent, ambitious woman committed to taking care and doomed by change and mortality to fail—even when her medium was her own living blood."[3] Thus, in many ways Welty recreated her mother's most distinctive qualities as she wrote *Losing Battles*. The daring, the forthrightness, the suffering, and the guilt—all those qualities that Welty knew so well live again in *Losing Battles*. This is not a nostalgic and therefore lifeless paean to the past, but a complex portrait that lives and that helped Welty to contend with the power of time.

Members of the Beecham-Renfro reunion are less tough-minded than Welty, more nostalgic, but they are engaged in the same story-telling enterprise that occupies her. These reunion members participate in a "continuous and never-ending recital." The past is not gone for the clan. It comes alive at least once a year

3. Romines, 290.

on Granny's birthday. Then the old stories are told, new stories are added to be retold in the future, and everyone participates in the telling—Percy with his "thready" voice, Etoyle who "embroiders," Aunt Beck with her "mourning dove's" voice (*LB* 22, 42), everyone. The death of Grandpa Vaughn is the reunion's newest story, and it is recounted with great sadness. Jack's rescue of the Moodys' Buick will be a story the next reunion can tell in high humor. The family members thus know that their lives are and will be part of the enduring family story, a story that seems to come alive in the telling. Granny momentarily believes Sam Dale Beecham to be alive after she has heard the reunion discuss him. And when the reunion members tell the story of Jack's trial and his time in the pen, they claim to be "bringing him" home (*LB*, 40). They unite Jack's past adventures and his current journey. Past events are an essential part of the family's present; they will never be dismissed as outmoded. The Beecham-Renfro stories, like the "Sacred Harp" singing Donald Davidson describes, are the invaluable art forms of a "somewhat traditional society," which "retains continuity with its past."[4]

Confronted with the changes that illness and death occasion, Welty thus chose to reexamine her family's past in *Losing Battles*, and that reexamination is integral to the novel's thematic contention that storytelling is a stay against the power of time.[5] But Welty reexamines far more than her family history in this novel. She also reexamines several of her earlier works of fiction. The plight of farmers during the Depression had early on been her subject in "Death of a Traveling Salesman" and "The Whistle" as it would again be in *Losing Battles*. The river-dragging procession of "The Wide Net," like the *Losing Battles* procession of school bus, truck, automobile, and mules into Banner, seems the ominous sort of procession that Welty has said typifies her fiction. And the night-blooming cereus and name Sojourner appear not only in *Losing Battles* but also in *The Golden Apples*. Writing during a time of change and loss, Welty seems to

---

4. Welty, "From Where I Live," 69; Donald Davidson, "The New South and the Conservative Tradition," *National Review* 9 (10 September 1960): 145.

5. Rosemary Magee in "Eudora Welty's *Losing Battles*: A Patchwork Quilt of Stories," *South Atlantic Review* 49 (May 1984), argues that *Losing Battles* is "a story about stories," a narrative about "the human impulse to give order and meaning to life through narrative" (72).

look back, to put the vision of her work to the test, and to reaffirm that vision in the face of personal tragedy.

Romines in her fine book *The Home Plot* looks at the relation of *Losing Battles* to Welty's first story, "Death of a Traveling Salesman." Romines suggests that Beulah Renfro parallels the farmwife in the early story and that her name recalls R. J. Bowman's search for the town of Beulah with all its allegorical associations. Romines later adds that Vaughn Renfro's late night encounter with Granny echoes Bowman's association of the farmwife with his own grandmother.[6] Yet *Losing Battles*, by virtue of being a novel and by virtue of being the work of a far more mature writer, is inevitably more complex, as Romines also argues, than the early story.

In the story, for example, Bowman discovers that his equating of the mysterious and the mystical has been misguided. He discovers that the simple and private relationship between a man and a woman offers the sort of fulfillment that he has believed to be remote and exotic:

> Bowman could not speak. He was shocked with knowing what was really in this house. A marriage, a fruitful marriage. That simple thing. Anyone could have had that.
>
> Somehow he felt unable to be indignant or protest, although some sort of joke had certainly been played upon him. There was nothing remote or mysterious here—only something private. The only secret was the ancient communication between two people. But the memory of the woman's waiting silently by the cold hearth, of the man's stubborn journey a mile away to get fire, and how they finally brought out their food and drink and filled the room proudly with all they had to show, was suddenly too clear and too enormous within him for response. (*CG*, 248)

Though Bowman at first tells himself that there is nothing mysterious or distinctive in what is not remote, he finally senses that the commonplace can itself be mysterious and enormous and beyond his capacity for words.

From the beginning of *Losing Battles*, Beulah knows what Bowman discovers. She knows the intricacies of ordinary human relationships, the mystery of even

6. Romines, 272, 288.

the most commonplace relationships, and, more tough-minded than Bowman, she knows that mystery often characterizes the tragic rather than the transcendent experience. When Aunt Cleo asks why Nathan attends the reunion, Beulah replies, "Just make up your mind you don't always know what a man's come for" (*LB*, 184–5). And when Lexie describes the torment she inflicted upon Miss Julia, Beulah tells her: "The littler you wish to see of some people, the plainer you may come to remember 'em. . . . Even against your will. I can't tell you why, so don't ask me" (*LB*, 283). More often than not, Beulah finds the mysterious nature of human experience to involve suffering, but she tells her husband, "I've got to stand it and I've got to stand it. And you've got to stand it. . . . After they've all gone home, Ralph, and the children's in bed, that's what's left. Standing it" (*LB*, 360). Julia Mortimer, of course, has no intention of standing it. She believes in change, in correcting the situation. She believes that any situation can be understood and improved, and she denies the inevitability of mystery. According to Gloria, Julia "said every mystery had its right answer—we just had to find it. That's what mysteries were given to us for" (*LB*, 252). Beulah is more realistic, yet her realism does not partake of despair. Her love for her family and their love for her gives her a life of meaning and purpose. It is Beulah who urgently calls for the family to form a circle as the reunion ends, and it is Beulah who begins singing "Blest Be the Tie that Binds" (*LB*, 348). Her vision of experience is affirmative in the face of woe; she is not R. J. Bowman. Bowman believes in the farm couple's fulfillment and despairs of his own. In *Losing Battles*, Welty transforms Bowman's dualistic view into Beulah's integrated vision of experience.

Just as *Losing Battles* looks back and reworks elements of Welty's first story, so too it looks back to her story "The Wanderers." Crucial episodes in both story and novel concern a night-blooming cereus. In "The Wanderers," Virgie Rainey associates the beautiful flower with all she has lost—her mother, her youth, her talent, her beauty—and she is temporarily reluctant to accept the message of urgency the flower conveys. In *Losing Battles*, the flower often proves to be similarly troubling. The flower's appearance disturbs Granny, who recognizes that its short life represents the brief time left to her. The insensitive Lexie later gives voice to the flower's ominous implications. When Granny asks Lexie to stay with her, Lexie "seemed not to hear, staring at the old cactus where another and still another bloom drifted white upon the dark. 'Yes, and those'll look like wrung chickens' necks in the morning,' she said. 'No thank you'" (*LB*, 356). Though the singular appearance of the bloom does not make Gloria think of death, it does suggest her separateness from Jack: "Everything love had sworn and done seemed to be already gone from him. Even its memory was a measure away from him and from her too, as apart as the cereus back there in its tub, that was itself almost a stranger now, having lifted those white trumpets" (*LB*, 362). To Vaughn as well the flower seems alien: "All of him shied, as if a harness had bloomed" (*LB*, 366), but Vaughn is the one member of his family most likely to bloom, to achieve the kind of distinction Julia Mortimer had sought from her pupils. His sense of the flower as alien seems sure to pass. And Welty's first description of the flower brings reassurance, not fear. The bloom arrives "like a member of the reunion who didn't invariably come when called" (*LB*, 349). Welty's metaphor suggests that this member of the reunion will appear again in its own good time. The family endures, generation succeeding generation and holding the previous generation in its memory, and the night-blooming cereus will also endure and bloom again. Such a description of the flower does not appear in "The Wanderers." But in *Losing Battles*, after actually facing the death of her mother as Virgie Rainey had in the earlier story, Welty uses the flower itself to sound a note of affirmation. As she faced the failing health of family members, as she endured a crippling grief, she nevertheless rediscovered a source of meaning and escaped the world of despair.

Writing at a crossroads of change in her own life, Welty uses her novel to reexamine both family history and her own history as a writer; she thereby gives her novel a private address. But *Losing Battles* has a public address as well, for Welty encountered major social changes even as she had to confront family tragedy, and she responds to those public events in her fiction. The civil rights movement and the violence in Mississippi had been Welty's concern in "Where is the Voice Coming From?" and "The Demonstrators." In *Losing Battles* she looks at a less dramatic but nonetheless significant social change. The completion of Mississippi's Balance Agriculture with Industry crusade, a program begun in the thirties that helped to decrease the percentage of farmers and farm workers in the labor force from more than 60 percent to less than 7 percent in 1970, invited Welty to use *Losing Battles* for a retrospective examination of the Depression. Times might have been more prosperous in the sixties as Welty wrote *Losing Battles*, but the destruction of an agrarian lifestyle must have also been in part a melancholy reminder of those earlier years. Indeed, in her *Delta Review* essay written just a year before *Losing Battles*, Welty sympathetically describes the "traditional value orientation" that has characterized agrarian life and Southern writing. Southern writers, Welty contends in the essay, feel "passionately about Place. Not simply in the historical or philosophical connotation of the word, but in the sensory thing, the experienced world of sight and sound and smell, in its earth and water and sky and in its seasons." And southern writers, she also asserts, have "watched and participated in" family stories; they know what it means to belong to a family, and they know that remembering and recounting are essential to a family's vitality.[7] Place, family, a communal past—these are the concepts that tie southern writers to the South, especially those writers known as the Nashville Agrarians, and these are the ideals that motivated generations of southerners who were literally agrarians.

Writing from the perspective of 1955–70 and looking back at farm life in the thirties, Welty deals sympathetically with traditional agrarian values that were threatened by urbanization and industrialization even as she recognizes that an agrarian life can be intellectually confining and physically debilitating.[8] In *Losing Battles* Welty suggests that the closeness to nature, the strong family ties, the sense of continuity inherent in an agrarian life are vital aspects of a meaningful existence, but she also recognizes that a traditional society may be blind to the strengths of a modern, more culturally diverse, more highly developed one. Welty's description of the ambiguity inherent in great fiction, in fact, seems a precise

7. See Howard Grasmick's definition of "traditional value orientation," "Social Change and the Wallace Movement in the South" (Ph.D. diss., University of North Carolina [Chapel Hill], 1973), 56; for population data see Loewen and Sallis, 329–30 and U.S. Bureau of the Census, *Census of Population: 1970*, vol. 1, *Characteristics of the Population*, Part 26, Mississippi (U.S. Government Printing Office, Washington, D.C., 1973), 176; Welty, "From Where I Live," 69.

8. In his essay "The Chosen People," *Southern Review* 6 (July 1970), Lewis P. Simpson notes that "the traditional drama of Agrarian versus Industrial" appears "obliquely and yet in a completely significant way" in *Losing Battles* (xxii).

description of the ambiguity in *Losing Battles*. "Great fiction," she writes, ". . . abounds in what makes for confusion; it generates it, being on a scale which copies life, which it confronts. It is very seldom neat, is given to sprawling and escaping from bounds, is capable of contradicting itself, and is not impervious to humor. There is absolutely everything in great fiction but a clear answer. Humanity itself seems to matter more to the novelist than what humanity thinks it can prove" (*ES*, 149). The intentional ambiguity of *Losing Battles* arises because Welty has created two foes, both of whom command our affection and respect. On the one hand, Granny Vaughn, her grandsons surnamed Beecham and granddaughter Beulah Beecham Renfro, their spouses, children, grandchildren, and in-laws live a traditional agrarian life as subsistence farmers. The retired school teacher Julia Mortimer, on the other hand, is an individual the sociologists would label a modernist: She believes in man's ability to harness or control nature; she emphasizes individual freedom and social duty as more desirable than family loyalty; and she believes in a philosophy of progress.[9] Granny Vaughn and her descendants stand in sharp contrast to Julia Mortimer, but Welty has not chosen between these opponents. Instead she has presented two modes of coping with a world that resists systematization of any sort.

The family that gathers each year to celebrate the birth of Granny Vaughn and the fact of kinship certainly seems to live in harmony with nature. The novel's opening chapter establishes this harmony; repeatedly Welty describes the family in terms of the natural world. Beulah treats Granny as if the old woman's shoulders "might be fragile as butterfly wings." Lady May Renfro's hair stands up on her head "straight as a patch of oats." And when her father Jack returns from Parchman Penitentiary just in time for the reunion, his face has "burned to a red even deeper than the home clay" (*LB*, 5, 47, 71).

But such imagery alone does not establish the family's reliance upon and reverence for nature. This family is engaged in the subsistence farming that Welty saw vanishing from contemporary Mississippi; the family relies upon the land for its physical survival. The Renfros raise chickens, cows, and a pig or two; they grow beans, peas, potatoes, and watermelons in addition to their cash crops of cotton and corn (*LB*, 189–90). They must buy "coal and matches and starch.

9. See Grasmick's definition of modernism, 51–3.

. . . And flour and sugar and vinegar and salt and sweet-soap. And seed and feed"
(*LB*, 90), but they provide other necessities for themselves. Perhaps because they
are so dependent upon the land, the Beechams and Renfros tend to worship it.
"Right here in the world is where I call it plain beautiful" (*LB*, 102), Jack tells
his wife Gloria, and the older generation nostalgically recalls a time when Banner, Mississippi, seemed even more desirable. Jack's Uncle Noah Webster tells
his wife: "Cleo, the old place here was plum stocked with squirrel when we was
boys. It was overrun with quail. And if you never saw the deer running in here,
I saw 'em. It was filled—it was filled!—with every kind of good thing, this old
dwelling, when me and the rest of us Beecham boys grew up here under Granny
and Grandpa Vaughn's strict raising. It's got everlasting springs, a well with
water as sweet as you could find in this world, and a pond and a creek both. But
you're seeing it today in dry summer" (*LB*, 193). Similarly, Jack's parents fondly
remember the dense forest of Banner and rue the time when loggers demolished
it as they did virtually all of Mississippi's virgin forests. Though Beulah's dislike
for the loggers has a provincial racist dimension, her overriding concern is for
the sanctity of the landscape: "Dearman is who showed up full-grown around
here, took over some of the country, brought niggers in here, cut down every
tree within forty miles, and run it shrieking through a sawmill." And even Jack's
father, who dynamited Dearman's tree stumps from the ground and who on occasion will still blow up a tree, bemoans the "nation of stumps" that Dearman
bequeathed to Banner (*LB*, 341, 342).

Though the clan reveres the beauty and fecundity of nature, they also feel
victimized by nature. Drought and land erosion endanger their farming existence: "'It's the same old story,' said Uncle Dolphus. 'It's the fault of the land
going back on us, treating us the wrong way. There's been too much of the substance washed away to grow enough to eat any more. 'Now well's run dry and
river's about to run dry. Around here there ain't nothing running no more but
snakes on the ground and candidates for office'" (*LB*, 194). Farmers like Dolphus, of course, are primarily at fault for the soil's condition and for erosion, but
these farmers are truly the victims of drought. They recognize, as did the Nashville Agrarians, that nature is a power man cannot ultimately control. As John
Crowe Ransom wrote in "Reconstructed but Unregenerate," "Nature wears out
man before man can wear out nature; only a city man, a laboratory man, a man

cloistered from the normal contacts with the soil, will deny that."[10] Dolphus's complaint indicates this kind of respect for the power of nature more than it does a rejection of the natural world. "Farmers still and evermore will be" (*LB*, 194), Dolphus proclaims of the Beecham boys, and Jack Renfro will follow in his uncles' footsteps, accepting nature's bounty and its severity.

Though the Beechams and Renfros have a respect for natural forces, their sense of impotence in the face of those forces is as much the result of ignorance as of painful experience. Their failure to heed the agricultural advice of Banner's former teacher is a case in point. Gloria reports that Miss Julia "had fruit bushes and flower plants for sale, and good seed—vegetables. She had a big yard and plenty of fertilizer" (*LB*, 243). And Gloria adds, "One year, she sent out more little peach trees than you can count, sent them free. . . . Came out of her orchard. She wanted to make everybody grow as satisfying an orchard as hers" (*LB*, 243). The Beechams and Renfros, however, are indifferent to her improved seeds and superior trees. As Dolphus reports in another context, "She thought if she told people what they ought to know, and told 'em enough times, and finally beat it into their hides, they wouldn't forget it. Well, some of us still had her licked" (*LB*, 240).

Though Miss Julia's scientific approach to agriculture seems totally sensible and though this approach would inevitably prevail, many of her encounters with nature are at once hilarious and foolishly heroic. When a flood threatened Banner school, Uncle Curtis recalls, Miss Julia taught the students to swim, refusing to dismiss class. And when a cyclone struck Banner school, Aunt Birdie declares, "Miss Julia got on her knees and leaned against it, and we all copied her, and we held the schoolhouse up" (*LB*, 237–8). Julia, it seems, if these exaggerated tales can be trusted, has always refused to acknowledge human limitation. The reunion folks, when not in her schoolroom, have been more realistic.

If *Losing Battles* examines the traditional agrarian reverence for the beauty and power of nature, the novel even more fully examines the strengths and weaknesses of traditional family life as it had existed in the rural South. More than place, more than the rural community of Banner, Mississippi, the Beechams and

10. John Crowe Ransom, "Reconstructed but Unregenerate," in *I'll Take My Stand* (1930; reprint, Baton Rouge: Louisiana State University Press, 1977), 9.

Renfros value each other. For them the extended family is the most important institution in life because that institution, though they would not think in these terms, gives each of them a secure sense of identity. They live in what Lyle Lanier feared a modern urban and industrial society would destroy—"the natural biological group, the normal milieu of shared experiences, community of interests, and integration of personality." The shared experiences of the Renfro-Beecham clan are, in fact, the basis of the novel. The rollicking story of Jack's battle with Curly and of his undeserved stint in Parchman, the story of Sam Dale Beecham, the story of Miss Julia, the story of the Beecham parents and their tragic death—all these stories have been or will be repeated year after year at the family reunion. Moreover, the family serves to establish the integrated personality Lanier described. The family members do not feel fragmented, split, at conflict with themselves. Indeed, Welty has said, "the feeling of the solidity of the family, which is the strongest thing in the book, is certainly not a battle of identity. The battle for identity is not even necessary. It's a sticking together. It involves both a submerging and a triumph of the individual, because you can't really conceive of the whole unless you *are* an identity. Unless you are very real in yourself, you don't know what it means to support others or to join with them or to help them."[11] Jack certainly knows both the submerging and the triumph of the individual. He loves his family and undertakes innumerable tasks for them. He breaks out of Parchman one day before his scheduled release because he knows he is expected at the family reunion. He refuses to criticize Uncle Homer Champion, who arrested him and who has repeatedly failed to come to his aid. And Jack, who ran the family farm before he went to prison, after the reunion will run the farm once again. Jack will never, as his wife wishes, move away from home; home ties are too strong. But Jack is not an automaton. Love and duty tie him to the family, but knowing that he belongs and always will, Jack feels free to act in ways his family cannot understand. He marries Gloria Short. He refuses to forgive Judge Moody for sending him to the pen when his family indulges itself in this act of condescension. He is able to "love" Miss Julia Mortimer, though he has known her only through stories told at the reunion

11. Lyle Lanier, "A Critique of the Philosophy of Progress," in *I'll Take My Stand* (1930; reprint, Baton Rouge: Louisiana State University Press, 1977), 146; Bunting, 48–9.

and though his family views her with a mixture of scorn and awe (*LB*, 361). Jack can act independently. He is an individual because he is a family man. He is not racked by inner conflict, pulled between the demands of family and of self. Those demands complement each other and coexist harmoniously within him.

The family, however, has a worthy foe who has seen its flaws and called for a wider loyalty than the family requires. Miss Julia Mortimer, Beulah reports, "wanted us to quit worshiping ourselves quite so wholehearted" (*LB*, 236). Because the family worships itself, Julia has realized, because it cannot see beyond itself, it is unable to view its own difficulties as part of a larger problem. Free of family ties, Miss Julia can take the larger view, and she once urged Gloria to share this perspective, to refuse Jack's proposal of marriage, and to turn herself "into a better teacher and do him and the world some good" (*LB*, 250).

Though Miss Julia's commitment is to the world at large, to the family of man, she seeks to meet this commitment by improving the state of Mississippi: "'A state calling for improvement as loudly as ours? Mississippi standing at the foot of the ladder gives me that much more to work for,' she'd say. I don't dream it was so much palaver, either," comments Miss Beulah. "She meant it entirely" (*LB*, 240). Julia has clear goals, and her teaching has been remarkably successful on occasion. Yet her attempts to move Mississippi up the economic and social ladder meet only limited success in her lifetime. Judge Moody tells the reunion that Julia "made her a Superior Court judge, the best eye, ear, nose, and throat specialist in Kansas City, and a history professor somewhere—they're all scattered wide, of course. She could get them started, lick 'em into shape, but she couldn't get 'em to stay" (*LB*, 305). Julia has broadened the horizons of Mississippians as Banner's new teacher will broaden the horizons of Vaughn Renfro, but she has not typically provided them with a sense of duty to the abstract concept of the state's welfare. Instead, she has encouraged the "brain drain" that had long plagued the South by the time Welty wrote *Losing Battles*. The loyalty of bright, young people has been diverted from family to self, not to society. Even Judge Moody, who has stayed in Mississippi to do his duty, confesses that he never "fully forgave" Miss Julia for denying him the chance for personal advancement. Miss Julia's knowledge, her openness to experience, her desire to cope with the state's problems are admirable, but they help to create a modern, fragmented society. Such a consequence is perhaps as dangerous as the insularity that family loyalty produces. Miss Julia's final years exemplify this danger. Though she spends hours waiting for visitors, her only companion is the insensitive, cruel Lexie Renfro. And when Miss Julia dies, she dies alone. Of course, even Granny Vaughn, whose family worships her, feels isolated at times. The children she has reared have moved away, all save one; her husband has died; and she realizes how inevitably separate human beings are. But her isolation is meliorated by the love that Beulah and Jack show her. No such love comes to Julia. If the family, embodied in the Renfro-Beecham clan, produces a confined view of experience, it provides the emotional support that neither loyalty to an "abstract social ideal" nor a focus upon the separate individual can generate.[12]

Family solidarity, in addition, gives rise to a concept of time that the reunion unconsciously accepts, that the modernist Julia Mortimer wholeheartedly opposes, and that Welty, as she wrote her novel, must have felt was endangered.[13] An unswerving loyalty to the people and place that constitute home creates a sense of continuity, and the Beechams and Renfros assume that time is continuous. The past for the family is not something to be forgotten or transcended; it is something to be remembered and retold.

Such an emphasis upon the past, a modernist might argue, may retard a society's necessary growth and development. Davidson insists that a society can turn to tradition "without being encumbered by it," but Welty shows that this scenario does not always occur. Most citizens of Banner, Mississippi, mindlessly resist Miss Julia Mortimer's focus upon the future. Her faith is in renewal and progress, and as a young teacher, Miss Julia is confident that she can overcome more than one individual's resistance to change: "I always thought if I could marshal strength enough of body and spirit and push with it, every ounce, I could change the future" (*LB*, 298). With strength of body and spirit, she has sought to improve the quality of agricultural produce, has lengthened the school

12. In "More Trouble in Mississippi: Family vs. Antifamily in Miss Welty's Losing Battles," *Sewanee Review* 79 (1971), Thomas Landess sees *Losing Battles* as a struggle between the Beecham-Renfro family and the antifamily, led by Miss Julia and held together by a "bond of mutually shared ideas" (626–34).

13. For pertinent discussions of time, see Kreyling, *Eudora Welty's Achievement of Order*, 140–52, and Daniele Pitavy, "La Guerre du Temps dans *Losing Battles* et *The Optimist's Daughter*," *Recherches Anglaises et Américaines* 9 (1976): 182–96.

term by more than three months, has attempted to provide her recalcitrant students with milk, and has desired "a doctor and a lawyer and all else we might have to holler for some day, to come right out of Banner" (*LB*, 235). By the time Julia comes to retire, these efforts have produced a few notable successes, even in Boone County. The hapless Willy Trimble has a profession of sorts because Miss Julia has capitalized on his one talent as a carpenter. Under Julia's instruction, Uncle Nathan has made guilt a source of good works. Overcome by remorse for having killed Dearman and having allowed a "sawmill nigger" to hang in his place, Nathan once felt only despair in facing his sin against the common humanity of black and white. Yet when Julia told him "Nathan, even when there's nothing left to hope for, you can start again from there, and go your way and *be good*" (*LB*, 344), Nathan began living his life of atonement. And Miss Julia has convinced Judge Moody and Dr. Carruthers (the doctor who brought Jack Renfro into the world) to remain in Mississippi. These achievements notwithstanding, most of Julia's efforts to improve agriculture, education, and public health have met with failure. As she writes in a final letter to Judge Moody, "All my life I've fought a hard war with ignorance. Except in those cases that you can count off on your fingers, I lost every battle" (*LB*, 298). Miss Julia seems aware that Depression-era Mississippi still stands "at the foot of the ladder" from which she has tried to move it: In 1930 Mississippi's farmers were poverty-stricken, its children inadequately educated and fed, and its populace without sufficient access to medical care.[14] Enamored of tradition, Banner, Mississippi, has resisted Julia's efforts to improve such a portrait. In this sense, Banner is encumbered by its past.

Yet Miss Julia's effort to transform the present into her image of the future is itself fraught with perils. Ransom has described these perils: "The concept of Progress is the concept of man's increasing command, and eventually perfect command, over the forces of nature; a concept which enhances too readily our conceit, and brutalizes our life. I believe there is possible no deep sense of beauty,

---

14. Davidson, 145; in 1930 Mississippi had the nation's lowest ten-year average for farm income and the nation's lowest average for days spent in school; in the thirties 50 to 90 percent of children in large areas of the South suffered from an inadequate diet; and in 1930 Mississippi had fewer than ten physicians for every 10,000 citizens (Odum, 20, 51–53, 103, 370).

no heroism of conduct, and no sublimity of religion, which is not informed by the humble sense of man's precarious position in the universe."[15] Miss Julia's belief that she can change the future certainly enhances her conceit. Blinded by this conceit, she cannot see the importance of leisure, of humor, or of family tradition. And blinded by this conceit, she would change the future in totally inappropriate ways. Confident that Sam Dale Beecham is actually Gloria's father and that Jack and Gloria Renfro are cousins, Miss Julia would have Judge Moody dissolve their marriage. Julia, in these efforts to alter the course of history, fails to recognize her own inherently clouded vision. She proves herself to be, in the words of Mrs. Moody, "a tyrant, if there ever was one. Oh, for others' own good, of course" (*LB*, 325). Julia's faith in her own infallible judgment has been misplaced, and Welty suggests that any plan for the future may be similarly flawed.

Thus, in *Losing Battles*, Welty allies herself with traditional agrarian values while at the same time she sympathetically depicts modernist opposition to them. The Renfros and Beechams' awareness of natural beauty and power, commitment to family, and sense of time's continuity are set against Miss Julia's love of knowledge, commitment to society, and belief in progress; each value system illuminates the deficiencies and virtues of the other. By 1970, then, the southern value orientation has proved both a chastened and an enduring one for Welty. History and modernists like Miss Julia have trampled a bit upon this philosophy, but Welty seems still to have found much that is "general, far-reaching, and profound" implicit in the lives of Depression-era Mississippians.

As a writer who was facing and coping with change, Welty revised *Losing Battles* in accord with her own shifting vision of experience. During the fifteen or so years in which she worked upon the novel, anxiety, exhaustion, and tragedy were often her companions, and the novel seemed about to become a rather dark comedy. But as Welty wrote scene after scene and draft after draft, she created a novel stressing the meaningfulness of life in the face of loss. Revisions of both characterization and plot reveal this metamorphosis as well as documenting Welty's craftsmanship.

15. Ransom, 10.

In her essay "Words into Fiction," Eudora Welty has written, "What its own author knows about a novel is flexible till the end; it changes as it goes, and more than that, it will not be the same knowledge he has by the time the work ends as he had when it began" (*ES*, 138). The flexibility of Welty's own knowledge during the composition of *Losing Battles* is a case in point. The Jack Renfro of the novel is not the Jack we see in its earlier drafts. In Part 2 of the novel, Jack Renfro sets out to obey the will of his family reunion and to wreak vengeance on Judge Oscar Moody, the man who had sentenced him to two years in Parchman penitentiary. Jack hopes to force Moody's "luxurious" Buick into a ditch; instead, when Jack's wife and daughter appear inopportunely in the road, Moody swerves to avoid hitting them and drives up Banner Top, the highest hill in Boone County. Jack, in gratitude, resolves to become Moody's savior, not his tormentor, and embarks upon a hilarious rescue mission. So perfectly is this episode composed, so rapidly and inevitably does it move, that critics have tended to compliment Welty's comic talent but to ignore the thematic significance with which she invests Jack's instantaneous choice. He chooses to save Judge Moody, and the basis of his decision is absolutely central to the novel's meaning.

The importance of Jack's decision becomes clearer if we try to imagine him acting from a motive other than gratitude. And we can easily imagine such a scenario, for Welty wrote at least three early drafts of Part 2. In a 1961 draft, Jack, or Joe Quick Bunting as he was then called, sets out to save the auto because his crying wife Willowdene asks him to and because he is unwilling to leave Judge and Mrs. Moody "standing out in the road all night." In a 1963 draft, Joe Quick has become Buford Bunting, but his motives for helping the judge are very similar. And in a 1965 draft, Jack acts to help the judge because Mary Jane, previously Willowdene, insists that he should and because the car belongs to a lady, to Mrs. Moody. The vengeance Jack seeks does not extend beyond nightfall, and his treatment of women is always chivalrous, but Jack in the 1961/63 drafts and to a lesser extent in the 1965 draft seems a rather superficial, even "aggravating" individual. He thrives on "a diet of commotion and fanfare"; he revels in the judge's predicament and in the opportunity to perform for an audience of neighbors and family once the rescue mission begins.[16]

16. Eudora Welty, "Losing Battles," Incomplete Drafts, Welty Collection, MDAH: Part 2, 1961, p. 36; Part 2, 1963, ul, 8.

210

By 1969, however, Welty had changed Jack's motivation to the motivation we see in the novel published by Random House; by doing so she transformed his character.[17] The new basis for Jack's decision, his gratitude to Moody, ensures that the plot will be more than comic, that it will serve as a metaphor for the novel's ultimate meaning, as a "device," in Welty's words, "organic to human struggle designed for the searching out of human truth" (*ES*, 167). Family solidity, individualism, mortality—these might serve as labels for the major concerns of *Losing Battles*, and Jack's decision as it stands in the Random House text illuminates each of these concerns.

Family solidity is an accurate but somewhat pale term to describe Jack's ultimate reason for helping Judge Moody. Indeed, when Jack shouts, "He saved my wife and baby!" (*LB*, 120), we see the great depth of his love for Gloria and Lady May. Joe Quick, Buford, and the Jack of 1965 never consider the possibility that wife or daughter could have perished under the Moody auto. They see only that the car has been happily diverted to Banner Top. For the moment, at least, a love of commotion rules their minds. This is not true of the Jack Renfro who exists in the published novel. Jack's motivation there is consistent with, not antithetical to, the love he has proclaimed and demonstrated in all previous versions. It stands, in fact, as an emblem of that love. Moreover, Welty has further altered the Random House text in ways that complement Jack's decision and emphasize the value he places upon the "living presence" of those he loves (*LB*, 362). In the early drafts of the novel, Jack visits Grandpa Vaughn's grave and remembers him with reverence and respect. But in the final version, Jack says: "I miss him! I miss his frowning presence" (*LB*, 102). Jack also misses Uncle Nathan and hopes Nathan will once again settle in Banner. In Part 6 of the 1970 novel, though not in the only extant early version (1964) of this section, Jack even hopes his own undeserved time in the pen will atone for the murder Uncle Nathan once committed: "'I'm glad Uncle Nathan didn't ever have to go to the pen. They would never have let him put up his tent and bring his own syrup. Or be an artist,' said Jack presently. 'As long as I went and took my turn, maybe it's

17. In late 1968 and early 1969, Welty completed a draft of the novel that, except for fine-tuning and a very few substantive changes, was identical to the novel that was published by Random House in 1970. For the convenience of readers, I shall therefore refer to the Random House text rather than the 1968–69 draft.

evened up, and now the poor old man can rest'" (*LB*, 431).[18] In this passage Jack's love proves to be a generous love, a love which looks outward, not inward. And in the novel, though not in early drafts, Jack extends the generosity of his love even to his horse Dan. Discovering that Dan is the property of Curly Stovall and has not been sent to the renderer's, Jack asserts: "I rather he's alive and fickle than all mine and sold for his hide and tallow" (*LB*, 435). In Welty's final version of *Losing Battles*, therefore, Jack's desire to be near those he loves, human or animal, and his willingness to sacrifice self-interest for their sakes emerge in incident after incident. But perhaps these qualities are most clearly seen when Jack, in gratitude, forgoes revenge and begins to help Moody. Without this basis for the car's rescue, *Losing Battles* would be far less charitable in its view of human nature.

Paradoxically, just as Jack's love for family is implicit in the cry "He saved my wife and baby!" so too is Jack's ability to act independently of the family. In early drafts of the novel, little sister Elvie assumes that Jack would help Moody only if Willowdene/Mary Jane insisted upon it; Elvie does not believe Jack's actions could be self-directed. And Elvie is right. Jack acts in defiance of the reunion only to be in compliance with his wife. But in the final text this is no longer the case. Jack makes his own instantaneous decision. And though Gloria thinks Jack's family will "kill" him for it (*LB*, 172), such a possibility never occurs to Jack. He sends for help from the family, and his sisters and father offer their ineffectual aid. He invites Judge Moody home for dinner and overnight accommodation, confident that "Mama knows what to do" (*LB*, 167). Jack knows that his family will accept his judgment, will acquiesce in his decision. He knows that he will always be treasured by his family, and secure in that knowledge, Jack need not worry about eccentric behaviors. In the published novel, Jack Renfro is both individualist and family man, and his decision to help Judge Moody embodies both aspects of that dualism and gives shape to the novel.

Finally, in *Losing Battles* Jack's desire to save Judge Moody springs from his growing recognition that life is as brief as it is precious. When Moody's car comes perilously close to killing Gloria and Lady May, Jack knows fear. Love

18. A 1964 draft of Part 6 of *Losing Battles* is part of the Welty Collection, MDAH.

comes not merely to involve communion but also to involve the possibility of heartfelt loss. Because Judge Moody has spared him that loss, Jack vows to be Moody's Good Samaritan.

Jack's awareness of human mortality is first prominent in the 1965 draft of Part 2. In 1965, as in the final text, his stint at Parchman has accustomed Jack to "a time that ages and changes people." After being away from home for a year and a half, Jack returns to find that his mother's health is getting "frailer, getting frailer all the time," that Uncle Nathan will "look older'n all of 'em" when he arrives, and that Grandpa Vaughn has died. And such intimations of mortality anticipate Jack's more articulate assertion that love involves both a fear of and a consolation for life's fragility. As Jack and Willowdene walk past his grand-parents' grave, Jack muses, "My own grandma wasn't but ten years older'n you, Willowdene, when she went under." Then he adds, "Yet will you look at the reunion today and count how many her and him managed to leave behind! Like something whispered to 'em and they was smart enough to take heed." Jack is aware that he "ain't for always," yet he suggests that the family is a source of immortality, a way of transcending death: The reunion folks live on, and they preserve the memory of those who have died.[19] Jack Renfro of 1965 thus has a very real sense of human transience, and he recognizes the "irreducible urgency" to counteract that transience (*ES*, 168).

Although Jack's varied confrontations with mortality date from Welty's 1965 draft of Part 2, they are not in this draft balanced on the fulcrum of his gratitude to Judge Moody. In the 1965 version, Jack still sees nothing to fear when Moody almost runs over his wife and child. And such a stance is particularly inappropriate in 1965, for Welty has by that date made Jack very conscious of time's inexorable movement. Her decision to transform his motivation is thus essential, for it completes a key pattern in the novel and ensures that the novel's major events are integral to its thematic concerns. When Jack in the 1970 novel vows to help the man who has saved Gloria and Lady May, he is a far more consistent and perhaps more self-conscious character than his predecessor. He recognizes that many events are beyond his control, that he is personally open

19. Kreyling, *Eudora Welty's Achievement of Order*, 147; "Losing Battles," Welty Collection, MDAH: Part 2, 1965, pp. 43, 23, 22, 50.

to tragic experience. And in the published novel this awareness tempers even one of Jack's most confident assertions. When Gloria tells Jack that he has lost everything—his truck, his horse, his shirttail—Jack replies, "They can't take away what no human can take away. My family. . . . My wife and girl baby and all of 'em at home. And I've got my strength. I may not have all the time I used to have—but I can provide" (*LB*, 434). Jack here acknowledges time and the limits it imposes upon our accomplishments. Although he sees family as a source of strength, although he hopes for "a string of other little chaps to come along behind" Lady May and ensure his family's continuity (*LB*, 435), he knows that he does not personally have "all the time" he might want. In the novel, Jack's decision to save the Moody car is based on just this realization: He knows that his limited time with Gloria and Lady May has been extended by the Judge's trip to Banner Top.

The most crucial moment in *Losing Battles* may therefore be that moment when Jack decides to save Judge Moody's Buick. In Jack's decision the novel's major issues converge, and the rescue of the judge's car becomes an important metaphor. Jack's love for his family, his ability to act independently, and his sense of human mortality are implicit in his resolve to become Moody's Good Samaritan. The novel's most profound concerns and its most comic action are truly one, and Jack Renfro is a character who commands our admiration and respect—no longer is he the irritating redneck protagonist who fails to recognize the meaning of his experience.

Welty's drafts of *Losing Battles* reveal a similar transformation in the character of Judge Oscar Moody. By carefully comparing three early drafts of *Losing Battles*, Part 2 (1961, 1963, 1965), with the novel, we can see the shifting concept of Judge Moody and of the values he represents.

In the 1961 and 1963 drafts of the novel, Welty treats Judge Moody with a good deal of irony. When Moody runs his car off the road and up a cliff, his first concern is not the welfare of young Lady May Bunting, whom he has swerved to avoid hitting, but the welfare of his car. Subsequently, Moody displays a rhetorical disregard for the laws he has sworn to uphold. Unable to phone for a wrecker because the only local telephone lies inside a closed store, the 1961 judge shouts "Break the door down!" And unable to travel to another town because all local vehicles seem unavailable, the Moody of both early drafts proclaims, "I'll Shanghai the first thing on wheels that dares to come along here!" The judge, frequently and ironically masked against the dusty roads, talks more like a highwayman than a law enforcement officer. In addition, Moody is emotionally out of control during this automotive crisis. He never shows the rational personality one would expect in a judge. Welty repeatedly introduces Judge Moody's speeches with words like "cried," "shouted," "roared," "burst wildly out," "bellowed," and "yelled," and at one point she writes that the judge "was raving." A final irony lies in the judge's clear reluctance to reach his destination, the home of Miss Florence Hand, alias Miss Vera Thrasher. The 1961 judge, we learn late in Part 2, has been in sight of the house where Miss Florence lies dead and has failed to recognize it. And in the 1963 draft, Mrs. Moody tells her husband, "I don't believe you wanted to get where you're going in the first place."[20] Judge Moody in these early drafts is thus a self-centered, overwrought, hypocritical, and self-deceived individual.

By 1965, however, the characterization of Judge Moody is less ironic and more sympathetic. Knowing that he "might have run over and killed" Mary Jane, Lady May's mother, this Judge Moody inquires of her, "Where did you come from? . . . Are you harmed?" His first concern here is human. He worries about his car only after assuring himself that Mary Jane is safe. Moreover, though he covers his face with a handkerchief and looks like a "bank robber," this judge respects the law.[21] Nowhere does he threaten to break into the store, and his threat to shanghai a vehicle is more obviously an idle one. Lastly, this judge is far less emotional than his predecessors of 1961 and 1963. He speaks less often, and he speaks in a more restrained fashion. He is, nevertheless, like them in his reluctance to reach the home of Miss Ida Moorehead, his former tutor who lies near death, for he has passed within sight of her house without recognizing it. In 1965, then, Judge Moody remains somewhat unaware of his own motivation, but he seems more humane and more rational than he had in previous drafts.

Welty builds upon this 1965 characterization in creating her ultimate charac-

20. "Losing Battles," Welty Collection, MDAH: Part 2, 1961, pp. 42, 51; Part 2, 1963, r16, r20.

21. Ibid., Part 2, 1965, p. 67; Part 1, 1965, j17.

ter. The judge of the published novel worries first about Gloria (formerly Mary Jane) and Lady May's welfare and only afterward about his car. He displays an active respect for the law: Mrs. Moody urges him to break into the local store and to shanghai a church bus, but the judge tells her that breaking into the store would be trespassing and ignores her command to hijack the bus. The masked judge still looks like a "bank robber" to Jack (*LB*, 82), but he is a scrupulous officer of the court. And this judge is an even stronger advocate of rationality, of system, of knowledge than his 1965 predecessor. He refrains from emotional tirades, and he encourages the use of logic. Although Jack's "system" for saving the Moody auto is to "be ready for what comes to me in a good strong flash," the judge prefers "calling up my own garageman, even if we have to wait a little longer on him" (*LB*, 128). The judge wants not a "Good Samaritan," but a "man with some know-how"; he wants not a "good strong flash" but a man with expertise and "a good piece of road equipment" (*LB*, 125).

The judge of *Losing Battles*, as I have described him so far, seems a humane, ethical, sensible man. He seems self-possessed and self-assured, but this is not totally the case. He is in conflict with himself, and his physical health is one indication of this conflict. When he seeks to climb Banner Top and examine the plight of his auto, Mrs. Moody says, "Oscar Moody, come back here. You're fifty-five years old, had a warning about your blood pressure, suffer from dust and hay fever" (*LB*, 124). When the judge persists in his intentions, she adds, "Come back, you heard me. I don't want to lose you *and* the car" (*LB*, 124). And finally she threatens her husband, "Don't set your foot an inch up that bank, or I'll tell Dr. Carruthers on you the minute we get home" (*LB*, 126). Three times in rapid succession Welty tells us that the judge suffers from high blood pressure, a clear sign of stress and frustration. And Miss Julia Mortimer is once again a notable source of stress for the judge. Indeed, he is subconsciously unwilling to answer her summons, to help her enforce laws that the citizens of Banner cannot comprehend, and to witness the physical and mental decline she has undergone. Mrs. Moody recognizes this reluctance, just as she recognizes the judge's physical woes, and she tells him, "You've still got to prove it to me you want to *get* where you're going" (*LB*, 143). But the judge ultimately overcomes his desire to escape from unpleasant duties. He deals with the legal issues Miss

Julia raises, though not as she might have wished, and he attends Julia's funeral as his 1964 forebear did not.

Judge Moody, it is clear, changes dramatically during the composition of *Losing Battles*, Part 2; Welty's "knowledge" of this character when she finished *Losing Battles* was certainly not the same "knowledge" with which she began. The early drafts of the novel satirize blatant hypocrisy. The judge of these drafts is scarcely more ethical than the lawbreakers he judges, and Welty laughs at a legal system that is inconsistently, even capriciously administered. But this is not an issue in the final text. There Welty, though her method is objective, examines the inner life of a very different Judge Moody. This judge values the law and defines himself as a member of the judiciary. Even in Banner, off-duty, standing on an isolated dirt road, Moody refers to himself as the "court" (*LB*, 164). But the very system that is the source of his identity undermines the judge's efforts to create respect for the law. The individuals he sentences to prison terms, for example, are routinely and prematurely set free from Parchman Penitentiary when they plead home ties. As a result, the judge in his last incarnation is inwardly distraught. Though he does not roar, rant, or bellow, though he holds "back a coming groan" as his predecessors have not (*LB*, 164), the judge feels terrible frustration and resentment. In Part 4 of the published text, Moody is able to discuss these emotions that have produced his high blood pressure. There, as Mrs. Moody worries about his blood pressure, the judge confesses to blaming Miss Julia for his own career of losing battles: "'I'm where I am today because she talked me into staying, doing what I could here at home, through the Boone County Courts.' After a pause he said, 'Well, and I never fully forgave her'" (*LB*, 305). The judge's many defeats and few victories have brought him a quiet despair. But, of course, acknowledging his previously repressed anger is a courageous act and a sign that the judge has come to forgive Miss Julia and to accept the nature of his own career. In the novel as published, Welty thus depicts the judge as a man who is coming to terms with the inherent limitations of his profession.

In a more important pattern of revisions, Welty transforms Moody into a man who ultimately confronts and comes to terms with the fact of human mortality. In all versions of Part 2, the judge flees this knowledge. In the 1961 and 1963 drafts, Judge Moody does not wish to pay his last respects to Florence

Hand or Vera Thrasher, in the 1965 draft he is loath to visit Ida Moorehead who lies near death, and in the novel he isn't "anxious enough" to visit the ailing Julia and "find out what had happened to her" (*LB*, 305). Moreover, the mask each judge wears against the dust serves as an emblem of his reluctance to face his former mentor and the death which has or soon will claim her. Mary Anne Ferguson has persuasively argued that an "association of dust and death" pervades *Losing Battles*, and Judge Moody in 1961 and 1963 dons a dust mask when he learns of the teacher's death.[22] In the novel, however, he removes the mask when her death is announced: "Judge Moody, out in the road, put his hands to his cheeks and rolled the tied-on handkerchief up into a ring around his forehead, and there was his naked face" (*LB*, 162). The announcement of Julia's death brings this judge out from behind his mask and forces him to acknowledge life's transience, to acknowledge man's inevitable return to the dust from which he came. Judge Moody does put the mask back on as he and his wife proceed to the Renfro-Beecham reunion, but this judge, unlike his predecessors, has recognized "time's deepest meaning" (*ES*, 168). He has not allowed "death in its reality" to pass him "right over" (*OD*, 131). He will go on to read Miss Julia's will to the assembled reunion, to recount the story of his relationship with her, and sorrowfully to recall the ways in which he "betrayed" her. And paradoxically these wounding memories are a mark of triumph for Moody. As Laurel Hand and Eudora Welty know, "The memory can be hurt, time and again—but in that may lie its final mercy. As long as it's vulnerable to the living moment, it lives for us, and while it lives, and while we are able, we can give it up its due" (*OD*, 179).

As she wrote *Losing Battles* in fits and starts over a fourteen or fifteen year period, then, Eudora Welty radically altered her concept of Judge Oscar Moody. Beginning with a two-dimensional figure and a satiric purpose, Welty gradually transformed the judge into a human being and transformed her own purpose from satire to understanding. Her vision of Judge Moody is ultimately both ironic and affirmative.

Welty's revisions of plot show a parallel shift in purpose. The action of *Losing*

---

22. Mary Anne Ferguson, "Losing Battles as a Comic Epic in Prose," in *Eudora Welty: Critical Essays*, ed. Peggy W. Prenshaw (Jackson: University Press of Mississippi, 1979), 316.

*Battles* forms the "kind of metaphor" which Welty believed characterized "every well-made plot" (*ES*, 167). Comparing Welty's early draft of Part 6 (1964) with the published text of 1970 reveals how thoroughly emblematic the novel's action is, how the details of that emblematic action changed inevitably as theme and character evolved, and how plot is indeed well made.

The early typescript of *Losing Battles*, Part 6, as well as two early drafts of Part 2 and one of Part 1 (early drafts of Parts 3, 4, and 5 seem not to be extant), presents an ironic picture of willful and successful resistance to the forces of modernism. A modernist, in the words of sociologist Joseph Kahl, believes "in making plans in advance for important parts of his life, and he has a sense of security that he can usually bring those plans to fruition." And Kahl further notes that "the modern man is willing to move away from his relatives and to depend upon his own initiative." But the Pembrokes, sometimes called Buntings, those characters who will be Renfros in the final version of *Losing Battles*, focus their lives upon the family and refuse to plan for the future. They will not even contemplate the future. They will not face the nature and extent of the Depression that lies before them, nor will they face the prospect of death. What Louis Rubin writes of the Renfros and Beechams thus might more accurately be said of the 1964 Pembrokes or Buntings: "What all these generations of men and women want to do—do, indeed, succeed in doing for the most part—is to go about their lives and their family and community doings innocently and unthinkingly, meeting birth, life, love and death as they arise, without the dread and the knowledge of anticipating or asking why. In so doing, they are not only helpless against time and change, but unable to deal with their circumstance."[23] The plot of Welty's 1964 version of Part 6 serves as a metaphor, albeit an imperfect one, for the helplessness Rubin notes. The insistence upon meeting difficulties as they arise, the refusal to anticipate or plan, are most clearly seen in the method which Buford Bunting, alias Jack Renfro, uses to rescue Judge Moody's car. Buford improvises. When Curly's truck cannot tow the car down from Lover's Leap but can only hold it suspended on a rope hanging over the edge of the cliff, Buford

23. Joseph Kahl, *The Measure of Modernism* (Austin: University of Texas Press, 1968), 133; Louis D. Rubin, "Everything Brought Out in the Open: Eudora Welty's *Losing Battles*," *Hollins Critic* 7 (1970): 4–5.

grabs the rope and pulls, calling for help. His wife, his mother, Judge Moody, and Mrs. Moody answer the call. And when this "human chain" breaks, Buford sizes up the situation, levels the car that has fallen on its nose, hitches it behind two mules, a school bus, and Curly's truck , scrounging trace chains, fence wire, a well rope, and the rope from his sister's swing to do so. Buford reacts by assembling groups, be they human or vehicular; he does not plan. His brother, who loves school and who seems destined to leave the family, does anticipate the future and prepare for it. As no one else in his family would think of doing, Hunter George readies the school bus the night before he must drive the local children to school, and he does so on his own. Buford, the family hero, never undertakes such advance planning, does not anticipate and prepare for problems that could arise, and as a result his rescue of the car is hardly a rescue at all. The Buick which Buford saves has "its crest gone, its nose broken in, its bumper swallowed up, both headlights blinded, and its cracked back window flashing with numerous rainbows."[24] Buford's refusal to anticipate the future, to anticipate the consequences of his actions and be prepared for them, does leave him unable to deal adequately with his circumstance. His unplanned and ineffectual rescue mission is thus metaphoric, an emblem of his family's unsuccessful coping with time and change.

If Buford's reliance upon improvisation is in itself metaphoric, so are the specific aspects of his car rescue scheme. A pair of mules appropriately pulls the truck and car "down the hill from Mount Prospect and Lover's Leap" to Curly's store in Pickway; the symbols of tradition and stubborn resistance lead this procession. And events in Pickway are also emblematic: Aycock's father, angry because Curly helped send Aycock to Parchman and thereby damaged the family name, dumps a load of cement on Curly's truck.[25] Curly, resolving to make a virtue out of this misfortune, calls the truck a monument; certainly it is a monument to the somewhat petrified, foolishly consistent minds of the Pembroke/Buntings and Curly Yates, minds to which forethought and foresight are inimical.

Significant as the car rescue is, another incident in the 1964 plot is more cru-

---

24. Welty, "Losing Battles," Welty Collection, MDAH: Part 6, 1964, p. 50.
25. Ibid., Part 6, pp. 40, 53–7.

cially metaphoric and thematic. In 1964 Welty elected not to depict the funeral or burial of Miss Vera, as Miss Julia was then called. Judge and Mrs. Moody, in fact, leave town before the funeral takes place. Scarcely disciples of Miss Vera, they flee from the reality of her death. And when the funeral does occur inside a local church, Willowdene (Gloria to be), though grieved by the death of Miss Vera, remains outside with her husband. Miss Vera's battles seem to have been losing ones. Judge Moody and Willowdene, her two most prized students, fail to honor her in death. And the reality of her death does not touch Buford. He tenderly covers his wife's eyes when Vera's coffin passes them on its way to the church, and when the funeral is over and the mourners have filed past again, Buford says nothing about death. He merely tells Willowdene, "I believe nearly everybody by this time has found out, one way or another, that I'm back." Buford refuses to acknowledge that Miss Vera's death prefigures Willowdene's or his own, just as he had previously refused to acknowledge that his daughter might have perished under the Moody auto. This refusal to look ahead, to recognize how short his life or Willowdene's or Lady May's may be, blinds Buford to the preciousness of time and leaves him content to share "a diet of commotion and fanfare" with his family.[26]

Plot in this early draft of Part 6 is thus a rather consistent and elaborately developed metaphor. In some ways, nevertheless, it is subject to attack. The existence of a human chain, for instance, surely suggests a sort of reconciliation among those who constitute it. But Judge Moody is not reconciled to Buford. On the contrary, Buford knows that the judge "ain't ever going to care for me."[27] And Willowdene, though she does wholly capitulate to Buford, though she gives up all hope of moving away from his extended family, marks her capitulation by breaking the chain, an act one might expect to signify a break from Buford. It does not, and as a result the episode of the human chain cannot fully carry the burden of theme.

By 1970, however, Welty has built upon and improved the action of *Losing Battles*. She has made that action clearer in outline, while enabling it to convey themes which have become more complex. During the rescue mission, for exam-

26. Ibid., Part 6, p. 59; Part 2, 1963, ul, 8.
27. Ibid., Part 6, 1964, p. 50.

ple, Welty calls more explicit attention to the family's insistence upon meeting life "without the dread and the knowledge of anticipating or asking why," and she sets this insistence against the thoroughgoing futurism advocated by Judge Moody. In the published novel, Jack, who declares "Single-handed—that ain't the way we do it around Banner" (*LB*, 228), continues to form improvised human chains, but he also overtly states that improvisation is his principle of action: "I still believe I can handle trouble just taking it as it comes," he tells the judge (*LB*, 390). The judge, on the other hand, is reluctant to handle trouble in this way. He has by 1970 become a representative modernist and tells Jack, "It takes thinking! We've got to think!" He calls for conversation to cease and pleads for "just a single idea" (*LB*, 390). The judge in the final novel is a man of ideas, an intellectual, and he is a man who plans for the future. His career has been devoted to Mississippi's future, to creating a respect for the law. And he approaches the rescue of the car with the same desire to plan. Unfortunately for the judge, Jack's methods prevail as they did in the 1964 typescript, and the car once again comes down from Banner Top "streaked with clay, hung with briars, the emblem gone from its radiator top, its bumper swallowed up, both headlights blinded, . . . listing sideways and fanning up mud" (*LB*, 396). Jack's attempt to handle trouble "just taking it as it comes" prevents him from dealing effectively with it.

In the 1970 novel, then, Jack's spontaneous, intuitive approach to life has become, paradoxically, a conscious principle with him, but the very consciousness of this principle suggests his awareness of other approaches to experience and his ability in some ways to modify his own method, to look to the future and to act on the basis of what he sees ahead. Jack may typically refuse to anticipate the consequences of his actions, but the revised plot of 1970 confirms what Michael Kreyling has suggested: Jack is very aware of human mortality and of the urgency to love that mortality implies.[28] He insists that Gloria attend Julia's funeral; he does not place his hands over her eyes to prevent her from facing death's reality. And he, as we have already seen, recognizes that an awareness of mortality is at the heart of the family's existence and cohesiveness. Jack and his

28. Kreyling, *Eudora Welty's Achievement of Order*, 151.

family are aware of their own transience. Jack's decision to attend the funeral and his insistence that Gloria attend are actions that express his realization.

Just as the 1970 plot conveys Jack's more complex philosophical stance, it also suggests that the judge, the modernist who believes in making plans and in making them work, recognizes man's inability to control the future no matter how carefully he prepares for it. For most of the novel, the judge seeks to repress this knowledge. By Part 6 of the novel, however, he has accepted the limitations of his judicial power. He has, moreover, accepted the limitations inherent in any attempt, professional or otherwise, to shape the future. After the human chain has failed to save the car and it stands on its nose, he permits Jack to level it but then abruptly insists that he himself drive the car down from a ledge where it sits. Early in the novel, the judge would have been unable to act so spontaneously. In Part 2, Mrs. Moody had stopped him from attempting to save the car on his own; she commanded him to think of the possible consequences, to consider his blood pressure. And when Lady May was as perilously perched on Banner Top as was the auto, Mrs. Moody again stopped her husband from acting impulsively: "You'll just scare her, make her fall quicker" (*LB*, 161). But the judge will not be stopped a third time. He drives the car himself. Ever the modernist who acts on his own, he tells Jack, "I believe I can do better if you're not standing over me. I may be peculiar that way" (*LB*, 396). Nevertheless, he handles "trouble just taking it as it comes." He has no plan or system, and he acts without considering the negative consequences. This event is not present in the 1964 draft, for the original Judge Moody experiences neither the repression nor the dawning awareness of his 1970 counterpart. That awareness prompts the later Moody to act quickly. He recognizes the importance of planning for the future, but he also accepts the limits on his ability to make such plans, to chart his professional course in life or his private route down a hill.

In addition to accepting these limitations, he confronts the ultimate limitation, the one future event that he has sought not to face. Early in *Losing Battles*, he flees the reality of death, but in Part 6, as the plot clearly indicates, he has ceased running and bravely gazes upon human mortality. As the novel begins, Judge Moody roams Boone County's back roads, unable to find Miss Julia's home, and he later admits, "I wasn't anxious enough at all to see Miss Julia today, find out what had happened to her" (*LB*, 305). But in Part 6, when Mrs.

Moody asks if they in good conscience can fail to attend Julia's burial service, the judge replies, "Oh, we're going. . . . We always were" (*LB*, 421). His 1964 forebear avoided even the sight of the funeral procession, but this judge goes on literally to bear the weight of death—he is a pallbearer. And when the service has ended and the mourners have dispersed, the judge can laugh at the absurdities of that service: at the insincerity of mourners like Curly Stovall and Homer Champion, who have stood by the grave of Dearman, their spiritual patriarch; at the provinciality of his own wife, who has complained about the "jabber" of the priest who conducted the service; and even at his own reluctant attendance. The exploration of absurdity, Richard Boyd Hauck writes, "is a grim and hilarious game; the explorer wins when he can laugh and loses when he cannot."[29] At the reunion Judge Moody had seemed destined to lose; he had not laughed but had said in a still, stubborn voice, "I don't care quite the same about living as I did this morning" (*LB*, 307). In the cemetery on the following day, however, he does laugh. He accepts the reality of death and the absurdities of life that death makes evident, and he still cares about living. He can face the burial, but can laugh nonetheless.

Though the judge feels that modernists like himself can accomplish very little within a lifetime, the 1970 plot suggests that the forces of progress, for better and for worse, are encroaching upon the family's more traditional way of life. No longer do mules, as they did in the 1964 typescript, lead the caravan that pulls the judge's Buick down from Banner Top; now the school bus heads the procession. And no longer does Miss Julia appear to have lost almost every battle. By 1970, Welty has granted her a considerable number of victories. In the 1969 galleys of the novel, Julia feels totally defeated and admits, "I lost, they won."[30] But Welty altered these galleys, and in the published novel Julia says, "Mostly, I lost" and admits only that she "never could win for good" (*LB*, 298). Here Julia's defeat, even in her own mind, is qualified. And the novel's 1970 plot suggests that though Julia's teaching has convinced very few students to work for the improvement of Depression-era Mississippi, it has convinced many that they can change their own futures. In gratitude, therefore, former students

29. Hauck, 14.
30. Welty, "Losing Battles," Welty Collection, MDAH: Galleys, 119.

from across the country assemble to honor Miss Julia Mortimer, and both Judge Moody and Gloria pay their mentor appropriate homage. Such victories for Julia, victories absent from the 1964 typescript, suggest that her attempts to keep the family from "worshiping [themselves] quite so wholehearted" (*LB*, 236) may one day prevail. Her triumphs surely prefigure the decline of the extended agrarian family so content to abide by tradition and to handle trouble as it arises, the decline Welty had observed by the time she began writing *Losing Battles* in the mid-1950s.

Thus, Welty's more sharply defined plot in the 1970 novel serves as an effective metaphor for more complexly rendered themes. No detail seems inappropriate or insignificant. The 1964 human chain episode is subject to such a charge; the 1970 episode is not. Gloria no longer breaks the chain. She holds tight to both Jack and her faith in the future. And the human chain in the completed novel is in truth a chain. It does indeed serve as an emblem of reconciliation. Jack calls for the chain out of a sincere desire to help Judge Moody. In the 1964 typescript, Buford feels no affection for Moody, but in the 1970 novel Jack credits the judge with saving Gloria and Lady May. Gratitude thus motivates Jack's rescue attempt. Similarly, in 1964 the judge has no faith in Buford. Before the rescue attempt begins, Mrs. Moody asks, "Do you reckon we've got a chance?" The judge looks at Curly's truck and replies, "Tied to a rattletrap like that?' [sic] Up on the edge of nowhere."[31] But in 1970 the judge's reply is rather different. He tells his wife, "I should say what chance we have depends on Jack" (*LB*, 382). He admires Jack as Miss Julia had stubbornly refused to do. Julia had been unable to see beyond the abstractions in which she placed her faith; Jack was, according to the proof she had assembled, Gloria's cousin and therefore should not be the young woman's husband. Julia did not even want to meet Jack. The judge has met Jack, however, and now he sees beyond abstractions. He shares Julia's faith in the law's wisdom—on the basis of that faith he sent Jack to Parchman—but he recognizes the generosity of Jack's love, Jack's commitment to people and to place, the appropriateness of Jack's marriage. He thus concludes, even before all of the so-called evidence is in, to let the marriage stand. The judge combines wisdom with mercy, a loyalty to Julia's principles with a fond-

31. Ibid: Part 6, 1964, p. 16.

ness for Jack. These two character traits both manifest themselves in the human chain episode. As his car hangs over Banner Top, the judge calls for a plan, for an idea, but he is also part of an impulsively formed chain. He is linked to Jack by bonds of affection as well as those of circumstance. In the completed novel when the chain has broken and the car has been rescued by other means, the judge and Jack still shake hands, and the judge expresses his hope that Jack will save the family's hay. The human chain functions metaphorically as it did not in the earlier version of the novel; the individuals who constitute the chain clearly see the virtues of their philosophic antagonists and are reconciled to those antagonists.

Beyond doubt, then, Welty's revisions of plot reveal her own changing knowledge during the composition process. Her revisions suggest a growing faith that modernists can understand and appreciate the best of traditional life, that traditionalists can benefit from forward-looking modernist thought without sacrificing the essence of their values, and that the significance of each human life deserves to be celebrated.

*Losing Battles* is clearly the product of Eudora Welty's encounters with change and loss, encounters that would have left many emotionally bereft. But in the course of writing this novel, Welty found that her resources as an individual and a writer enabled her to keep the quality she attributes to the novel's characters— "a courage, a joy of life, even, that's unquenchable." Writing between 1955 and 1970, Welty looked back at the Great Depression and created, to use Allen Tate's words, "a literature conscious of the past in the present" even as she celebrated the courage of a forward-looking modernist like Julia Mortimer.[32] In doing so, she asserted that family, memory, storytelling, as well as commitment to the future, can enable us not merely to endure, but also to prevail over time. Tested by tragedy and attrition, Eudora Welty and her characters— traditionalists and modernists alike—thus stand victorious in *Losing Battles*.

32. Bunting, 48; Tate, 545.

IX

## "The Old and the Young, the Past and the Present, the Living and the Dead"

Confluence in *The Optimist's Daughter*

Like *Losing Battles*, *The Optimist's Daughter* was written in a season of change, and change may be the source of its being. Within a year after the January 1966 deaths of her mother and her brother Edward, Welty felt compelled to write *The Optimist's Daughter*. She would complete a version of the story in 1967, see it published in the *New Yorker* in 1969, and then revise it for book publication in 1972. The result of this process was a novel unlike any other Welty had written. Only in this novel do Welty family members figure so explicitly and so prominently as sources for the novel's central figures. Though the present action of the novel is wholly of Welty's making and owes but little to Welty family experiences, Welty drew upon the life of her mother and upon her own life in creating Becky McKelva and her daughter Laurel McKelva Hand. Moreover, the past events that define these characters' values and beliefs and the settings in which these characters move often have a factual basis. Of course, that factual basis is only the starting point from which Welty works in *The Optimist's Daughter*. Her characters have an existence of their own; events and settings drawn from actual experience become fictional metaphors. But Welty's reliance upon autobiography is itself central to her novel. In writing of her personal losses to time, Welty defies time's power. She asserts the continuity of her love in the face of death, and in doing so she discovers her novel's most profound meaning.

*The Optimist's Daughter* tells the story of Laurel McKelva Hand, a woman in her mid-forties who has long since lost both her husband and her mother to death. As the novel opens, Laurel has joined her father, Judge Clinton McKelva, and his new wife in New Orleans so that her father may have the specialized eye surgery unavailable in his Mount Salus, Mississippi, home. When her father dies after the surgery, Laurel returns with his body to Mount Salus, attends the funeral arranged by the new wife, and stays for three additional days so that she may set the family home in order before returning to her job in Chicago. During those days, Laurel finds herself driven into the past, confronting memories long repressed, memories of her mother, her father, and her husband, memories of pain and of the joys it has been painful to lose. The process is a harrowing one, but it allows the past to come alive for Laurel, to be more than a record of loss. Laurel is thus able to leave Mount Salus with a sense of fulfillment as well as grief.

Of all of these characters, the one most closely allied to an actual person is Laurel's mother, Becky McKelva, for Becky's attitudes and experiences often resemble those of Chestina Andrews Welty. Welty dedicated *The Optimist's Daughter* to her mother, and the novel is one way Welty grieved for her mother's death. When Charlotte Capers asked if writing this novel had helped Welty work through her emotions, Welty replied, "I think it did; although, I did not undertake it for any therapeutic reasons, because I don't believe in that kind of thing. I believe in really trying to comprehend something. Comprehension is more important to me than healing; but, I suppose the by-product of that was being able to understand something better—my own feelings about it. It was helpful to me."[1] *The Optimist's Daughter* certainly reveals Welty's attempts to understand the patterns of her mother's life, not to romanticize that life but to understand and celebrate it nonetheless. Welty's approach to change and loss

---

1. Charlotte Capers, "An Interview with Eudora Welty," in *Conversations with Eudora Welty*, ed. Peggy W. Prenshaw (Jackson: University of Mississippi Press, 1984), 116.

was thus a movement toward understanding the past, not a retreat into an idealized past.

Chestina Welty and Becky McKelva are perhaps most alike in their pessimism and their courage. "You're a good deal of a pessimist, sweetheart," Eudora Welty recalled hearing her father say to her mother. And her mother's response was unequivocal: "I certainly *am*" (*OWB*, 45). But though she expected the worst, Chestina Welty was a "daredevil" who "when there *was* a fire, had broken loose from all hands and run back—on crutches, too—into the burning house to rescue her set of Dickens which she flung, all twenty-four volumes, from the window before she jumped out after them" (*OWB*, 45–6). As she defied fire, she would defy the weather itself: "Why, I always loved a storm! High winds never bothered me in West Virginia! Just listen at that! I wasn't a bit afraid of a little lightning and thunder! I'd go out on the mountain and spread my arms wide and *run* in a good big storm!" (*OWB*, 4). Both Mrs. Welty's attitudes and her experiences are reborn in Becky McKelva, but they are also transformed. Mrs. Welty's willingness to challenge a storm, for instance, becomes an important metaphoric pattern in the novel, for Becky yields "to the storms that began coming to her out of her darkness of vision" (*OD*, 145). The storm that literally darkens the sky becomes in the novel a figurative storm that darkens Becky's vision of life. Like Chestina Welty, Becky McKelva finds herself almost blind as she approaches death, and like Mrs. Welty, Becky has difficulty coping with this limitation. Laurel, of course, must face both a literal and a figurative storm of her own. Laurel is alone in her parents' house on her last night in Mount Salus when a storm hits. She doesn't rush out into the actual storm as her mother might have, but she does confront the storm that comes from the darkness of her own vision. She confronts the reality of her parents' lives together; she confronts the torment as well as the love that constituted their marriage; and she confronts the loss of her husband Philip, a loss she had previously sealed away. The next morning Laurel awakes to clear skies and a clearer view of experience than Becky had known. Welty thus uses Chestina Welty's boast about the storm, but she transfigures that boast, finds in it a clue to the emotional plight of her mother's final years, and makes it part of her novel's metaphoric structure.

Other patterns in Chestina Welty's life became clear to Welty as she wrote *The Optimist's Daughter* and were similarly transformed. Old and almost blind and unable to read for herself, Mrs. Welty, for instance, would recite poems from McGuffey's Readers, the poems she had recited as a young teacher traveling on horseback to and from a remote West Virginia school: "She could still recite them in full when she was lying helpless and nearly blind, in her bed, an old lady. Reciting, her voice took on resonance and firmness, it rang with the old fervor, with ferocity even. She was teaching me one more, almost her last, lesson: emotions do not grow old. I knew that I would feel as she did, and I do" (*OWB*, 52). *The Optimist's Daughter* recounts the same events in almost the same terms. As a young West Virginia teacher going to and from school, Becky tells her daughter, "To make the time pass quicker, I recited the whole way, from horseback—I memorized with no great effort, dear" (*OD*, 137). And as an old woman, Becky would recite "The Cataract of Lodore" from McGuffey's Fifth Reader: "Whatever she recited she put the same deep feeling into. With her voice she was saying that the more she could call back of 'The Cataract of Lodore,' the better she could defend her case in some trial that seemed to be going on against her life" (*OD*, 147). Immobile, unable to see or act, Becky attempts "to make the time pass quicker," to get through this difficult time, by turning to the past. When talking about her own mother, Welty stressed the similarity between the old woman reciting and the young woman reading. But when writing about her character, Welty's emphasis is more sharply defined. Here we sense that Becky is engaged in a desperate and doomed effort to assert the continuity of her identity in the face of age and illness. Perhaps that too was part of Chestina Welty's experience, and perhaps *The Optimist's Daughter* complements the analysis of Mrs. Welty's character in *One Writer's Beginnings*.

In *One Writer's Beginnings*, Welty reports that blindness threatened the very core of Chestina Welty's identity—her sense of independence and self-reliance. Her mother's "fierce independence," Welty writes, "was what we shared, it made the strongest bond between us and the strongest tension. To grow up is to fight for it, to grow old is to lose it after having possessed it. For her, too, it was most deeply connected to the mountains" (*OWB*, 60). Mrs. Welty's idealization of her West Virginia origins was allied to the sense of self-sufficiency and self-reliance she could feel there. That self-reliance gave her the strength at age fifteen to take her desperately ill father to a hospital in Baltimore and to return alone with his body. That sense of self-reliance was a painful loss when Mrs. Welty found herself old and weak and blind.

In writing *The Optimist's Daughter*, Welty clearly drew upon her mother's symbolic view of West Virginia. Like her forebear, Becky McKelva loves to be "up home" in the Mountaineer State: "Sometimes the top of the mountain was higher than the flying birds. Sometimes even clouds lay down the hill, hiding the treetops farther down. The highest house, the deepest well, the tuning of the strings; sleep in the clouds; Queen's Shoals; the fastest conversations on earth—no wonder her mother needed nothing else!" (*OD*, 141) Like her forebear, the Becky of West Virginia is sufficient for any task. "You don't know anybody in Baltimore?" the doctors ask Becky. "But," Welty writes, "Becky had known herself" (*OD*, 144). And like her forebear, Becky finds the loss of this independence almost unbearable. Becky, blind and nearing death, longs to go "up home," but her husband cannot understand her despair, and Becky dies in exile and humiliation. Becky feels betrayed by her husband precisely because she loves him so deeply and because he loves her deeply in return: "He loved his wife. Whatever she did that she couldn't help doing was all right. Whatever she was driven to say was all right. But it was *not* all right! Her trouble was that very desperation. And no one had the power to cause that except the one she desperately loved, who refused to consider that she was desperate. It was betrayal on betrayal" (*OD*, 150). This betrayal is not part of Welty's description of her mother—Christian Webb Welty died thirty-five years before his wife. But a sense of betrayal helps to deepen Welty's fictional investigation of love and separateness, an investigation which goes beyond the bounds of individual experience but which also must draw upon the helplessness Welty felt when she, despite the ability to recognize and consider her mother's desperation, was unable to assuage it.

Chestina Welty's death thus clearly prompted Eudora Welty's attempt to understand and celebrate her mother's life and to find in her mother's life a vehicle for understanding experience more generally. The 1966 loss of her mother also prompted Welty to look for patterns or continuities in her own life. Eudora Welty never thought of herself as a model for Laurel McKelva Hand; she did, however, draw upon her personal experience to develop selected aspects of this character's life.

The differences between Welty and Laurel are clear. The marriage of Laurel and Philip Hand is one, for Eudora Welty, of course, never married. And there are other significant differences between the author and her creation. Though Welty her entire life called Jackson, Mississippi, home, Laurel lives in Chicago—she has chosen to remain in the North, away from her roots, even though her husband has been dead for twenty years or more and even though the elders of Mount Salus urge her to return. In Chicago is her work and in Chicago she will remain. Granting Laurel a base outside of Mississippi is an important choice for the meaning of the novel, for Laurel must be in exile from her family home. Laurel's trip to Mississippi, like her mother's annual trips to West Virginia, must seem a trip into the past. When Laurel leaves Mount Salus, therefore, she is returning not only to Chicago, but also to life in the present. She is leaving with "freed hands—pardoned and freed" (*OD*, 179). But she is not abandoning the past—it exists for her in memory. She simply does not need the family home, the books and furniture, the town itself in order to recall those she has loved. In creating Laurel Hand, Welty creates a character who will serve the purposes of the novel; she does not write veiled autobiography.

In important ways, nevertheless, Eudora Welty and Laurel Hand are very much alike. They are both artists, they hold similar values, they even share common experiences. *The Optimist's Daughter* is a novel about the significance of love, the difficulties inherent in loving, and the continuity of love that ultimately memory alone can provide. The deaths of her immediate family members surely made these themes especially important to Welty, and she draws upon memories of love to develop them. *The Optimist's Daughter* is as much an account of Welty's encounter with memory as it is of Laurel Hand's. In this novel, Welty and her protagonist recover a common past and simultaneously learn that memory gives life to what is past.

One element of this common past involves the love of parents for each other and for their children. As a young child with a "fast-beating heart," Welty was allowed to spend all day in her parents' double bed. Then at night, she reports,

My parents draped the lampshade with a sheet of the daily paper, which was tilted, like a hat brim, so that they could sit in their rockers in a lighted part of the room and I could supposedly go to sleep in the protected dark of the bed.

> They sat talking. What was thus dramatically made a present of to me was the secure sense of the hidden observer. As long as I could make myself keep awake, I was free to listen to every word my parents said between them.
>
> I don't remember that any secrets were revealed to me, nor do I remember any avid curiosity on my part to learn something I wasn't supposed to—perhaps I was too young to know what to listen for. But I was present in the room with the chief secret there was—the two of them, father and mother, sitting there as one. I was conscious of this secret and of my fast-beating heart in step together, as I lay in the slant-shaded light of the room, with a brown, pear-shaped scorch in the newspaper shade where it had become overheated once. (*OWB*, 20–1)

Welty as a child sensed that her parents were "as one." Their love bound them inextricably together, and she felt herself "included in" this love because of "what I could hear of their voices and what I could see of their faces in the cone of yellow light under the brown-scorched shade" (*OWB*, 21).

Laurel Hand has a similar sense of the love between her parents and of the way that love includes her. Laurel's memory of her parents reading is much like Welty's of her parents talking:

> When Laurel was a child, in this room and in this bed where she lay now, she closed her eyes like this and the rhythmic, nighttime sound of the two beloved reading voices came rising in turn up the stairs every night to reach her. She could hardly fall asleep, she tried to keep awake, for pleasure. She cared for her own books, but she cared more for theirs, which meant their voices. In the lateness of the night, their two voices reading to each other where she could hear them, never letting a silence divide or interrupt them, combined into one unceasing voice and wrapped her around as she listened, as still as if she were asleep. She was sent to sleep under a velvety cloak of words, richly patterned and stitched with gold, straight out of a fairy tale, while they went reading on into her dreams. (*OD*, 57–8)

Laurel hears her parents voices combine "into one unceasing voice" and she feels wrapped in the beauty of their common voice and their uncommon love. Years before she would write *One Writer's Beginnings*, Welty thus depicted the powerful impact of her parents' love upon her. For Welty, listening to her parents read while she supposedly slept was a way of "exercising as early as then the turn of mind, the nature of temperament, of a privileged observer; and owing to the way I became so, it turned out that I became the loving kind" (*OWB*, 21). Laurel too is an observer, though a less astute and generous one than Eudora Welty. She speaks very little in the course of the novel, but she records detail after detail in her memory. And on the stormy night she spends alone in her family home, her effort, like Welty's in writing *The Optimist's Daughter*, is to understand her parents and herself, to place a lifetime of observations into a comprehensible and credible pattern.

Some memories that Welty and Laurel hold in common quite naturally have rather different implications for author and for character. Laurel's memories of feeding her grandmother's pigeons, for instance, are identical to Welty's memories of the same activity:

> Laurel had kept the pigeons under eye in their pigeon house and had already seen a pair of them sticking their beaks down each other's throats, gagging each other, eating out of each other's craws, swallowing down all over again what had been swallowed before: they were taking turns. The first time, she hoped they might never do it again, but they did it again the next day while the other pigeons copied them. They convinced her that they could not escape each other and could not themselves be escaped from. So when the pigeons flew down, she tried to position herself behind her grandmother's skirt, which was long and black, but her grandmother said again, "They're just hungry, like we are." (*OD*, 140–1)

Laurel's youthful revulsion is young Eudora Welty's own (*OWB*, 56–7). And Laurel's refusal to admit a fear that might shame her mother betokens Eudora Welty's realization that "parents and children take turns back and forth, changing places, protecting and protesting each other" (*OD*, 141). Nevertheless, the character Laurel responds to this memory in a way unique to her fictional experience. She associates this ritual of the pigeons, as Mary Hughes Brookhart has noted, with her widowed father's marriage to the much younger, cheaply attractive Fay Chisom.[2] As Judge McKelva lies immobile in a New Orleans hospital

2. See the discussion of bird imagery in Mary Hughes Brookhart's "The Search for Lost

bed, Fay passes a cigarette from her mouth to the mouth of the judge, an act that repels Laurel because it suggests sexual intimacy. Laurel is reluctant to acknowledge her father's need for Fay; she flees this knowledge when, on the train from New Orleans to Mount Salus, Fay awakens saying "Oh no, no, not any more" and when the ladies of Mount Salus allude to it (*OD*, 45, 116). Similarly, Laurel's fear of the swift in her house is a fear of Fay—both defile the house, yet both must be confronted and dealt with. Only late in the novel through her memory of the pigeons does Laurel overcome fastidiousness and acknowledge with sympathy and understanding her father's hunger. Welty's own father did not survive her mother, did not remarry, did not create such a crisis for his daughter. But from her personal life Welty has found an action capable of conveying Laurel's dilemma.

Another actual memory conveys Welty's and Laurel's recognition and acceptance of human limitation. Welty remembered, as does Laurel, hearing the story of her mother's ill-fated trip by raft down a frozen river and then on by train to Baltimore, a trip taken in hope of saving her father. But that memory in *One Writer's Beginnings* establishes only Chestina Welty's great courage. At age fifteen Mrs. Welty had been able to brave the elements, to face her father's death, and to return his body to their mountaintop home. For Laurel in *The Optimist's Daughter* this memory has more to say. Laurel feels that she has not made a courageous attempt to save her father; she feels she has countenanced Fay's abuse of him and has failed to interest him in living. And Laurel also recalls her ineffective attempts to help Becky deal with illness and despair. The memory of her mother's youthful strength as compared to her own inaction thus troubles her. But that memory also tells her that human beings are inevitably separate, that we cannot totally understand and support each other no matter how great our love, that we certainly cannot overcome the final separation of death: "Baltimore was as far a place as you could go with those you loved, and it was where they left you" (*OD*, 151). Eudora Welty herself made a courageous trip to a metaphorical Baltimore as she cared for her mother during the last years of Chestina Welty's life. She declined a Ford Fellowship, restricted her journeys to New York and to

---

Time in the Early Fiction of Eudora Welty" (Ph.D. diss. University of North Carolina [Chapel Hill], 1981), 205.

visit friends, turned down many offers from universities across the country, taught at a local college—all in order to see that her mother was as content, safe, and secure as possible. Diarmuid Russell worried about the physical, emotional and artistic toll such self-denial was taking upon Welty, and he urged her to find a professional facility where her mother would be comfortable.[3] Ultimately, professional care was the only answer, but Welty, unless she was traveling to academic or literary engagements, daily made the 100-mile round trip to visit her mother in a Yazoo City nursing center. Despite all her daughter's endeavors, however, Chestina Welty passionately desired to return home, and when confronted by her mother's unhappiness, Welty must have learned in a very personal and painful way that she had reached her own version of "Baltimore" and could go no further.

If Welty and her character share individual memories, they also share an attitude toward the importance of memory itself. Memory, Welty writes, "is the treasure most dearly regarded by me, in my life and in my work as a writer. Here time, also, is subject to confluence. The memory is a living thing—it too is in transit. But during its moment, all that is remembered joins, and lives—the old and the young, the past and the present, the living and the dead" (*OWB*, 104). Laurel Hand comes to a similar realization in *The Optimist's Daughter*. We are separate, she knows. Time will create rifts and misunderstandings; time will eventually bring death to those we love. But memory, Laurel realizes, can provide the continuity we require. She learns that life is "nothing but the continuity of its love" (*OD*, 160) and that "the memory can be hurt, time and again—but in that may lie its final mercy. As long as it's vulnerable to the living moment, it lives for us, and while it lives, and while we are able, we can give it up its due" (*OD*, 179). In this realization, Eudora Welty and Laurel McKelva Hand are most truly one. They each recognize that the past is to a considerable extent the construction of a "living moment," but because the past is vulnerable to the "living moment," to the construction that memory puts upon it, the past is truly alive. There is a truth to be known about the past—both Laurel and Welty believe in that truth and in the importance of avoiding falsification—but they also

---

3. Russell to Welty, 4 March 1963, 5 March 1963, 3 December 1963, 9 December 1963, restricted papers, Welty Collection, MDAH.

acknowledge and affirm the way an individual's understanding of the past changes and evolves.

Personal tragedy and the dramatic changes it produced in her life prompted Welty's quest for continuity, and in writing *The Optimist's Daughter*, she seems to have fulfilled that quest. There is a sense of resolution about *The Optimist's Daughter* that is missing in Welty's early fiction. In the stories published before 1955, as Reynolds Price has noted, "the last note is almost invariably rising, a question; the final look in the onlooker's eyes is of puzzlement—'Anyone could have had that. Should I have tried?' Not in *The Optimist's Daughter* however. The end clarifies. Mystery dissolves before patient watching—the unbroken stare of Laurel McKelva Hand, the woman at its center."[4] In a sense then, *The Optimist's Daughter* seems to look back at Welty's early work and attempt to comment upon it. The changes in her life and her attempts to cope with them seem to have prompted a rethinking of her thematic vision, especially of the autobiographical vision in "The Winds" and "The Bride of the Innisfallen."

In creating Josie of "The Winds," as in creating Laurel, Welty drew upon her memories of childhood. But the import of those memories predictably had changed in the thirty years between publication of "The Winds" and of *The Optimist's Daughter*. In particular, the devastating events of January 1966 must have pushed Welty to rethink the attitudes and priorities advanced in that early story. In "The Winds," young Josie's experience at the Redpath Chautauqua makes her long for "all that was wild and beloved and estranged" (*WN*, 139); Josie longs to leave the protection of home, to be estranged, to be free to follow her passion. Whether she will find that freedom, however, remains in doubt as the story closes. Josie is, after all, still a child. When she does find a note written by the "big girl" Cornella, a note that expresses a desire for romance and freedom, that note literally ends with a question—"When?" (*WN*, 140) In *The Optimist's Daughter* this question has been answered. In some ways, Laurel may seem the adult incarnation of Josie, for Laurel has followed her passion. She has left home, married Phil, and made a career for herself as a designer. As a child

---

4. Reynolds Price, "The Onlooker Smiling," in *A Common Room*, 57. Price wrote his essay about "The Optimist's Daughter" as it appeared in the *New Yorker* in 1969, but his comments seem to describe the novel in its final form more accurately than they do the periodical version.

Laurel "grew up in the kind of shyness that takes its refuge in giving refuge," and before she met Phil, "she thought of love as shelter" (*OD*, 161). It is Phil who has taught her that love can liberate rather than protect. But it is here that Laurel's similarity to Josie ends, for Laurel ultimately does not want to be estranged; she wants to be connected to her lost family and to her past. Only when Laurel faces the tormented nature of her parents' marriage and Phil's "craving for his unlived life" (*OD*, 154) can she truly be free. Only when memory brings her a sense of continuity with the past can she truly live in the present. Laurel leaves Mount Salus as Josie longs to leave her home town, but she is not estranged; her memory can still "be hurt, time and again," and she will still give memory its due (*OD*, 179).

*The Optimist's Daughter* thus provides, as Price has suggested, a sense of resolution that is missing from early stories like "The Winds." It also provides the resolution that is missing from *The Bride of the Innisfallen* (1955). In the title story of that volume, for instance, a young woman journeys away from her past, from a bad marriage and a sense of confinement. In the no man's land of a boat train from London to Ireland, amid travelers who relish their freedom from rigidly defined roles, the young woman observes the joy that freedom brings. And as the story ends, she enters an unknown pub, walking without protection "into the lovely room full of strangers" (*BI*, 83). There is no resolution here; there is instead anticipation, an embracing of mystery and openness. In *The Optimist's Daughter*, Laurel journeys from Chicago to New Orleans, only to find her father in the no man's land of a hospital. In "The Bride of the Innisfallen," being cut off from a defining place allows one to create the self, but in *The Optimist's Daughter*, a missing sense of place threatens rather than enhances identity. Judge McKelva, cut off from home and tied down in a New Orleans hospital, loses all will to live:

> This was like a nowhere. Even what could be seen from the high window might have been the rooftops of any city, colorless and tarpatched, with here and there small mirrors of rainwater. At first, she did not realize she could see the bridge—it stood out there dull in the distance, its function hardly evident, as if it were only another building. The river was not visible. She lowered the blind against the wide white sky that reflected it. It seemed to her that the grayed-

238

> down, anonymous room might be some reflection itself of Judge McKelva's "disturbance," his dislocated vision that had brought him here. (*OD*, 14–5)

The dislocated vision that prompted the judge to marry the selfish and superficial Fay and that ultimately destroys him is also reflected in the new part of the Mount Salus cemetery where Fay elects to bury him. There graves are "dotted uniformly with indestructible plastic Christmas poinsettias" (*OD*, 90–1). And there graveside services are conducted "upon the odorless, pistachio-green of Mr. Pitts' portable grass" (*OD*, 91). This is a nowhere that leaves the dead without context or identity. In the old part of the cemetery, however, there are "winged angels and life-sized effigies of bygone citizens in old-fashioned dress, standing as if by count among the columns and shafts and conifers like a familiar set of passengers collected on deck of a ship, on which they all knew each other—bona-fide members of a small local excursion, embarked on a voyage that is always returning in dreams" (*OD*, 89). And it is the sense of place and community and involvement represented by the life-sized effigies and by the dreams and memories they evoke that can save Laurel from the dislocated vision that afflicted her father. At the end of the novel, Laurel knows that the past has not only done everything to her, it has also done everything for her. She embraces not the freedom that anonymity can bring, but the freedom that comes from accepting, not repressing, the power of the home place. And that acceptance allows her to leave Mount Salus and any physical reminders of it. She puts down her mother's breadboard and leaves her parents' house, knowing that "memory lived not in initial possession but in the freed hands, pardoned and freed, and in the heart that can empty but fill again, in the patterns restored by dreams" (*OD*, 179). Ann Romines believes that in "this passage, Laurel has become one of Welty's voyaging brides, having internalized at last all that her mother and grandmother could give her, through their domestic culture and their valiant individual lives."[5] Romines's description of Laurel is a perceptive one. Insofar as she carries memories of home and "up home" with her, Laurel might be compared to the voyaging bride Gabriella, who at the end of "Going to Naples" is united with mother and grandmother, but there is a settled quality

5. Romines, 269.

about Laurel's future that neither the young wife who has escaped her past in "The Bride of the Innisfallen" nor Gabriella ever feel. As a result, *The Optimist's Daughter* ends with a sense *not* of anticipation, but of acceptance and completion that is absent from the earlier stories. Laurel is not a bride or a young wife; she is a mature woman who has confronted life's horrors and emerged with a chastened but affirmative vision of experience.

Just as profound change prompted Welty to write about her mother and herself and to rethink the vision of her earlier autobiographical fiction, her evolving response to the deaths of her family members prompted Welty to rewrite and rethink *The Optimist's Daughter* itself. This novel, begun in the aftermath of loss and completed as a story in 1967, was published in the *New Yorker* two years later and in an expanded, book form by Random House in 1972. The Mississippi Department of Archives and History, in addition, holds three short story drafts that precede the *New Yorker* version and one draft of a novel that succeeds it. The 1972 novel thus exists in five earlier versions, four written before June 1967 and one written in 1971. The years that elapsed between these versions surely allowed Welty to reevaluate her situation; she had lived with the magnitude of her loss, had come through the paralyzing nature of first grief, and had discovered the power of memory to defy time. The result is a novel that conveys a sense of loss more forcefully than did earlier versions, but that also is more affirmative than those versions. The result is, moreover, a novel that focuses not only upon private relationships, but also upon the social change through which Mississippi and the nation were going. The passage of time between her mother's and brother's deaths and publication of *The Optimist's Daughter* thus broadened Welty's vision as well as deepened it, enabling her to see the personal in context of the social and to produce a novel in which "there is at the end . . . a complicated sense of joy."[6]

In both the *New Yorker* story and the Random House novel, grief threatens

---

6. *The Optimist's Daughter* typescripts were opened for research at the Mississippi Department of Archives and History in April 1986, and include the typescript setting copies used by the *New Yorker* and Random House in addition to drafts of the story and novel; Price, "The Onlooker Smiling," in *A Common Room*, 67.

to destroy Laurel McKelva Hand as despair has destroyed her parents, but Laurel ultimately believes in the value of life and in the urgency human transience brings to it. In *The Optimist's Daughter*, as in its *New Yorker* predecessor, all three McKelvas seek or have sought to fill their days in a creative and generous fashion. Becky's creative endeavors—her gardening, her reading, her homemaking—sustain her; only when these activities are no longer possible is she afflicted with despair. Similarly, Judge McKelva's varied activities as lawyer, as civic leader, and as husband sustain him. Only when he is immobile and in the hospital does he languish in "a *dream* of patience" (*OD*, 23–4). And Laurel needs her work in Chicago, needs to live fully in the present moment, but after her father dies as her mother had years earlier, that need is threatened by the grief that holds Laurel suspended in time. In 1966, Welty's grief had threatened to leave her without words,[7] and she well knew the danger in which she had placed each of the McKelvas.

In fact, Welty's revisions increasingly emphasize the common danger each of the McKelvas must face. When Judge McKelva has eye surgery and is confined to a hospital bed in "An Only Child," Welty's second draft of the story, Laurel tells Fay that they'll both be needed to care for her father, noting only that "It's pretty hard to get used to being helpless, don't you think." This line was still in the story when Welty made a key holograph revision to the *New Yorker* typescript setting copy: She crossed out the word "helpless" and penned in a rather evocative phrase. When Fay, as she had in all previous drafts, tells Laurel to return to Chicago because "It's not like you'd come on a matter of life and death," Laurel replies, "Why, I'm staying for my own sake" and adds, "Father'll need all the time both of us can give him. . . . He's not used to being tied down." Laurel in *The Optimist's Daughter* uses the same expression, and there the phrase "tied down" is immediately and much more tellingly followed by Fay's retort, "O.K., that's not a matter of life and death, is it" (*OD*, 16). Yet in both the *New Yorker* story and the novel's final version, being tied down certainly is a matter of life and death. Late in both Laurel recalls her mother's last eye operation: "'Don't let them tie me down,' her mother had whispered on the evening before the last of the operations. 'If they try to hold me, I'll die'" (*OD*, 142–3). Laurel

---

7. Welty to Engel, 2 March 1966, Millsaps College.

knows that her mother is quoting her own father, who had said that very thing before he died on the operating table. And in a New Orleans hospital Laurel has linked Clinton and Becky McKelva by using the phrase "tied down" to describe him. She clearly is fearful that her father will die just as her mother had and in just as much psychological pain. Laurel recognizes that her parents share the need to use time creatively, and she knows that being tied down by illness has destroyed her mother and may destroy her father. She does not recognize her own danger, but Welty makes that danger clear to us when she describes Laurel herself as being "tied." From her first draft of the story Welty depicts Laurel's reaction to her father's imminent death in the same words: "A thousand pack-threads seemed to cross and criss-cross her skin, binding her there."[8] In the 1972 novel, however, these words appear in a more resonant context: Though Fay insists that being "tied down" is not a matter of life and death, it has been so for both Becky and Clinton McKelva, and it threatens to mean death, a death in life, for Laurel.

Other revisions intensifying Laurel's alienation came haltingly. In early versions of the story, the experience of loss does not threaten to be so debilitating as it does in the 1972 novel. In those early typescripts, Laurel thinks about her life in Chicago even as she focuses upon her father's plight. And these thoughts suggest that consoling voices and productive endeavors await Laurel in Chicago, where she will again be able to push time forward. In a passage Welty ultimately excluded from "An Only Child," Laurel thinks of a friend in Chicago as she tries to decide how she should have responded to Fay's final abuse of the judge, and she hears the friend's voice say that silence has been her only option. In the *New Yorker* Laurel recalls having been out with a friend when her father phoned to say he needed medical attention: "Her father, in the old home in Mount Salus, took pleasure in telephoning instead of writing, but this had been a late hour for him—she'd been saying goodnight to a friend after the theater." And in all early drafts, Laurel phones a friend, not just her office, when she realizes she won't be returning for some time. Even in the typescript setting copy of the

8. Eudora Welty, "An Only Child," Welty Collection, MDAH, 9; Eudora Welty, "Poor Eyes," *New Yorker* typescript setting copy, Welty Collection, MDAH, 13; Eudora Welty, "The Optimist's Daughter," *New Yorker* 45 (15 March 1969): 40; Eudora Welty, "Baltimore," Welty Collection, MDAH, 17.

Random House novel, Welty for a time retained material added in 1971 and emphasizing the emotional commitment of Laurel's life in Chicago: As Laurel looks after her father and as she brings his body home for burial, she is able to think of her work as a designer, of her passion for her profession. In the hospital, for instance, Laurel's mind wanders from her father: "As upon the stealthy opening of a door, the thought of her own work came into her mind—the design for a curtain for a new repertory theatre she'd spent recent time sketching on. She could see it as rows of small baroque figures in ones and twos, holding mandolins or swords or scarves or tambourines, bowing or dancing or dueling on their shadows in a long flowing line, black and white on a silver-gray background." And when this Laurel brings her father's body home to Mount Salus, she again thinks of her work: "The train slowed all in a moment or two for the Mount Salus stop. Laurel got to her feet, swaying with the curve, and in doing so, she got a better idea for the color of her theatre." Laurel's work gives her life focus and meaning, and she anticipates returning to it. Laurel "loved her hard work," Welty tells us. This Laurel finds that "her true gratification was in finding how each new commission opened up a new and different experience in learning, with its own beginning, middle, and end."[9] But Laurel in *The Optimist's Daughter* thinks none of these thoughts. Clearly, Welty crossed out these passages in the Random House typescript setting copy and dropped references to Laurel's Chicago friends in order to suggest how thoroughly worry and then grief cut Laurel off from life. And though leaving Mount Salus and returning to Chicago will allow her to look to the future, she may do so without the zest for living she once possessed.

Welty's revisions thus ultimately emphasize Laurel's alienation from her friends and career, from her life in the present, but revisions also emphasize that worry and grief alienate Laurel from her past. In early versions of parts 1 and 2 of the story, Laurel is not thoroughly removed from the past. In the very early typescript titled "An Only Child," when Laurel decides to read *Nicholas Nickleby* to her father, she remembers her mother: "Perhaps what was in his mind

9. Welty, "The Optimist's Daughter," *New Yorker*, 37; Welty, "The Optimist's Daughter," Random House typescript setting copy, 22, 41, 16, 16 (Welty Collection, MDAH)—each of these passages has been crossed out by hand.

243

was what had been in hers: that set of Dickens at home. It had been rescued from her burning house by Laurel's mother, and brought back to Mount Salus after her last trip 'up home'—stiff all through and water-spotted, some of the spines scorched. This would be a part of home."[10] But in later versions this reference to Laurel's mother is postponed. By 1972 Laurel may hope to reach her father's memory by reading *Nicholas Nickleby*, but she does not think back to the Dickens' volumes her mother saved. That memory comes to her only much later in the novel.

In "An Only Child," Laurel again thinks of the past, this time of a painful episode, as Missouri goes to wake Fay before the funeral. Laurel watches Missouri go to Fay with a breakfast tray, and she sees "the tray go out as if it were loaded with the memory of her mother's last years in bed, unable to help herself, when food brought to her on a tray was simply a punishment." Here Laurel is not cut off from the past, but in all subsequent versions of the story and novel, this passage has been deleted. Laurel at this point in *The Optimist's Daughter* is not ready to dredge up such painful memories. In the *New Yorker* story, Welty has revised to emphasize Laurel's inability to deal with the past, but that inability is not so thoroughgoing as it would become in the full-length novel. Indeed, in the *New Yorker* Laurel's first night in her childhood room brings her a flood of memories: "Now that she lay in her old room in her own bed, Laurel found that with a surrender she had forgotten about, and was unprepared for, she let memory take charge of her mind."[11] But by the time Welty had revised her *New Yorker* story and published it separately as *The Optimist's Daughter*, this sentence had disappeared. In the final text, Laurel is very loath to let memory take charge. She represses floods of memory, protecting herself from the sense of loss that they would intensify and avoiding the dark memories which must come with surrender.

Indeed, in the first two sections of the 1972 novel, Laurel's conscious memories of the past are few. Numbed by the shock of her father's vulnerability, illness, and death, Laurel, like Joel Mayes in "First Love," recalls the past "frugally, almost stonily" (*WN*, 6) and lives in a kind of timelessness. She is like the sea

10. Welty, "An Only Child," Welty Collection, MDAH, 13–4.
11. Ibid., 32 (hand-numbered page); Welty, "The Optimist's Daughter," *New Yorker*, 54.

gull flying beside the train that returns the judge's body to Mount Salus—"like a stopped clock on a wall" (*OD*, 45). As she drifts off to sleep in her childhood room, Laurel does think of her young parents, reading aloud to each other. But this memory is idealized. Laurel thinks not about the discord and despair that came to dominate her parents' marriage; she recalls only the harmony of their lives together. During the hours before her father's funeral, Laurel objects to the way her Mount Salus neighbors distort the past, telling stories about the judge that are not wholly accurate. But Laurel's own highly selective memory is also unreliable, its unreliability signaled by her difficulty in identifying the people who come to pay their last respects. It is only in the novel's closing pages that Laurel will find "it was no effort any longer to remember anybody" (*OD*, 163).

The degree of consistency with which Laurel blocks out the past makes her encounter with it in Part Three of the Random House novel far more dramatic than that encounter had been in earlier versions. The flood of memories that comes to Laurel during her long night in her parents' house is overwhelming in its impact, freeing her to live.

Becky's Climber, the climbing rose named after Laurel's mother, is a key emblem of memory in all versions of the story and novel, but only in the novel's final form does this emblem prefigure Laurel's complex encounter with memory. From the time of the story's second draft, Welty tells us that the judge "recalled himself" at Becky's Climber—he remembered as he came to this rose that he was pruning the climbing roses at the wrong time. Figuratively, of course, this marks the beginning of his memories of Becky, of his seeing things behind himself, and of his journey into a past he had chosen to repress in favor of being an "optimist." Laurel also recalls herself at Becky's Climber. In all but the two earliest drafts of the story, Laurel remembers her mother as she digs in her mother's garden surrounded by her mother's friends. She recognizes intellectually what in the Random House novel she will go on to accept emotionally—she recognizes the nature of memory. Laurel knows that memory, like Becky's Climber, will flourish when it has "the room it asked for" (*OD*, 114). She knows that memory has "the character of spring. In some cases, it was the old wood that did the blooming" (*OD*, 115). Becky makes room for the rose that may be a hundred years old, and it returns to bloom. Laurel will make room in her life for memory, and it will blossom. Her mother, though her recollections of the past remain vivid, does not have this sense of continuity and feels cut off from the experiences she recalls in such ideal terms. Though she tells Laurel that the rose will bloom again, if not this year then the next, she regrets the inevitability of delay: "'That's how gardeners must learn to look at it,' her mother would say" (*OD*, 114). Clearly Welty has constructed this passage to emphasize the 1972 Becky's *reluctant* patience. In the *New Yorker* story, Laurel remembers her mother saying, "That's how gardeners look at it," not "must learn to look at it."[12] And the flowering of memory cannot bring Becky in either incarnation even a resigned hopefulness; it cannot provide her with sufficient compensation for loss. In the Random House novel, however, it does so for Laurel. After the night in which she is trapped alone in her parents' bedroom, Laurel, like Eudora Welty, will accept memory as life's most reliable source of continuity, as life's most secure defense against loss, as her "treasure most dearly regarded" (*OWB*, 104).

In *The Optimist's Daughter* (1972), the issues involved in her dark night of the soul are a matter of grave consequence to Laurel. If she does not gain full access to the past, she may continue to be tied down and to lack faith in the significance of her own endeavors; she may continue to believe that love is lost through time. Welty thus changed the *New Yorker* version of the text to make this scene in Part Three of the Random House novel far more intense. And in the final version of the novel, Welty makes Laurel's recovery of lost time far more complete. In the hospital Laurel breaks free from the packthreads that bind her and runs to her father; during her night alone in the house, she moves toward memory, the past, and freedom. Story versions of the novel scarcely mention Laurel's dead husband Philip, but the published novel deals with Philip and with Laurel's recollections of him. And in doing so, the novel develops major ideas not present in its earlier forms.

Welty had evidently once worked on a short story about a young woman who was widowed during World War II, but she never completed or published this story. Instead she used that concept in *The Optimist's Daughter*. In an incomplete typescript that dates from 1967, Welty attempted to incorporate Phil into the story she would publish in the *New Yorker*, but unable to do so, she put the

---

12. Welty, "An Only Child," Welty Collection, MDAH, n. pag.; Welty, "The Optimist's Daughter," *New Yorker*, 93.

material into a folder with a note instructing herself to "omit this part for now." In these omitted pages, Philip is an artist who fills his sketchbook with drawings of the birds he loves; Laurel too is an artist, but she gives up painting for design after her husband, who has become a wartime pilot, is shot down over the Pacific Ocean. Though this Laurel's recollections of Phil are idealized, they are not locked away. "The reminder of loss was still a part of her conscious effort to live," Welty writes, "but was familiar now, almost in the nature of a comfort. Losing your love was like being given a compass, though too late for the journey." For this Laurel, memory seems to provide understanding and consolation but never joy. Neither her constant openness to the memory of Philip nor her response to that memory is appropriate to the Random House novel. Welty thus had to alter her concept of Philip and his effect upon Laurel, but in expanding the *New Yorker* text, Welty included much more information about the new Phil than she could ultimately keep.[13] An excited, portentous meeting of Laurel and Phil at the Art Institute in Chicago, specific examples of Phil's practical abilities—these are passages that Welty later omitted. The cut passages would have framed the richness of Laurel's life with Phil rather than stressing her need to recognize the meaning of loss and memory. With Philip, Welty tells us, Laurel has falsified the past—refused to acknowledge what pain might have come their way, refused to recognize how desperately Phil would have wanted life instead of a perfect past. Only when she is able to remember how much Phil relished the challenges of living, how much he valued process over product, will Laurel's acceptance of the past be complete. Only when she confronts the death of her young husband as well as that of her elderly father will she be able to see finally the true importance of memory, the continuity it provides.

In Part Four of *The Optimist's Daughter*, its final section and the section immediately following her night of memory, Laurel comes to such a realization. In the *New Yorker* version of the novel, Laurel's access to the past has been more selective, and as a consequence, the prospects for her future seem less sanguine

13. Eudora Welty, "An Only Child" 1967, omitted pages, Welty Collection, MDAH, n. pag.; see Sally Wolff's essay "'Among Those Missing': Phil Hand's Disappearance from *The Optimist's Daughter*," *Southern Literary Journal* 25 (1992): 74–88, for a full discussion of the way Welty added and then deleted information about Phil Hand as she rewrote the *New Yorker* version of the novel.

than they do in the 1972 novel. Part IV of the *New Yorker* story begins with Laurel restored to time after facing harrowing memories of her mother and father only. Having put her parents' house in order and having gone through their effects, Laurel chooses to take one memento back to Chicago. As would be the case in the novel, Laurel takes the stone boat her father had made for her mother, but she keeps the object here as an artificial spur to memory:

> She had dropped the little stone boat, just as she'd found it, into her big Chicago handbag for her fingers to come upon some busy day. It was stolen from this house; she was a thief now. At the same time, having it there in her bag was a way to go back to Chicago. It was one of her ways to live—storing up to remember, putting aside to forget, then to find again—hiding and finding. Laurel thought it a modest game that people could play by themselves, and, of course, when that's too easy, against themselves. It was a game for the bereaved, and there wasn't much end to it.

For this Laurel memory does not flower naturally as Becky's Climber does; memory is something to be manipulated. It is a kind of game, and a rather sad one at that. Laurel is in retreat. She burns her mother's papers, and that act in the *New Yorker* and earlier versions marks Laurel's attempt to protect her mother from Fay. Laurel realizes this fact when she discovers Becky's breadboard and sees the way Fay has misused and defaced it:

> As she held it there, all the pride she had felt in the cleaning, the polishing, the burning of evidence, in all she had driven herself to do, changed suddenly and wholly into shame. Shame beat inside her, thudded against her chest.
>
> She had conspired with silence, when she ought to have shouted "Abuse!" And perhaps shouted also "Love!" There was nothing in the whole house now to show for her mother's life and her mother's happiness and suffering, and nothing to show for Fay's harm; her father's turning between them, holding onto them both, then letting them go, was without its meaning. She herself had made it all shining surface, sweet smells, a drift of smoke. The house itself, in that moment, seemed to have died.

In this passage from the *New Yorker* story, we see that Laurel, after confronting the past the previous night, has gone on the next day to falsify it. She does finally accuse Fay of never loving her father, and she does finally leave the breadboard and walk away from the house. Tish says Laurel has made it by the skin of her teeth, but Laurel has not realized that the past is invulnerable and that memory need not rely upon objects like the little boat. Laurel in this version seems to be saving her integrity and dignity in the face of Fay's challenge, but she also seems unable to come to terms with her experience. The more appropriate ending to this version of the story might be the one Welty rejected after writing "An Only Child": "'We can still make it,' said Tish when Laurel was seated between her and Gert and the car was rolling into the leaf-hung street. 'There, now.' And Gert said, 'What a day to leave Mount Salus! Listen to the mocking bird.'" The mocking song of the bird suggests the very limited victory Laurel has achieved. She has repressed thoughts of her husband's death, she has not asked Fay about the judge's death, and she flees in the face of Fay's challenge to her memories. Life in the present, disconnected from the "whole solid past" (*OD*, 178), seems to be all Laurel can salvage.[14]

The final section of the Random House novel, however, is more hopeful than that of the story. After Laurel has recalled the agony of losing Philip and has acknowledged Phil's "craving for his unlived life" (*OD,* 154), she gains full access to her past. She also gains full access to her emotional life. Part Four of *The Optimist's Daughter* begins as Laurel awakes with a sense of joy from the dream she has just had, the dream of a train journey with Philip, a journey from Chicago to Mount Salus, a journey past the confluence of the Ohio and Mississippi Rivers. And on waking Laurel knows that the confluence of rivers is like the confluence of lives, and she knows that a growing and evolving, not a static, understanding of the past is the source of a vital connection with her lost husband.

---

14. Welty's actual father made just such a stone boat for his future bride, Chestina Andrews; Welty, "The Optimist's Daughter," *New Yorker*, 125–6, 127; Welty, "An Only Child," n. pag.; both Michael Kreyling and Helen Tiegreen share this view of the *New Yorker* version of Laurel. Kreyling writes that "Laurel leaves Mount Salus, in the story, without affirming the continuity in life" (*Eudora Welty's Achievement of Order,* 172). And Tiegreen asserts that "the Laurel of the original story confronts her crisis and works through it, but she does not reach a point of comprehension; one imagines her returning to Chicago to nearly the same life she had before" ("Mothers, Daughters, and One Writer's Revisions," in *Welty, A Life in Literature*, ed. Albert Devlin [Jackson: University Press of Mississippi, 1987], 192).

Life, she realizes, is "nothing but the continuity of its love" (*OD*, 160). In her early incarnations, Laurel had never confronted her loss of Philip and had never come to this realization. But Laurel in her last incarnation feels sure that whether death comes early or late, to the young or the old, love's continuity can provide a sort of immortality. The novel's final section thus begins on a victorious note—this Laurel has suffered more deeply from memory than have her predecessors, but her rewards are already far greater. And this Laurel will not only accept memory's double legacy, but will also confront Fay. When Fay enters the house, Laurel asks, as she had in the *New Yorker*, why Fay has dirtied and gouged Becky's breadboard. But in the novel Philip has made the breadboard. It is an emblem of his love for Becky, of his creativity, of his respect for order and form; it is an emblem for values Fay cannot comprehend. Laurel's concern with the breadboard seems far more significant here than it had in earlier versions. Moreover, Laurel's confrontation with Fay here is a far more honest one. This Laurel asks the big question about Fay's attempt to pull the judge from his hospital bed, an attempt that precipitated the judge's death: "What were you trying to scare Father into—when you struck him" (*OD*, 175). No longer does Laurel conspire with silence and stifle her anger. She shouts "Abuse!" through her question. And when Laurel leaves the house and the breadboard to Fay, she is not in retreat. Like Phil, she recognizes that, though the work of an artist or craftsman may be physically defaced, the memory of the creative act endures. She leaves knowing that the ability to face the past as openly as possible, to recognize that an understanding of the past is not fixed but is "vulnerable to the living moment," and to bear the pain a comprehensive vision will inevitably bring ensures that the past continues to live, that love can be continuous. And Laurel further knows that no object, no stone boat, no breadboard is necessary to prompt the memory. Laurel may have burned her mother's papers in a wrongheaded effort to protect the past from Fay, but her burning of them affirms the freedom of her hands and the self-sufficiency of her memory. "Experience," she has realized in another context, "did, finally, get set into its right order, which is not always the order of other people's time" (*OD*, 174). Welty thus modifies the implications of events that she had included in previous story versions of the novel— Laurel's burning of her mother's papers, the encounter between Laurel and Fay,

Laurel's relinquishment of the breadboard—and these modifications complement Welty's revised concept of the nature and power of memory.

Distance in time from devastating personal losses thus seems to have enabled Welty to make *The Optimist's Daughter* at once more tough-minded and more affirmative. It also seems to have widened her vision, for many revisions suggest that memory may guide the direction of public as well as private change. As Welty rewrote *The Optimist's Daughter*, traditionally southern ways of life were undergoing radical transformation, and she chose quite naturally to deal with a social change that emphasized a need for the continuity of love rather than hate. With the rise of the civil rights movement and the push for racial justice in the 1960s, the degree of black activism and the virulence of white racism destroyed the facade of gratitude and concern that had characterized the South. That facade, like the facade of a building, was destined to change with time, but Welty clearly hoped that tolerance and openness would become heartfelt commitments. In *The Optimist's Daughter* Judge McKelva clearly has opposed white racists throughout his legal career, and the memory of his actions ensures that his commitment to justice has not died with him. In all typescripts of the story, Major Bullock lionizes the judge for facing down Klansmen who wanted to take the law into their own hands. Probably he is distorting the past—the judge has not been a crusader—but this distortion tells us that Judge McKelva never accepted the methods of white supremacists and that the judge's values endure, though in melodramatic clothing. In the final version of *The Optimist's Daughter*, Welty adds a conversation indicating that Laurel too recalls her father's immunity from racism. When Bullock tells the story of a "got shot witness" the judge had located for a trial, Laurel identifies the witness as the McKelvas' maid Missouri and comments: "He brought her here afterwards and kept her safe under his own roof" (*OD*, 81). Laurel's vision of her father is still selective at this point in the novel, but this memory is an important part of the judge's legacy to his daughter. She knows that he did not feign concern for Missouri; he truly cared about her welfare. He saw the common humanity of blacks and whites and never embraced a politically expedient racism. In the novel's final form, Welty has the black citizens of Mount Salus remember this all too unusual quality in the judge, for when he dies, they dress themselves in black and attend the funeral (*OD*, 89). Perhaps they sense that white people like the judge have

251

provided the civil rights movement with a strategic "moral and political re-source," to use David Chappell's words and concept[15]; perhaps they feel that white people like the judge have enhanced the prospects for a more egalitarian political and social system, for overcoming the Fays of the world who do not wish to note their presence even at a funeral. Perhaps by living a life of love and fairness and by having those principles remembered, Welty thus suggests, indi-viduals like the judge can help to effect needed change.

Race is not the only public issue of continuity and change that Welty ad-dresses in the novel's final version. She also depicts the decline of small-town ways of life. When Laurel returns to Mount Salus, the old-fashioned town she once knew has become quite modern in its appearance and its customs. Not all of its modern developments are necessarily objectionable to Laurel or to Welty, but many of them do show a concern with speed and convenience as opposed to order and tradition. Though in all versions of the novel the cemetery's new and old sections are sharply different, only in the final version is the cemetery set on the edge of an interstate highway. And only in the final version does Lau-rel hear the highway traffic from her bedroom. Other ugly monuments to mo-dernity adorn Mount Salus in the 1972 novel. Dr. Woodson tells mourners at Judge McKelva's funeral about a youthful adventure in the woods outside town and then adds that the adventure took place "where the Self-Serve Car Wash is now" (*OD*, 74). In the 1972 novel, suburban sprawl has come to Mount Salus, and Laurel's bridesmaids have mostly moved into the town's new additions. And only in the novel's ultimate form does Welty stress the changing sexual mores of the modern South, for only in this version does Tish's son have his girl friend arrive for visits through his bedroom window. The altered face and the new cus-toms of her hometown endanger Laurel's sense of continuity with her past. She needs to live in the present, to move on with her life, but she also needs to be-lieve that "passionate things, in some essence, endure" (*ES*, 299). Neither the physical world nor the social scene can provide that sense of continuity—only an evolving, living memory can. And by 1972 Laurel has come fully to under-stand, and Welty to reaffirm, the nature and the importance of memory. They know, as Welty wrote in 1944, that "new life will be built upon" the memory

15. Chappell, xxv.

of "whatever is significant and whatever is tragic"—"regardless of commerce and the way of rivers and roads, and other vagrancies" (*ES*, 299).

*The Optimist's Daughter* as it now exists is thus a far more affirmative and more carefully built work than it had been in any of its earlier incarnations. In her final version Welty looks at time, at the fragility of human life, at the importance of memory in more complex ways than she had in earlier drafts, yet her conclusions are more positive than the conclusions she had earlier reached. And in her final version Welty alters plot and setting, establishing their integral relationship to her revised concepts of character and theme. As a photographer Welty realized that "trouble, even to the point of disaster, has its pale, and these defiant things of the spirit repeatedly go beyond it, joy the same as courage" (*OTOP*, 6). *The Optimist's Daughter* bears witness to the triumph of "these defiant things of the spirit" in the life of Laurel Hand and to the triumph of artistry in the life of her creator, Eudora Welty.

X

# One Writer's Imagination

In 1984 when Eudora Welty revised and published her Harvard University William E. Massey Lectures in the History of American Civilization, she titled her book *One Writer's Beginnings*. In that book, as in her lectures, she attempted to explain how and why she became a writer. She discussed her family life and the influence of her parents and brothers upon her. She wrote of family tragedies and of good times, of love and of tension. She talked about her community and her state, her friends, her education, and her travels. Welty's comments about her beginnings as a writer are perceptive and instructive, and they place her somewhat in the tradition of the modernist creators Howard Gardner discusses in his book *Creating Minds*. But ultimately, neither Welty nor Gardner can explain why one individual becomes a creator and another does not. As both would acknowledge, the source of creativity remains a wonderful mystery. What artists and scholars can do, however, is to describe both the way creative individuals find their imaginations sparked and the course the creative imagination takes once it has been lit. Thanks to Welty's autobiography, her critical essays, her many published interviews, and her generous discussions with me, we know

254

a good deal about her imagination as it operated between 1936 and 1972 and thanks to psychological studies of creativity, we know that Welty's imaginative process is a rather representative one.

In her earliest stories, Welty responded most strongly to the world around her, to its sights and sounds, its personalities and its conversations. In a phrase or an image, in a "fractal chip of vision," Welty repeatedly discovered the metaphors that animated the stories to be collected in *A Curtain of Green*. Soon, however, stories began to emerge from memory, and Welty realized what Elizabeth Bowen would say in 1945, "Remote memories, already distorted by the imagination, are the most useful."[1] Such memories are crucial to *The Robber Bridegroom*, *The Wide Net*, and *Delta Wedding*. In *The Golden Apples*, of course, Welty found herself most fully able to unite the two major sources for her imagination as she wrote during years of pivotal change for Mississippi and herself. Once she had achieved that union, she cast herself adrift in new territory: In *The Bride of the Innisfallen*, Welty rendered personal experiences, especially travel experiences, more extensively than she ever had before, and she wrote of characters who were not rooted in time or place, as they had typically been in her earlier works, and who were consequently able to create themselves. In "Where is the Voice Coming From?" and "The Demonstrators," Welty confronted political issues explicitly rather than obliquely. And in both *Losing Battles* and *The Optimist's Daughter*, Welty relied upon the sort of personal experiences and memories she had begun to use in *The Bride of the Innisfallen*, but she also returned to the very specific times and places that had characterized her work before 1955. Writing at the end of the 1960s, Welty knew that her life, her profession, and her culture were undergoing tremendous changes, and her sense of being once again at "a crossing of the ways" seems to have prompted her to write and to reassess the importance of rootedness.

Welty's imagination thus traveled along a varied route during her almost forty years as a fiction writer, but there were constants in her imaginative course. Throughout her career, from the publication of *A Curtain of Green* to the con-

---

1. Briggs, 282; Bowen, "Notes on Writing a Novel," 40.

clusion of *The Optimist's Daughter*, whether she was writing about the contemporary world or about times past, whether she found her inspiration in travel or at home, Welty's imagination thrived upon polarities that characterized her personal life and her perceptions of the society at large. Frank Barron's contention that "the strife between opposites is an important source of energy for an evolving new synthesis" certainly describes the energy that led to synthesis after synthesis in Welty's fiction.[2] The opposites that Virgie Rainey knows to be "of the closest blood" are the opposites of Powerhouse's simultaneous connection and alienation, the contradictory elements that Clement Musgrove sees in Jamie Lockhart, the birth and death associated with Aunt Studney's sack, the joy and sorrow of Gabriella's arrival in Naples, the doubling and redoubling portraits of the Beecham-Renfro clan and Miss Julia Mortimer, and the converging duality of love and loss in Laurel Hand's memory.

This much we know of one writer's imagination. Much, much more remains unknown and unknowable, and that very mystery is at the heart of Eudora Welty's fiction.

2. Barron, 81.

# Bibliography

## Works by Eudora Welty

*The Bride of the Innisfallen and Other Stories*. New York: Harcourt, Brace and Company, 1955.

"The Bride of the Innisfallen." *New Yorker* 27 (1 December 1951): 53–56, 58, 60, 62, 64, 66, 68, 70–4, 77–84.

*Bye-Bye Brevoort*. Jackson: New Stage Theatre, 1980.

*A Curtain of Green*. New York: Doubleday, Doran and Company, 1941.

"Clytie." *Southern Review* 7 (Summer 1941): 52–64.

"Death of a Traveling Salesman." *Manuscript* 3 (May–June 1936): 21–9.

"The Demonstrators." In *The Collected Stories of Eudora Welty*, 608–22. New York: Harcourt Brace Jovanovich, 1980.

*Delta Wedding*. New York: Harcourt, Brace and Company, 1946.

"Elizabeth Bowen's *Pictures and Conversations*." In *The Eye of the Story*, 169–76. New York: Random House, 1979.

"Fairy Tale of the Natchez Trace." In *The Eye of the Story*, 300–14. New York: Random House, 1979.

"From Where I Live." *Delta Review* 6 (1969): 69.

*The Golden Apples*. New York: Harcourt, Brace and Company, 1949.

"Golden Apples." *Harper's Bazaar*, September 1947, 216–17, 286, 288–90, 295–302, 305–7, 311–20.

"The Hitch-Hikers." *Southern Review* 5 (Autumn 1939): 293–307.

*Losing Battles*. New York: Random House, 1970.

"Looking Back at the First Story." *Georgia Review* 33 (1979): 751–55.

"Must the Novelist Crusade?" In *The Eye of the Story*, 146–58. New York: Random House, 1979.

"Old Mr. Grenada." *Southern Review* 3 (Spring 1938): 707–13.

*One Time, One Place*. New York: Random House, 1971.

*One Writer's Beginnings*. Cambridge, Mass.: Harvard University Press, 1984.

"The Optimist's Daughter." *New Yorker* 45 (15 March 1969): 37–46, 48, 50, 53–4, 56, 61–2, 64, 67–8, 70, 75–6, 78,81–2, 84, 86, 88, 93–5, 98, 100, 103–6, 111–4, 117–20, 125–8.

*The Optimist's Daughter*. New York: Random House, 1972.

*Photographs*. Jackson: University Press of Mississippi, 1989.

"A Piece of News." *Southern Review* 3 (Summer 1937): 80–4.

"Place in Fiction." In *The Eye of the Story*, 116–33. New York: Random House, 1978.

*The Ponder Heart*. New York: Harcourt, Brace and Company, 1954.

"Put Me in the Sky!" *Accent* 10 (Autumn 1949): 3–10.

*The Robber Bridegroom*. New York: Doubleday, Doran, and Company, 1942.

"A Sketching Trip." *Atlantic Monthly* 175 (June 1945): 62–70.

"Some Notes on River Country." In *The Eye of the Story*, 286–99. New York: Random House, 1979.

"Some Notes on Time in Fiction." In *The Eye of the Story*, 163–73. New York: Random House, 1979.

"Voice of the People." *Jackson Clarion-Ledger*, 28 December 1945.

"What Stevenson Started." *New Republic*, 5 January 1953, 8.

"Where is the Voice Coming From?" In *The Collected Stories of Eudora Welty*, 603–7. New York: Harcourt Brace Jovanovich, 1980.

"The Whistle." *Prairie Schooner* 12 (Fall 1938): 210–15.

"The Whole World Knows." *Harper's Bazaar*, March 1947, 198–9, 332–8.

*The Wide Net and Other Stories*. New York: Harcourt, Brace and Company, 1943.

"Words into Fiction." In *The Eye of the Story*, 134–45. New York: Random House, 1979.

*A Writer's Eye: Collected Book Reviews*. Ed. Pearl Amelia McHaney. Jackson: University Press of Mississippi, 1994.

"Writing and Analyzing a Story." In *The Eye of the Story*, 107–15. New York: Random House, 1979.

## Manuscripts, Unpublished Correspondence, and Other Archival Materials

Adams, John Quincy. Papers and Audio Tapes. Faculty Papers, Series F. Millsaps College Archives, Jackson, Mississippi.

Aswell, Mary Louise. Letters to Eudora Welty, restricted papers. Welty (Eudora Alice) Collection. Mississippi Department of Archives and History, Jackson, Mississippi.

Finger, H. E. Administrative Papers, Series A1. Millsaps College Archives, Jackson, Mississippi.

Jackson, Jesse. Letter to the *New Yorker*, restricted papers. Welty (Eudora Alice) Collection. Mississippi Department of Archives and History, Jackson, Mississippi. Photocopy.

Minutes of Faculty Meeting, 24 January 1963, Series B. Millsaps College Archives, Jackson, Mississippi.

Robinson, Nancy McDougall. Diaries 1832–1873. Mississippi Department of Archives and History, Jackson, Mississippi.

Russell, Diarmuid. Letters to Eudora Welty, restricted papers. Welty (Eudora Alice) Collection. Mississippi Department of Archives and History, Jackson, Mississippi.

Social Sciences Forum Announcements. Tougaloo College Archives, Tougaloo, Mississippi.

"Waverley." Subject file. Mississippi Department of Archives and History, Jackson, Mississippi.

Welty, Chestina. "The Perfect Garden." Unpublished essay. Marrs's personal collection.

Welty, Eudora. Letters to Elizabeth Bowen. Bowen (Elizabeth) Collection. Harry Ransom Humanities Research Center, University of Texas, Austin, Texas.

———. Letters to Lehman Engel. Engel (Lehman) Papers. Millsaps-Wilson Library, Millsaps College, Jackson, Mississippi.

———. Letter to Suzanne Marrs, n.d. Marrs's personal collection.

———. Letters to Katherine Anne Porter. Papers of Katherine Anne Porter, Special Collections, University of Maryland Libraries, College Park, Maryland.

———. Manuscripts: Fiction ("Beautiful Ohio," "The Children," "Delta Cousins," "The Flower and the Rock," various drafts of *Losing Battles*, various drafts of *The Optimist's Daughter*, "Stories," and an untitled draft of "Where is the Voice Coming From?"); Drama ("What Year Is This?"); Non-Fiction (William E. Massey Lectures, Southern Literary Festival Speech [23 April 1965]); Correspondence (Letters to Mary Louise Aswell [restricted], John F. Robinson, Diarmuid Russell [restricted], John Woodburn); Photographs. Welty (Eudora Alice) Collection. Mississippi Department of Archives and History, Jackson, Mississippi.

———. Written comments on draft of an unpublished lecture by Suzanne Marrs. Marrs's personal collection. 19 September 1990.

Woodburn, John. Letters to Eudora Welty. Welty (Eudora Alice) Collection. Mississippi Department of Archives and History, Jackson, Mississippi.

## Interviews

### Interviews with Eudora Welty

#### Published

Prenshaw, Peggy W., ed. *Conversations with Eudora Welty*. Jackson: University Press of Mississippi, 1984. Interviews by Charles T. Bunting, Charlotte Capers, Walter Clemons, *Commentary* magazine, Scot Haller, John Griffin Jones, and Linda Kuehl.

————. *More Conversations with Eudora Welty*. Jackson: University Press of Mississippi, 1996. Interviews by Hunter McKelva Cole and Seetha Srinivasan, and Charles Ruas.

#### Unpublished

Marrs, Suzanne. Personal interviews, 19 September 1985, 7 December 1985, 14 November 1986.

Marrs, Suzanne, and Mary Hughes Brookhart. Personal interview, 23 July 1983.

### Other Interviews

Marrs, Suzanne. Interview with Richard Ford. Public Radio in Mississippi. 4 March 1986.

————. Interview with Barry Hannah. Public Radio in Mississippi. 4 March 1986.

————. Personal interviews with Patti Carr Black, March 1997.

————. Personal interviews with R. Edwin King, 20 March 1997, 7 April 1997, 19 June 1997.

————. Personal interview with Ann Morrison, September 1999.

————. Personal interviews with Jane Reid Petty, March 1997.

————. Personal interview with Reynolds Price, 25 October 1998.

## Books, Articles, Dissertations, and Other Sources

Adkins, Howard Glenn. "The Historical Geography of Extinct Towns in Mississippi." Ph.D. diss. University of Tennessee, 1972.

Appel, Alfred. *A Season of Dreams: The Fiction of Eudora Welty*. Baton Rouge: Louisiana State University Press, 1965.

Audubon, John James. *Journal of John James Audubon, Made during his Trip to New Orleans in 1820–1821*. Ed. Howard Corning. Cambridge, Mass.: Business Historical Society, 1929.

Baker, Jean. *The Stevensons: A Biography of an American Family*. New York: W. W. Norton & Co., 1996.

Barron, Frank. "Putting Creativity to Work." In *The Nature of Creativity: Contemporary Psychological Perspectives*, ed. Robert J. Sternberg, 76–98. Cambridge and New York: Cambridge University Press, 1988.

"Bilbo and Rankin Get Blessings of Former Huey Long Chieftain." *Jackson Clarion-Ledger*, 20 December 1945.

Black, Patti Carr, ed. *Eudora*. Jackson, Mississippi: Mississippi Department of Archives and History, 1984.

Bowen, Elizabeth. "Book Shelf." Review of *Delta Wedding*. *The Tatler and Bystander*, 6 August 1947, 183.

———. "Notes on Writing a Novel." In *The Mulberry Tree: Writings of Elizabeth Bowen*, ed. Hermione Lee, 35–48. San Diego, New York, London: Harcourt Brace Jovanovich, 1986.

———. "Out of a Book." In *The Mulberry Tree: Writings of Elizabeth Bowen*, ed. Hermione Lee, 48–53. San Diego, New York, London: Harcourt Brace Jovanovich, 1986.

Briggs, John. *Fire in the Crucible: The Alchemy of Creative Genius*. New York: St. Martin's Press, 1988.

Brookhart, Mary Hughes. "The Search for Lost Time in the Early Fiction of Eudora Welty." Ph.D. diss. University of North Carolina (Chapel Hill), 1981.

Brooks, Cleanth. "American Literature: Mirror, Lens, or Prism?" In *A Shaping Joy: Studies in the Writer's Craft*, 166–80. New York: Harcourt Brace Jovanovich, 1971.

Bullock, Alan. *Hitler: A Study in Tyranny*. New York: Harper and Row, 1962.

Burger, Nash K. "Eudora Welty's Jackson." *Shenandoah* 20, no. 3 (1969): 8–15.

———. "Eudora Welty's Monsieur Boule and Other Friends: A Memoir of Good Times." *Southern Quarterly* 32, no. 1 (1993): 40–48.

Burrus, John N. "Urbanization in Mississippi, 1890–1970." In *A History of Mississippi*, ed. Richard Aubrey McLemore, vol. 2, 346–74. Hattiesburg: University and College Press of Mississippi, 1973.

Carson, Franklin D. "'The Song of Wandering Aengus': Allusions in Eudora Welty's *The Golden Apples*." *Notes on Mississippi Writers* 6 (Spring 1973): 14–7.

Carter, Hodding. *So the Heffners Left McComb*. New York: Doubleday, 1965.

Chappell, David L. *Inside Agitators: White Southerners in the Civil Rights Movement*. Baltimore: Johns Hopkins University Press, 1994.

Chengges, Catherine. "Textual Variants in 'Old Mr. Marblehall.'" *Eudora Welty Newsletter* 10, no. 2 (1986): 1–6.

Claiborne, J.F.H. *Mississippi as a Province, Territory and State*. Jackson: Power and Barksdale, 1880.

Clark, Charles. "*The Robber Bridegroom*: Realism and Fantasy on the Natchez Trace." *Mississippi Quarterly* 26 (Fall 1973): 625–38.

Clark, Thomas D. "Changes in Transportation." In *A History of Mississippi*, ed. Richard Aubrey McLemore, vol. 2, 274–311. Hattiesburg: University and College Press of Mississippi, 1973.

"Cloud-Cuckoo Symphony." *Time*, 22 April 1946, 104, 106, 108.

Coates, Robert. *The Outlaw Years: The History of the Land Pirates of the Natchez Trace.* New York: Macaulay, 1930.

Cole, Hunter McKelva. "Windsor in Spencer and Welty: A Real and Imaginary Landscape." *Notes on Mississippi Writers* 7 (Spring 1974): 2–11.

Creekmore, Hubert. "That Man Bilbo." *Time*, 22 October 1934, 2.

———. *The Welcome.* New York: Appleton-Century-Crofts, 1948.

Cunningham, W. J. *Agony at Galloway: One Church's Struggle with Social Change.* Jackson: University Press of Mississippi, 1980.

Curley, Daniel. "Eudora Welty and the Quondam Obstruction." *Studies in Short Fiction* 5 (Spring 1968): 209–24.

Davidson, Donald. "The New South and the Conservative Tradition." *National Review* 9 (10 September 1960): 141–6.

DeLaughter, Jerry. "Miss Welty Opens Literary Festival." *Jackson Clarion-Ledger*, 19 April 1963, sec. A.

Devlin, Albert J. *Eudora Welty's Chronicle: A Story of Mississippi Life.* Jackson: University Press of Mississippi, 1983.

———. "Eudora Welty's Historicism: Method and Vision." *Mississippi Quarterly* 30 (Spring 1977): 213–34.

———. "From Horse to Heron: A Source for Eudora Welty." *Notes on Mississippi Writers* 10, no. 2 (1977): 62–9.

———. "The Making of *Delta Wedding*." In *Biographies of Books*, ed. James Barbour and Tom Quick, 226–61. Columbia: University of Missouri Press, 1996.

———. "Meeting the World in *Delta Wedding*." In *Critical Essays on Eudora Welty*, ed. Craig Turner and Lee Harding, 90–109. Boston: G. K. Hall, 1990.

*Dictionary of American Biography.* s.v. "Rankin, John."

Dorsey, L.C. *Freedom Came to Mississippi.* New York: Field Foundation, 1977.

Dow, Lorenzo. *History of Cosmopolite: Or the Writings of Lorenzo Dow.* 6th ed. Cincinnati and Philadelphia: Rulison, 1856.

East, Charles. "The Search for Eudora Welty." *Mississippi Quarterly* 26 (Fall 1973): 477–82.

Eliot, T. S. *The Waste Land: A Facsimile and Transcript of the Original Drafts Including the*

*Annotations of Ezra Pound*, ed. Valerie Eliot. New York: Harcourt Brace Jovanovich, 1971.

Emerson, Ralph Waldo. "Self-Reliance." In *Selections from Ralph Waldo Emerson*, ed. Stephen E. Whicher, 147–68. Cambridge, Mass.: Riverside Press, 1957.

Emmerich, John. "McComb Editor Sought Moderation in Explosive Summer." *Jackson Clarion-Ledger*, 1 July 1984, sec. H.

Engel, Lehman. *This Bright Day: An Autobiography*. New York: Macmillan, 1974.

Ethridge, Tom. "Mississippi Notebook." *Jackson Clarion-Ledger*, 29 May 1963.

Faulkner, William. "William Faulkner's Speech of Acceptance upon the Award of the Nobel Prize for Literature." In *The Faulkner Reader: Selections from the Works of William Faulkner*, 3–4. New York: Random House, 1954.

Ferguson, Mary Anne. "Losing Battles as Comic Epic in Prose." In *Eudora Welty: Critical Essays*, ed. Peggy W. Prenshaw, 305–24. Jackson: University Press of Mississippi, 1979.

Friedman, Susan Stanford. "Women's Autobiographical Selves: Theory and Practice." In *The Private Self: Theory and Practice of Women's Biographical Writings*, ed. Shari Benstock, 34–62. Chapel Hill: University of North Carolina Press, 1988.

Gardner, Howard. *Creating Minds: An Anatomy of Creativity Seen Through the Lives of Freud, Einstein, Picasso, Stravinsky, Eliot, Graham, and Gandhi*. New York: Basic Books, 1993.

"Giant Soviet Dam Again is Reported Blasted by U.S.S.R." *Jackson Clarion-Ledger*, 28 August 1941.

Goodman, Walter. *The Committee: The Extraordinary Career of the House Committee on Un-American Activities*. New York: Farrar, Straus, Giroux, 1968.

Grasmick, Harold. "Social Change and the Wallace Movement in the South." Ph.D. diss. University of North Carolina (Chapel Hill), 1973.

Griffin, Dorothy. "The House as Container: Architecture and Myth in *Delta Wedding*." In *Welty: A Life in Literature*, ed. Albert J. Devlin, 96–112. Jackson: University Press of Mississippi, 1987.

Hains, Frank. "On Stage—Eudora Welty's 'Ponder Heart': A Message of Love Needed Now." *Jackson Daily News*, 17 May 1970, sec. C.

Halberstam, David. *The Fifties*. New York: Villard Books, 1993.

Hamblin, Robert W. "Robert Penn Warren at the 1965 Southern Literary Festival: A Personal Recollection." *Southern Literary Journal* 22 (Spring 1990): 53–62.

Hammond, Martha H. "Dialogue: New Stage Theatre and Jackson, Mississippi." Ph.D. diss., University of Southern Mississippi, 1994.

Hauck, Richard Boyd. *A Cheerful Nihilism: Confidence and "The Absurd" in American Humorous Fiction*. Bloomington, Indiana: Indiana University Press, 1971.

Heilbrun, Carolyn. *Writing a Woman's Life*. New York: W. W. Norton & Co., 1988.

Hickman, Nollie W. "Mississippi Forests." In *A History of Mississippi*, ed. Richard Aubrey McLemore, vol. 2, 212–32. Hattiesburg: University and College Press of Mississippi, 1973.

Hills, Charles. "Affairs of State." *Jackson Clarion-Ledger*, 6 June 1963, sec. A.

Homer. *The Odyssey*. Translated by E. V. Rieu. Baltimore: Penguin Books, 1946.

Howard, H. R., comp. *The History of Virgil A. Stewart*. Reprint, Spartanburg, S.C.: Reprint Company Publishers, 1976.

"Jackson Is Unique in its Unity." Editorial. *Jackson Clarion-Ledger*, 29 May 1963.

Jones, Anne Goodwyn. *Tomorrow Is Another Day: The Woman Writer in the South, 1859–1936*. Baton Rouge: Louisiana State University Press, 1981.

———. "Every Woman Loves a Fascist: Writing World War II on the Southern Home Front." In *Remaking Dixie: The Impact of World War II on the American South*, ed. Neil R. McMillen, 111–30. Jackson: University Press of Mississippi, 1997.

Kahl, Joseph. *The Measurement of Modernism: A Study of Values in Brazil and Mexico*. Austin: University of Texas Press, 1968.

Kazin, Alfred. *On Native Grounds: An Interpretation of Modern American Prose Literature*. New York: Reynal and Hitchcock, 1942.

Kreyling, Michael. *Author and Agent: Eudora Welty and Diarmuid Russell*. New York: Farrar, Straus, and Giroux, 1991.

———. *Eudora Welty's Achievement of Order*. Baton Rouge: Louisiana State University Press, 1980.

Landess, Thomas H. "More Trouble in Mississippi: Family vs. Antifamily in Miss Welty's *Losing Battles*." *Sewanee Review* 79 (1971): 626–34.

Lanier, Lyle. "A Critique of the Philosophy of Progress." In *I'll Take My Stand: The South and the Agrarian Tradition*, 122–54. 1930; Reprint, Baton Rouge: Louisiana State University Press, 1977.

Loewen, James W., and Charles Sallis. *Mississippi Conflict and Change*. Rev. ed. New York: Pantheon Books, 1980.

Magee, Rosemary M. "Eudora Welty's *Losing Battles*: A Patchwork Quilt of Stories." *South Atlantic Review* 49 (May 1984): 67–79.

Mark, Rebecca. *The Dragon's Blood: Feminist Intertextuality in Eudora Welty's* The Golden Apples. Jackson: University Press of Mississippi, 1994.

Marrs, Suzanne. *The Welty Collection: A Guide to the Eudora Welty Manuscripts and Documents at the Mississippi Department of Archives and History*. Jackson: University Press of Mississippi, 1988.

———. "Eudora Welty's Snowy Heron." *American Literature* 53, no. 4 (1982): 723–5.

———. "The Metaphor of Race in Eudora Welty's Fiction." *Southern Review*, n.s. 22 (1986): 697–707.

May, Rollo. *The Courage to Create.* New York: W. W. Norton & Co., 1975.

Mayne, Richard. *The Recovery of Europe 1945–1973.* Rev. ed. Garden City, New York: Anchor Press, 1973.

McCaleb, W. F. *The Aaron Burr Conspiracy.* New York: Dodd, Mead, 1903.

McDonald, W. U. "Eudora Welty's Revisions of 'A Piece of News.'" *Studies in Short Fiction* 7 (Spring 1970): 232–47.

———. "Welty's 'Social Consciousness': Revisions of 'The Whistle.'" *Modern Fiction Studies* 16, no. 2 (1970): 193–98.

McGillis, Roderick. "Criticism in the Woods: Fairy Tales as Poetry." *Children's Literature Association Quarterly* 7, no. 2 (1982): 2–8.

McHaney, Thomas. "Eudora Welty and the Multitudinous Golden Apples." *Mississippi Quarterly* 26 (Fall 1973): 589–624.

———. "The Tishomingo of Welty's Imagination." Unpublished ms. 1–21.

McKinley, Laura G. "Millsaps College and the Mississippi Civil Rights Movement." Honors Thesis, Millsaps College, 1989.

McMillen, Neil R. *Dark Journey: Black Mississippians in the Age of Jim Crow.* Urbana and Chicago: University of Illinois Press, 1989.

———. "Fighting for What We Didn't Have: How Mississippi's Black Veterans Remember World War II." In *Remaking Dixie: The Impact of World War II on the American South,* ed. Neil McMillen, 93–110. Jackson: University Press of Mississippi, 1997.

"Millsaps President and Wright Protest." *Jackson Clarion-Ledger,* 9 March 1958, sec. A.

Minter, David. *William Faulkner: His Life and Work.* Baltimore: Johns Hopkins University Press, 1980.

"Miss Eudora Welty Honored at Beautiful Bridge Party of Eight Congenial Tables." *Jackson Daily Clarion-Ledger,* 22 June 1930.

Moody, Anne. *Coming of Age in Mississippi.* New York: Dial Press, 1968.

Moore, Carol. "Aunt Studney's Sack." *Southern Review,* n.s. 16 (1980): 591–6.

Mortimer, Gail L. *Daughter of the Swan: Love and Knowledge in Eudora Welty's Fiction.* Athens: University of Georgia Press, 1994.

"The New Cotton Kingdom." Exhibition Text. Old Capitol Museum, Jackson, Mississippi.

O'Brien, Michael. "A Heterodox Note on the Southern Renaissance." *Perspectives on the American South* 4 (1987): 1–17.

Odum, Howard. *Southern Regions.* Chapel Hill: University of North Carolina Press, 1936.

Percy, Walker. "Novel-Writing in an Apocalyptic Time." In *Signposts in a Strange Land,* 153–67. New York: Farrar, Straus, Giroux, 1991.

Pierpont, Claudia Roth. "A Perfect Lady." *New Yorker* 5 October 1998, 94–104.

Pitavy, Daniele. "La Guerre du Temps dans *Losing Battles* et *The Optimist's Daughter*." *Recherches Anglaises et Américaines* 9 (1976): 182–96.

Prenshaw, Peggy W. "Coates' *The Outlaw Years* and Welty's 'A Still Moment.'" *Notes on Modern American Literature* 2, no. 2 (1978): Item 17.

———. "Sex and Wreckage in the Parlor: Welty's 'Bye-Bye Brevoort.'" *Southern Quarterly* 33 (Winter/Spring 1995): 107–16.

———. "A Study of Setting in the Fiction of Eudora Welty." Ph.D. diss. University of Texas, 1970.

———. "Woman's World, Man's Place." In *Eudora Welty: A Form of Thanks*, ed. Louis Dollarhide and Ann J. Abadie, 46–77. Jackson: University Press of Mississippi, 1979.

Price, Reynolds. "The Onlooker, Smiling." In *A Common Room: Essays 1954–1987*, 54–69. New York: Atheneum, 1987.

———. "The Thing Itself." In *A Common Room: Essays 1954–1987*, 9–14. New York: Atheneum, 1987.

Ransom, John Crowe. "Reconstructed but Unregenerate." In *I'll Take My Stand: The South and the Agrarian Tradition*, 1–27. 1930; Reprint, Baton Rouge: Louisiana State University Press, 1977.

Raper, Julius Rowan. "Inventing Modern Southern Fiction: A Postmodern View." *Southern Literary Journal* 22 (Spring 1990): 3–18.

"A Reaffirmation of Principle." *New York Times*, 26 October 1988, sec. A.

Reed, John Shelton. *One South: An Ethnic Approach to Regional Culture*. Baton Rouge: Louisiana State University Press, 1982.

Richardson, Robert. *Emerson: The Mind on Fire*. Berkeley: University of California Press, 1995.

Robbe-Grillet, Alain. *For a New Novel: Essays on Fiction*. Translated by Richard Howard. New York: Grove Press, 1965.

Robinson, John Fraiser. "'. . . All this Juice and All this Joy.'" *Horizon* 18 (November 1948): 341–7.

———. "A Room in Algiers." *New Yorker* 22 (19 October 1946): 89–95.

Roland, Charles P. *The Improbable Era: The South Since World War II*. Rev. ed. Lexington: University of Kentucky Press, 1976.

Romines, Ann. *The Home Plot: Women, Writing and Domestic Ritual*. Amherst: University of Massachusetts Press, 1992.

Rothenberg, Albert. "The Process of Janusian Thinking in Creativity." In *The Creativity Question: Contemporary Psychological Perspectives*, ed. Albert Rothenberg and Carl Hausman, 311–27. Durham, N.C.: Duke University Press, 1976.

Rubin, Louis D. "Everything Brought Out in the Open: Eudora Welty's *Losing Battles*." *Hollins Critic* 7 (1970): 1–12.

———. *The Faraway Country: Writers of the Modern South*. Seattle: University of Washington Press, 1963.

Salter, John. *Jackson, Mississippi*. Hicksville, N.Y.: Exposition Press, 1979.

Schmidt, Peter. *The Heart of the Story: Eudora Welty's Short Fiction*. Jackson: University Press of Mississippi, 1991.

Shoemaker, W. C. "Mix Riders Lose Appetites in Jail." *Jackson Daily News*, 1 June 1961, sec. A.

Silver, James W. *Mississippi: The Closed Society*. New York: Harcourt, Brace and World, 1966.

Simpson, Lewis P. "The Chosen People." *Southern Review* n.s. 6 (July 1970): xvii–xxii.

———. "The Southern Aesthetic of Memory." *Tulane Studies in English* 23 (1978): 207–27.

Singal, Daniel J. *The War Within: From Victorian to Modernist Thought in the South, 1919–1945*. Chapel Hill: University of North Carolina Press, 1982.

Skates, John Ray. *Mississippi: A History*. New York: Norton, 1979.

Sulzberger, Cyrus L. "Dnieper Let Loose." *New York Times*, 29 August 1941.

Tate, Allen. "The New Provincialism" [1945]. In *Essays of Four Decades*, 535–46. Chicago: The Swallow Press, 1968.

Thompson, Victor H. "Aaron Burr in Eudora Welty's 'First Love.'" *Notes on Mississippi Writers* 8 (Winter 1976): 75–81.

———. "The Natchez Trace in Eudora Welty's 'A Still Moment.'" *Southern Literary Journal* 6, no. 1 (1973): 59–69.

Tiegreen, Helen Hurt. "Mothers, Daughters, and One Writer's Revisions." In *Welty: A Life in Literature*, ed. Albert Devlin, 188–211. Jackson: University Press of Mississippi, 1987.

Tolischus, Otto D. "Portrait of a Revolutionary." *New York Times Magazine*, 19 May 1940, 3, 21.

Trilling, Diana. "Fiction in Review." *Nation* 2 October 1943, 386–7.

U.S. Bureau of the Census. *Census of Population: 1970*, vol. 1, *Characteristics of the Population*, Part 26, Mississippi. U.S. Government Printing Office, 1973.

Warner, John M. "Eudora Welty: The Artist in 'First Love.'" *Notes on Mississippi Writers* 9 (Fall 1976): 77–87.

Warren, Robert Penn. "A Poem of Pure Imagination: An Experiment in Reading." In *Selected Essays*, 198–305. New York: Random House, 1958.

Weir, Sara Ann. "Miss Welty Tells Position of Southern Writers Today." *Purple and White* (Millsaps College), 8 December 1964.

Westling, Louise. *Sacred Groves and Ravaged Gardens: The Fiction of Eudora Welty, Carson McCullers, and Flannery O'Connor*. Athens: University of Georgia Press, 1985.

Weston, Ruth D. *Gothic Traditions and Narrative Techniques in the Fiction of Eudora Welty.* Baton Rouge: Louisiana State University Press, 1994.

Winter, William F. "New Directions in Politics, 1948–1956." In *A History of Mississippi,* ed. Richard Aubrey McLemore, vol. 2, 140–53. Hattiesburg: University and College Press of Mississippi, 1973.

Wolff, Sally. "'Among Those Missing': Phil Hand's Disappearance from *The Optimist's Daughter.*" *Southern Literary Journal* 25, no. 1 (1992): 74–88.

Yaeger, Patricia. "'Because a Fire Was in My Head': Eudora Welty and the Dialogic Imagination." In *Welty: A Life in Literature,* ed. Albert J. Devlin, 139–67. Jackson: University Press of Mississippi, 1987.

Yeats, W. B. *The Poems.* Ed. Richard J. Finneran. New York: Macmillan, 1983.

# Index

4230

AEE-7054

Gramley Library
Salem Academy and College
Winston-Salem, N.C. 27108